# 365
# With Self-Discipline

365 Life-Altering Thoughts on Self-Control, Mental Resilience, and Success

By Martin Meadows

# Download Another Book for Free

I want to thank you for buying my book and offer you another book (just as valuable as this one): *Grit: How to Keep Going When You Want to Give Up*, completely free.

Visit the link below to receive it:

http://www.profoundselfimprovement.com/365

In *Grit*, I'll tell you exactly how to stick to your goals, using proven methods from peak performers and science.

In addition to getting *Grit*, you'll also have an opportunity to get my new books for free, enter giveaways, and receive other valuable emails from me.

Again, here's the link to sign up:

http://www.profoundselfimprovement.com/365

# Table of Contents

Download Another Book for Free .................................................. 2

Table of Contents ............................................................................ 3

Prologue ........................................................................................ 25

WEEK 1 ........................................................................................ 30

Day 1: On Living the Hard Way .................................................. 30

Day 2: On Your Choices ............................................................... 32

Day 3: On Being a Human ........................................................... 33

Day 4: On Creating Systems ........................................................ 34

Day 5: On Enslavement to Self .................................................... 36

Day 6: On Superhumans ............................................................... 37

Day 7: On Poverty and Self-Discipline ....................................... 39

WEEK 2 ........................................................................................ 41

Day 8: On Unessential Necessities ............................................... 41

Day 9: On Your Future Self ......................................................... 43

Day 10: On Building Your Story ................................................. 45

Day 11: On Self-Discipline and Talent ....................................... 47

Day 12: On Calmness of Mind ..................................................... 49

Day 13: On What You Want Now
and What You Want Most ............................................................ 51

Day 14: On Long-Term Focus .................................. 53

WEEK 3 ................................................................. 55

Day 15: On Constant Improvement ......................... 55

Day 16: On Self-Reliance ........................................ 56

Day 17: On Rising from the Ashes of Failure ............. 57

Day 18: On Higher Standards .................................. 58

Day 19: On Fighting Well ........................................ 59

Day 20: On Taking Small Steps ............................... 60

Day 21: On the Importance of Habits ...................... 62

WEEK 4 ................................................................. 64

Day 22: On Self-Discipline as Freedom .................... 64

Day 23: On Disciplined Education ........................... 65

Day 24: On Happiness Through Self-Discipline ......... 67

Day 25: On Starting Today ...................................... 69

Day 26: On the Long-Term Consequences
of Your Choices ..................................................... 70

Day 27: On Following the Wrong Path ..................... 72

Day 28: On Living in Offensive Mode ...................... 74

WEEK 5 ................................................................. 76

Day 29: On Avoiding Effort ..................................... 76

Day 30: On Looking Like a Fool .............................. 78

Day 31: On Being "Normal" ..................................... 80
Day 32: On Cultivating Self-Discipline Like a Plant ..... 82
Day 33: On Things You Can't Rush ........................... 84
Day 34: On Enlightenment ....................................... 86
Day 35: On the Value of Difficulty ............................ 88

WEEK 6 .................................................................. 89

Day 36: On Pushing Your Limits Step by Step ........... 89
Day 37: On Initial Resistance ................................... 91
Day 38: On Moderation as a Good Thing .................. 93
Day 39: On Moderation as a Bad Thing .................... 95
Day 40: On Talking vs. Doing ................................... 97
Day 41: On Arrogance ............................................. 98
Day 42: On Diligent Practice .................................... 99

WEEK 7 ................................................................ 101

Day 43: On Making Continuous Efforts ................... 101
Day 44: On Optimism ............................................ 103
Day 45: On Honesty .............................................. 104
Day 46: On Looking Fear in the Face ...................... 106
Day 47: On the Folly of Loafing Around .................. 107
Day 48: On the Deadening of the Soul ................... 109
Day 49: On Obeying Lusts ..................................... 111

WEEK 8 .................................................................................... 113

Day 50: On Not Resting on Your Laurels ..................... 113

Day 51: On Taking Action,
in Spite of Potential Criticism ......................................... 114

Day 52: On Thinking for Yourself ................................. 116

Day 53: On Having a Burning "Yes" Inside ................ 118

Day 54: On Underestimating
the Long-Term Approach ................................................ 120

Day 55: On Bearing Misfortunes Nobly ....................... 122

Day 56: On Thinking You Can ...................................... 124

WEEK 9 .................................................................................... 126

Day 57: On Two Types of Happiness ........................... 126

Day 58: On Cultivating Physical Excellence ............... 128

Day 59: On Your Vices Masquerading as Virtues ....... 131

Day 60: On Pressing On .................................................. 133

Day 61: On Extreme Actions ......................................... 135

Day 62: On Moonshot Projects ...................................... 137

Day 63: On the Will Being Stronger Than the Skill .... 139

WEEK 10 .................................................................................. 141

Day 64: On Seeing Obstacles as Hurdles ..................... 141

Day 65: On Self-Discipline with Money ...................... 143

Day 66: On Pointless Complaints ................................. 145

Day 67: On Borrowing Money.................................... 147

Day 68: On Choosing the Right Motivator ................. 149

Day 69: On Climbing Steep Hills ............................... 151

Day 70: On Parkinson's Law ...................................... 152

WEEK 11 ................................................................... 154

Day 71: On Taking a Step Forward ............................ 154

Day 72: On the Value of the Struggle ......................... 156

Day 73: On Having Fun .............................................. 158

Day 74: On Acting Less and Thinking More .............. 160

Day 75: On Haters....................................................... 162

Day 76: On Changing Your Mind............................... 164

Day 77: On Hurting Yourself
with Your Own Judgments.......................................... 166

WEEK 12 ................................................................... 168

Day 78: On Collaboration ........................................... 168

Day 79: On Books ....................................................... 170

Day 80: On Cultivating Positivity
When Things Go Bad .................................................. 173

Day 81: On Identifying Your Resources..................... 175

Day 82: On Extreme Focus ......................................... 177

Day 83: On Changing Your Identity .............................. 179

Day 84: On Work and Chatter ...................................... 181

WEEK 13 ................................................................... 183

Day 85: On Experimenting to See What Happens ....... 183

Day 86: On the Spillover Effect of Success ................. 185

Day 87: On Attributing Failure to External Factors ..... 187

Day 88: On the Comfort Zone ...................................... 189

Day 89: On Not Making Excuses ................................. 191

Day 90: On Quitting in a Smart Way ........................... 193

Day 91: On Starting Now ............................................. 195

WEEK 14 ................................................................... 197

Day 92: On Pleasure Gained from Abstaining ............. 197

Day 93: On Connecting Dots ....................................... 199

Day 94: On Overidentifying With Your Emotions ...... 201

Day 95: On Early-morning Workouts .......................... 202

Day 96: On Silence ...................................................... 204

Day 97: On Treating Yourself Well ............................. 206

Day 98: On Society (Not) Holding You Back ............. 207

WEEK 15 ................................................................... 209

Day 99: On Applying Knowledge ................................ 209

Day 100: On Being a Leader ........................................ 211

Day 101: On the Ultimate Excellence
in Self-Discipline ................................................. 213

Day 102: On the Deeper Meaning
Behind Temptations ............................................. 215

Day 103: On Controlled Burn ............................... 217

Day 104: On the Past Predicting the Future ......... 219

Day 105: On Predicting When You'll Give In ...... 220

WEEK 16 ................................................................ 222

Day 106: On Valuing Your Own Opinion .............. 222

Day 107: On the Innocent Distractions ................. 224

Day 108: On Following a Routine ......................... 226

Day 109: On the Size of Containers ...................... 228

Day 110: On Moving Yourself
Closer to the Finish Line ....................................... 230

Day 111: On Patience With Mindset Changes ...... 232

Day 112: On Self-Licensing ................................... 234

WEEK 17 ................................................................ 236

Day 113: On a Lack of Time .................................. 236

Day 114: On Fulfilling Your Own Standards ........ 238

Day 115: On the Cost of Indulgence ..................... 240

Day 116: On Taking the Low Road ....................... 241

Day 117: On Dressing New Things in Old Habits ....... 243

Day 118: On Free Things ..................................................245

Day 119: On Hatching the Egg ........................................247

WEEK 18 ...........................................................................249

Day 120: On Handling Interruptions
to Your Routine ................................................................249

Day 121: On the Mark of a Champion ..........................251

Day 122: On Making Agreements With Yourself ........253

Day 123: On Doing This or Nothing .............................254

Day 124: On Daily Gratitude ..........................................255

Day 125: On Going Away From Work ..........................256

Day 126: On Shedding Light on the Dark Things .......257

WEEK 19 ...........................................................................258

Day 127: On Cold Exposure ...........................................258

Day 128: On Principles ....................................................260

Day 129: On Everyday Practice .....................................262

Day 130: On Working on Laziness ................................263

Day 131: On Building an Ark .........................................265

Day 132: On Being Willing to Be Bad ..........................266

Day 133: On Self-Caring .................................................268

WEEK 20 ...........................................................................269

Day 134: On Staying Congruent ....................................269

Day 135: On Staying in Love With Your Goals ..........271

Day 136: On the Desire for Happiness
Replacing the Need for Self-Discipline ......................273

Day 137: On Waiting for Ten Minutes ........................275

Day 138: On Nature Boosting Your Focus ..................277

Day 139: On Tolerating an Absence of Novelty..........278

Day 140: On Longing for Paradise ..............................280

WEEK 21 ......................................................................281

Day 141: On Punctuality ..............................................281

Day 142: On Keystone Habits......................................283

Day 143: On Falling in Love
With the Idea of Starting .............................................285

Day 144: On the Work of a Human Being...................287

Day 145: On Complicating the World for Profit..........289

Day 146: On Decision Avoidance................................291

Day 147: On Walking by Your Mistakes.....................292

WEEK 22 ......................................................................294

Day 148: On Fear .........................................................294

Day 149: On the Weak Point in Your Armor ..............296

Day 150: On Indulgences Charging You Interest ........298

Day 151: On Changing Your Character.......................300

Day 152: On the Future Value of Money ..................... 302

Day 153: On Spontaneity ............................................... 303

Day 154: On the Value of Doing Things Yourself ....... 305

WEEK 23 ....................................................................... 307

Day 155: On Broadening Your Horizons ..................... 307

Day 156: On Wanting What We Already Have ........... 309

Day 157: On Remembering Death ............................... 311

Day 158: On Learning From the Greats ....................... 312

Day 159: On Having Options ....................................... 314

Day 160: On Deliberate Practice .................................. 316

Day 161: On Addressing the Real Mistakes ................ 318

WEEK 24 ....................................................................... 319

Day 162: On Inverse Paranoia ...................................... 319

Day 163: On Angry Comebacks ................................... 321

Day 164: On Easing Yourself Into the Pain ................. 323

Day 165: On Not Living Up To Your Ideals ................ 325

Day 166: On Handling Emotions .................................. 326

Day 167: On Routines Overcoming a Bad Mood ........ 328

Day 168: On Wasting Your Energy
When You Don't Have Important Rituals ..................... 329

WEEK 25 ....................................................................... 331

Day 169: On Stopping at the Right Moment
to Help You Tomorrow .................................................. 331

Day 170: On Supply and Demand ................................. 332

Day 171: On Stress .......................................................... 334

Day 172: On Having More Than One Identity ............ 336

Day 173: On Eating Alone .............................................. 338

Day 174: On Experiencing Life ..................................... 339

Day 175: On Improving Self-Control
by Using Your Other Hand ............................................ 341

WEEK 26 ......................................................................... 343

Day 176: On Jotting Things Down ............................... 343

Day 177: On Sleep .......................................................... 345

Day 178: On Losing Momentum ................................... 347

Day 179: On Effort Generating Satisfaction ................ 348

Day 180: On Paying the Price as Fast as Possible ....... 350

Day 181: On the Disciplined Pursuit of Less ............... 352

Day 182: On Saying No .................................................. 354

WEEK 27 ......................................................................... 355

Day 183: On Shocking Your Body ................................ 355

Day 184: On Creating Value .......................................... 357

Day 185: On Staying With Problems Longer .............. 359

Day 186: On Simple Rules ............................................... 361

Day 187: On Not Judging Too Quickly ....................... 363

Day 188: On Pride ......................................................... 365

Day 189: On Adventures ............................................... 367

WEEK 28 ....................................................................... 369

Day 190: On Being Specific
About Your Resolutions ............................................... 369

Day 191: On Futile Determination ............................. 370

Day 192: On Being in It for the Long Term ................ 372

Day 193: On Becoming a New Person ......................... 374

Day 194: On Pain and Quitting ................................... 376

Day 195: On Procrastination as Your Ally .................. 378

Day 196: On Impermanent Motivation ....................... 380

WEEK 29 ....................................................................... 381

Day 197: On Eliminating a Negative Attitude ............ 381

Day 198: On Your Maxims ........................................... 383

Day 199: On Your Inaction Hurting Others ................ 385

Day 200: On Fretting About Yesterday's Problems .... 387

Day 201: On Teaching Others ..................................... 389

Day 202: On Accepting the Worst .............................. 391

Day 203: On Maintaining Composure ....................... 392

WEEK 30 ................................................................... 395

Day 204: On Psychological Limits ............................... 395

Day 205: On Treating Hate as an Exercise .................. 397

Day 206: On Vice Fasts ................................................. 398

Day 207: On Enthusiasm and Endurance..................... 399

Day 208: On Profiting From Your Losses ................... 401

Day 209: On Finishing Quick Tasks Right Away ........ 403

Day 210: On Deferring Happiness ............................... 405

WEEK 31 ................................................................... 407

Day 211: On a Simple Adherence Hack ...................... 407

Day 212: On Learning From Your Illness ................... 409

Day 213: On Sudden Trials........................................... 411

Day 214: On Fearing the Future................................... 413

Day 215: On Self-Determination ................................. 415

Day 216: On Accounting for Flexibility
in Your Plans................................................................. 417

Day 217: On Things Not Being Up to Us .................... 419

WEEK 32 ................................................................... 421

Day 218: On Protein in Your Diet ............................... 421

Day 219: On Dropping Unnecessary Tasks ................. 423

Day 220: On a Lack of Vision ...................................... 424

Day 221: On Antimodels ................................................ 425

Day 222: On Your Depleting Willpower ..................... 426

Day 223: On Clear Cues and Rewards ........................ 428

Day 224: On Juggling Five Balls ................................. 430

WEEK 33 ........................................................................ 432

Day 225: On Following Someone Else's Plan ............. 432

Day 226: On Waiting to Be Saved ............................... 434

Day 227: On Being Stuck in the Past .......................... 435

Day 228: On Going Where Your Eyes Go ................... 436

Day 229: On the Opportunity in Chaos ....................... 438

Day 230: On Laser-Focusing on Specific Aspects ....... 440

Day 231: On Minimizing What You Need .................. 442

WEEK 34 ........................................................................ 444

Day 232: On Going All In ............................................ 444

Day 233: On Obstacles as Filters ................................. 446

Day 234: On Forgiving ................................................. 447

Day 235: On Looking Only One Day Ahead .............. 448

Day 236: On Being a Normal Chap ............................. 450

Day 237: On Shifting Responsibility to Others ........... 452

Day 238: On Dividing Your Life
into 10-Minute Units ..................................................... 454

WEEK 35 ............................................................. 456

Day 239: On Imagining the Process
as a Litmus Test.................................................... 456

Day 240: On Separating Yourself From the Pain ........ 458

Day 241: On Enabling the Future ............................... 460

Day 242: On Selectivity ............................................. 461

Day 243: On the Crime of Aiming Too Low ............... 463

Day 244: On the Fun in the Impossible....................... 465

Day 245: On Following or Leaving a Path ................. 467

WEEK 36 ............................................................. 469

Day 246: On Learning the Big Ideas........................... 469

Day 247: On First-Order and
Second-Order Consequences...................................... 471

Day 248: On Reducing Your Targets.......................... 473

Day 249: On Working Backwards .............................. 475

Day 250: On Fluctuating Energy ................................ 477

Day 251: On Relaxing While Working....................... 479

Day 252: On Getting Older ........................................ 481

WEEK 37 ............................................................. 483

Day 253: On the Invisible Prison Bars........................ 483

Day 254: On Capitalizing on Your Talents................. 485

17

Day 255: On Self-Image ................................................. 487

Day 256: On Taking a Real Decision ........................... 489

Day 257: On Being Impeccable With Your Word ....... 490

Day 258: On Helping, With No Strings Attached ........ 492

Day 259: On the Motivation to Get Up Early .............. 494

WEEK 38 .................................................................... 496

Day 260: On Courage .................................................. 496

Day 261: On Giving Up the Last Word ...................... 497

Day 262: On Fragility Caused by Comfort ................. 498

Day 263: On Thinking for Yourself ............................ 500

Day 264: On Being Honest With Yourself
About Your Feelings .................................................... 502

Day 265: On Transformation Taking Place Now ......... 503

Day 266: On Temptations and
Your Decision What to Do About Them ..................... 504

WEEK 39 .................................................................... 506

Day 267: On Self-Monitoring ...................................... 506

Day 268: On Taking Ownership for Your Ideas .......... 508

Day 269: On Stretching ................................................ 510

Day 270: On Self-Reflection ....................................... 512

Day 271: On How to Use Books ................................. 513

Day 272: On Extinguishing Bad Habits ....................... 515

Day 273: On Reprogramming Your Brain .................. 517

WEEK 40 .................................................................... 519

Day 274: On Constant Movement ............................... 519

Day 275: On Staying a Champion ............................... 520

Day 276: On the Price of Personal Growth ................. 522

Day 277: On Making Things Convenient .................... 524

Day 278: On the Rent Axiom ...................................... 526

Day 279: On Learning With Age ................................ 528

Day 280: On Seeing Your Troubles
from the Proper Perspective ........................................ 529

WEEK 41 .................................................................... 531

Day 281: On the Hardships
Writing Your Life Story .............................................. 531

Day 282: On Analysis Paralysis .................................. 532

Day 283: On Being Hungry ........................................ 534

Day 284: On Habits as Handcuffs ............................... 536

Day 285: On Small Efforts at Self-Control ................. 538

Day 286: On Avoiding Problems ................................ 540

Day 287: On Reducing Procrastination
That Comes From Overwhelm .................................... 541

WEEK 42 .................................................................... 543

Day 288: On Routines and Relationships ..................543

Day 289: On Accounting for Taxes ..........................545

Day 290: On Letting Go of the Old Person................547

Day 291: On the How Instead of the Outcome ............549

Day 292: On Mental Resilience ................................551

Day 293: On Cutting Your Losses .............................553

Day 294: On the All-or-Nothing Mentality.................555

WEEK 43 ...............................................................557

Day 295: On Wandering Aimlessly ...........................557

Day 296: On Your Habitual Thoughts .......................559

Day 297: On the Best Time to Work..........................560

Day 298: On the Suffocating Mantras........................562

Day 299: On Generalizations ....................................564

Day 300: On Walking ...............................................566

Day 301: On the Power of Rituals .............................567

WEEK 44 ...............................................................569

Day 302: On Listening to Your Gut...........................569

Day 303: On Buddha's Counsel ................................571

Day 304: On the Unsexy Reality of Work ..................573

Day 305: On the Addiction to Electronics .................574

Day 306: On Ignorance .............................................576

Day 307: On Breaking Your Rules ............................... 577

Day 308: On Not Having Money ................................ 579

WEEK 45 ...................................................................... 581

Day 309: On the Matters of Right and Wrong ............. 581

Day 310: On Having Good Private Teachers ............... 583

Day 311: On Setting an Example .................................. 585

Day 312: On Learning Without a Desire to Learn ....... 586

Day 313: On What You Demand From Life ................ 588

Day 314: On Neatness .................................................. 590

Day 315: On the Cost of Education and Ignorance ...... 591

WEEK 46 ...................................................................... 593

Day 316: On Doing What You Love ........................... 593

Day 317: On Thinking You're Able ............................. 595

Day 318: On the Inconvenience of Change ................. 597

Day 319: On Learning From Refusal ........................... 599

Day 320: On Change as a Cold Bath ............................ 601

Day 321: On Being the Creator
of Your Circumstances ................................................. 603

Day 322: On Subtraction .............................................. 605

WEEK 47 ...................................................................... 607

Day 323: On Prolonged Sitting .................................... 607

Day 324: On Ignoring the World
When You're Down ..................................................609

Day 325: On Being the Child of Your Own Works .....611

Day 326: On Your Deeds Determining You ................612

Day 327: On the Biggest Person
Standing in Your Way ................................................614

Day 328: On Anger .....................................................616

Day 329: On a Change in Beliefs ................................618

WEEK 48 ....................................................................619

Day 330: On Turning Back Right at the Very End ......619

Day 331: On Finding an Easier Way ...........................620

Day 332: On a Lack of Variety ....................................622

Day 333: On Happiness as a Duty ..............................624

Day 334: On Self-Criticism .........................................626

Day 335: On Wishing ..................................................627

Day 336: On Remembering That
Your Time Is Limited .................................................628

WEEK 49 ....................................................................630

Day 337: On a Coin Flip .............................................630

Day 338: On "I Don't" vs. "I Can't" ............................631

Day 339: On Appreciating Your Body ........................633

Day 340: On Better Learning ......................................635

Day 341: On When Not to Make
Important Decisions ................................................... 637

Day 342: On Doing the Best You Can
With What You Have .................................................. 639

Day 343: On Turning Intentions into Actions ............. 641

WEEK 50 ........................................................................ 643

Day 344: On the Desire for Safety .............................. 643

Day 345: On Injecting Adventure
in Your Routines ......................................................... 645

Day 346: On Surpassing Yourself ................................ 647

Day 347: On Enduring Your Tyrants ........................... 648

Day 348: On Using Your Strength ............................... 650

Day 349: On Managing Energy .................................... 651

Day 350: On Doing Things Deliberately ..................... 653

WEEK 51 ........................................................................ 654

Day 351: On Admitting You're Struggling ................. 654

Day 352: On the Empowerment in Trade-Offs ........... 655

Day 353: On Glancing at Your Smartphone ............... 656

Day 354: On Focusing on the Good Things ................ 657

Day 355: On Luxuries .................................................. 659

Day 356: On Taking the Initiative .............................. 661

Day 357: On the Rare Indulgence ............................... 663

WEEK 52 ...................................................................664

Day 358: On Acting Differently From Others .............664

Day 359: On Treats vs. Rewards...................................666

Day 360: On Self-Myofascial Release .........................668

Day 361: On Smiling....................................................670

Day 362: On Professionalism.......................................672

Day 363: On Relying Upon Yourself...........................674

Day 364: On Books, Part Two .....................................676

WEEK 53 ...................................................................678

Day 365: On Sweeping the Floor.................................678

Epilogue ......................................................................679

Download Another Book for Free................................680

Could You Help?..........................................................681

About Martin Meadows .................................................682

# Prologue

Ouzouk woke up with the first rays of sunlight hitting his face. He scanned the interior of his dusty hut, constructed with twigs, mud and dry grass. He scratched his back, which, as always, had been bitten by insects over and over again throughout the night. Grateful that the night had passed without any danger to his family, he crawled out, careful not to make any sounds.

It was a crisp and clear morning. He would have loved to take his family for a walk around the waterfall and play with his little son, but there was work to do. It had been five days since the tribe ate something more substantial than a fistful of berries. Unfazed by the bloodthirsty mosquitoes buzzing by, Ouzouk walked over to the fire pit and warmed his calloused hands. The light scent of wood smoke filled his nostrils. He rubbed his hands together, still feeling the painful absence of his index finger lost during that fateful hunt many moons ago.

One by one, his fellow tribesmen crawled out of their huts and joined him at the fire. There was Dhizgab, his friend who was bitten by a snake and was left partly paralyzed on his left side. Gnokk limped along next, with his broken foot badly healed, and a part of his skull partly caved in after a stone thrown by an enemy tribesman hit him smack dab in the middle of his forehead. Rekknodd sauntered into the group next. So far, he was the luckiest of the band, with only a deep scar on his cheek, left from an attack by a tiger that had massacred a half of the tribe. Other men—some missing limbs, some having lost their entire families, some with even more horrible memories—joined the group.

When the men were ready, they separated into two groups and ventured out to secure food for the tribe. They made it back to the camp in the early afternoon, forced to make a hasty retreat after spotting a leopard resting in the thick bushes. Yet again, they had failed to obtain food, but at least they were grateful that (unlike two moons ago) this time nobody had been hurt.

With empty stomachs, the adults gathered around the fire pit while small children, supervised by teenagers armed with spears and bows, played by the creek a short distance from the camp.

They reluctantly decided that the area could no longer support them. While clean water was plentiful and predators rare, food was becoming increasingly scarce and successful hunts were few and far between.

The next day they would gather their belongings, put them on their backs, and walk for a long time until they would find another suitable place for a new temporary dwelling. Some would die along the way, some would get hurt, but such was life, Ouzouk thought to himself. A human being couldn't *ever* stop struggling and fighting to survive each day.

I can hear you thinking, "What a weird prologue to a book about self-discipline!" Bear with me, please...

Our basic human nature hasn't changed since the days of Ouzouk. While the vast majority of humans fortunately no longer have to live in constant discomfort and fear of death, we would still do well to possess even a fraction of mental toughness and self-discipline our ancestors had. In the modern world, it's easy to live without even a modicum of self-discipline.

Back then, nobody could avoid discomfort. It was a fact of life that one couldn't thrive unless they ventured into the world, facing unknown risks and possible death in a quest for a better life.

Today, most people are unable to wake up early without an alarm clock, and even then, it takes them thirty minutes just to crawl out of bed. Most would find it impossible to sleep on the bare floor, with insects crawling over them and biting their bodies the entire night. If they experienced just a slight ache, most would skip work and complain about how much pain they were in. Most wouldn't be able to fast for an entire day, let alone go without food for five days in a row.

Compared to our ancestors, we have it *easy*.

Yet, or perhaps because of it, so many people struggle with self-discipline today. A great majority of them do nothing to fix that, and the ones who try are often met with ridicule. If you belong to the group that is trying to better themselves or wanting to do so, the book you're now reading is for you.

I wrote *365 Days With Self-Discipline* with the intention of creating a daily companion to help you embrace self-discipline in your everyday life.

As the author of several bestselling books about self-discipline and being a personal growth junkie myself, self-control is a topic close to my heart. I believe that if a person wants to reach their full potential, he or she can't avoid discomfort. Doing things that might not be entirely pleasant is key to achieving long-term objectives.

In the following pages, I'll share with you one thought for each day of a year that is devoted to the topic of self-discipline, mental toughness, success, or self-improvement in general. The thoughts come from some of the world's brightest minds: successful entrepreneurs, athletes, bestselling authors, researchers, performers, bloggers, and more.

Since the entries are brief and get straight to the heart of the matter, you'll be able to quickly find ongoing inspiration to continue working on your most important long-term goals and on becoming an ever better person.

Due to the large number of days in a year, some themes will inevitably repeat, but I strove to address each subtopic from different perspectives. Please note that I have quoted various people from numerous sources, including books, articles, blogs, speeches, interviews, and more. By citing their words, I don't necessarily endorse their works or their persona.

(A note on quotes in the physical and ebook version of the book — whenever I could, I cited the source and included an endnote. Unfortunately, the exact source of a small number of quotes, particularly those by historic figures, was elusive to me. Whenever I couldn't find the author — as is often the case with many inspirational quotes circulating around the Internet — instead of risking misattribution I wrote "Unknown.")

Let's turn the page and start with Day 1 and the most important thought that defines the difference between a self-disciplined person and a weak-willed one.

# WEEK 1

# Day 1: On Living the Hard Way

*Life's easy when you live it the hard way... and hard if you try to live it the easy way.*

—*Dave Kekich*[1]

Self-discipline means living your life the hard way: resisting temptations and instant gratification, in order to receive bigger and better rewards in the future. It's certainly *easier* to avoid all kinds of discomfort and indulge yourself whenever you want, but in the end, all that you get from that approach is fleeting pleasure *now* at the expense of your future, which otherwise could have been much better.

Consider a weak-willed person who, when faced with a challenge, immediately opts out. How likely is this person to achieve anything substantial in life if their primary value is to feel comfortable? How is this person going to manage a crisis that they *must* face? Even a relatively insignificant problem can become an insurmountable obstacle for a person who's been living a sheltered life and always avoided what's difficult or disagreeable.

Now contrast that with a person who *voluntarily* makes his or her life harder. They seek out and welcome challenges as opportunities to grow. Each self-imposed affliction strengthens them, so that fewer and fewer difficulties in life overwhelm them. Day by day, they immunize themselves against problems, precisely because they seek them out. When life deals them an unexpected blow, they're ready to handle it because — thanks to living their lives the hard way — they're *always* ready for hardships.

# Day 2: On Your Choices

*Your choices are made in a moment, but their consequences will transcend a lifetime.*

—*MJ DeMarco*[2]

Eat this greasy, high-calorie hamburger or prepare a healthy salad? Sleep in and barely get to work on time or wake up at 5 a.m. to work on your side business before going to work at your day job? Stop trying the moment you get rejected or swallow your pride and keep going, despite hearing "no" dozens of times?

It takes only a moment to make the wrong choice and jeopardize your future. What feels like an insignificant decision today can have a great, lasting impact on your future.

Each choice sets a precedent — and when you make the same wrong choice several times in a row, it becomes your standard *modus operandi*.

While one hamburger every now and then isn't likely to ruin your overall efforts to lose weight, underestimating the impact of *repeatedly* making the wrong choice can profoundly affect you over the course of the rest of your life.

Each time you're faced with a decision between exerting self-discipline and taking it easy, remind yourself that the choice you're making today doesn't affect the present moment alone. A momentary decision can (and often will) reverberate for many years or even decades into the future.

# Day 3: On Being a Human

> *Willpower is what separates us from the animals. It's the capacity to restrain our impulses, resist temptation — do what's right and good for us in the long run, not what we want to do right now. It's central, in fact, to civilization.*
>
> —*Roy Baumeister*[3]

Humans have the capacity to act against their urges in exchange for a better future. Unfortunately, many people live by the principle of "if it feels good, do it, and if it doesn't, don't do it."

Caving in to your temptations whenever you feel them emerge is like relinquishing your humanity, in a way. As an intelligent human being, you have an ability — and I daresay an *obligation* — to make decisions that are based on rational thinking, not on your instincts alone.

Strive to be a better human and embrace your humanity by exercising your "willpower muscle," instead of succumbing to your most primal (and least helpful for your long-term goals) part of the brain. Your most primal instincts may provide temporary comfort, but seldom are good for the long term, except when there is a direct threat to your survival.

# Day 4: On Creating Systems

> *I value self-discipline, but creating systems that make it next to impossible to misbehave is more reliable than self-control.*
>
> —*Tim Ferriss*[4]

A lot of people think that being self-disciplined means that you can sit in front of a delicious piece of cake and stare at it for hours without eating it. They think of resisting temptations as being like a knight defending his kingdom against the invader.

If you go to seedy bars every week, your chances of getting punched in the face are higher than those of a person spending their evenings at home with a book. Likewise, the best way to protect yourself against temptations is to avoid them — and for that, plain old preparation is more valuable than self-control.

Your chances of cheating on a diet are higher if you have forbidden foods at home. Removing them from your house — a simple act that requires little willpower, as long as you're satiated while doing so — will protect you when you get hungry and the urge to gorge on them hits you like a ton of bricks.

Your chances of sleeping in are lower if you set three different alarms and place them away from your bed.

You'll be less likely to waste time at work when you block the most distracting websites instead of relying on your willpower to stop you before loading those funny cat pictures.

Prepare yourself for difficult situations by putting up roadblocks ahead of time, when your resolve isn't being tested. Your self-control *system* will do some of the heavy lifting for you, leaving your reserves of self-discipline to be used for the unplanned situations, when they arise.

# Day 5: On Enslavement to Self

> *Before complaining that you are a slave to another, be sure that you are not a slave to self. Look within; you will find there, perchance, slavish thoughts, slavish desires, and in your daily life and conduct slavish habits. Conquer these; cease to be a slave to self, and no man will have the power to enslave you.*
>
> —*James Allen*[5]

It's easy to delegate the responsibility for our lives and choices to other people.

It's not your fault that you can't stick to a diet — it's because your friends constantly tempt you to grab something to eat with them.

It's not your fault that you can't control your finances — it's those evil corporations that spend millions on advertising and leave you powerless to change.

It's not that you lack willpower to exercise — people always want something from you and you never have the time to develop this healthy habit.

In reality, nothing could be further from the truth. While external circumstances can affect you, in the end, whether or not they control your life depends on you. Just like James Allen said, when you achieve self-mastery, no one (and no thing) will have the power to enslave you.

The next time you blame an external factor for your lack of self-discipline, think again. Was it the person eating chocolate next to you who controlled what you put in your mouth, or was it you?

# Day 6: On Superhumans

*Life can be much broader once you discover one simple fact: Everything around you that you call life was made up by people that were no smarter than you and you can change it, you can influence it, you can build your own things that other people can use.*

—*Steve Jobs*[6]

Despite an enormous selection of movies about superhumans, they don't really exist. I know, it's shocking news, right?

Nobody — including the world's biggest geniuses — was, is, or ever will be a superhuman, infinitely better in all aspects than the average mortal.

It's easy to forget this fact when you look at the accomplishments of the people who are changing the world around you. After all, they appear to be so perfect — extremely productive, intelligent, beautiful, creative, persistent, strong... and the list goes on.

Behind the scenes, everyone struggles in some areas of their lives.

I'm an author of several books about self-discipline, but it doesn't mean that I never struggle with self-control. I deal with the same problems as every other person, and the only difference is that I've discovered how to handle some of them a bit more effectively. I've had my fair share of failures, found myself unable to resist some temptations, and I jeopardized some long-term goals because I succumbed to the allure of instant gratification.

This is the human condition. People whom you consider to be extremely successful aren't that different from you. Many of them in the past had less willpower than you exhibit now, and many of them might be more disciplined than you in one aspect, but less disciplined in another.

Becoming a self-disciplined person is within everybody's grasp. You don't need to have won the genetic lottery or get introduced to a country club to develop self-control — and neither you nor anybody else will ever achieve permanent, flawless self-mastery over every aspect of life. Accept that and accept yourself, as well.

# Day 7: On Poverty and Self-Discipline

> *A second line of research has shown that economic stress robs us of cognitive bandwidth. Worrying about bills, food or other problems, leaves less capacity to think ahead or to exert self-discipline. So, poverty imposes a mental tax.*
>
> —*Nicholas Kristof*[7]

Financial stress (or for that matter, all kinds of stress) diminishes your ability to delay gratification. Consequently, poor people find it harder to resist temptations. In the end, they get stuck in a vicious cycle — they can't escape poverty because it imposes constant mental stress on them, which then leads them to making bad decisions — not only the financial ones, but also those relating to their health, relationships, and general future.

Does it mean that if you're struggling financially, you're destined to have a bad life? Not necessarily. Taking personal responsibility and becoming conscious of the source of the problem can help you push ahead and overcome your circumstances.

Launching one of my businesses put me in debt. It exerted immense daily stress on me. No matter what I was doing, there was always the thought in the back of my head that I had a debt to repay. In some months, I was so close to not meeting my obligations on time that I would have been forced to close up shop if it weren't for some money I managed to make at the last minute.

This experience has made me realize that no matter what they say about money not bringing happiness, at least several months' worth of income kept as savings in the bank means the difference between a relatively stress-free life and the soul-crushing fear when you can't cover an urgent, important expense.

If you're struggling with finances, make it one of your priorities to get out of debt as quickly as you can and build an emergency fund covering at least three to six months of basic living expenses. In addition to improving your financial health, it will dramatically reduce stress and strengthen your ability to delay gratification and make more optimal choices favoring your future.

# WEEK 2

# Day 8: On Unessential Necessities

> *Epicurus wanted to examine the things he thought he needed so he could determine which of them he could in fact live without. He realized that in many cases, we work hard to obtain something because we are convinced that we would be miserable without it. The problem is that we can live perfectly well without some of these things, but we won't know which they are if we don't try living without them.*
>
> —*William B. Irvine*[8]

Ancient Greek philosopher Epicurus would have his hands full in modern times if he wanted to spread his philosophy. We live in the world in which you feel you *deserve* to have luxuries. In fact, they're no longer considered luxuries but necessities because most people mistakenly think they can't live without them.

The problem with mistaking luxuries for necessities is that it's impossible to develop powerful self-discipline if you *need* a lot just to function.

How is a person who believes that they *need* to eat empty calories in the form of burgers, pizzas, or white bread supposed to lose weight? How likely is that an individual who thinks that it's *necessary* to lease a new car every two years will exert enough self-discipline to save money and "deprive" himself or herself of what they consider a basic human need?

Periodically try living without something that you consider a necessity. You'll benefit in several ways.

First, you'll voluntarily put yourself in an uncomfortable situation that will help you expand your comfort zone and develop your mental resilience.

Second, you'll discover whether you really *need* this thing in your life — and if you find you don't, it will provide food for thought as to how many other things in your life are in fact not as important as you thought they were. This can then help you eliminate the unessential from your life and free up additional resources to focus on what's important.

Finally, you will increase your ability to feel happy with less — including being happy in a situation when you're deprived of something involuntarily.

# Day 9: On Your Future Self

> *In four studies, participants interacted with realistic computer renderings of their future selves using immersive virtual reality hardware and interactive decision aids. In all cases, those who interacted with virtual future selves exhibited an increased tendency to accept later monetary rewards over immediate ones.*
>
> —*Hal E. Hershfield*[9]

Studies suggest that people who are aided with technology to imagine their future selves are more likely to delay gratification. In the case of the cited study, they're more likely to save money for retirement.

This shows that your self-discipline is largely affected by your ability to feel empathy toward your future self. If the vision of you ten, twenty, or thirty years from now isn't particularly vivid, you'll have a hard time denying yourself pleasure today so that the stranger in the future can benefit.

For this reason, consider occasionally meditating on your future self. Ask yourself if today you're grateful for the choices you made several years ago, or if you wish that in the past you had been more concerned about your future. Are the choices you're making today choices that are only benefiting the present "you," but don't contribute to — or worse, jeopardize — your well-being in the future?

The person you'll become in ten years will most likely not be the same person you are today, but it will still be you — and it's in your hands whether, ten years from now you'll look back and feel glad you extended self-empathy well into the future, or find that you decided to be selfish and steal from your future for some fleeting pleasure today.

# Day 10: On Building Your Story

> *Words create sentences; sentences create paragraphs; sometimes paragraphs quicken and begin to breathe.*
>
> —*Stephen King*[10]

Writing a novel is a daunting task if you've never written one before. It's hard to write even a single paragraph, let alone write two or three hundred pages that will capture the attention of the reader and keep them reading until the last page. What's worse, after all this effort, you'll probably realize that your novel, when compared to a widely-acclaimed bestselling novel, is only good for kindling.

What you fail to see is that the author of that bestselling novel most likely has spent a decade or more mastering their craft. They started with words, which then became sentences, paragraphs, and eventually stories. Their first attempts — like those of everybody else — were unsuccessful. It took them hundreds of thousands of words' worth of practice to finally write a masterpiece.

Building self-discipline is similar to writing a novel. You might consider a disciplined person who always wakes up at four in the morning, is physically active every day, eats a healthy diet, is super productive, and is capable of balancing it all with their social life and family obligations as a superhuman. But in reality, this person, like the bestselling novelist, probably started with one simple change and kept building on top of it.

Whenever you get discouraged, or feel tired by how far you still have to go to accomplish your goals, remind yourself that everybody who has built self-discipline had to go through the same process — starting with little changes which then turned into habits, which then led to big lifestyle changes and identity shifts, and eventually, into successes.

# Day 11: On Self-Discipline and Talent

> *Self-discipline without talent can often achieve astounding results, whereas talent without self-discipline inevitably dooms itself to failure.*
>
> —*Sydney J. Harris*[11]

When you look at some of the most successful high-performers, it might be tempting to say that they were born this way. They're talented, end of story. In fact, talent — while undeniably makes life easier — is but one part of the equation.

I used to be a shy and fearful person. If you compared me, the awkward outsider, with the most successful guys at school, you could say they were born talented to be popular, liked and as alpha male as you could get, while I didn't have such luck.

However, my apparent misfortune turned out to be a source of strength because it provided a spark to introduce big changes in my life. By continuously pushing my comfort zone, I not only overcame social shyness and improved my communication skills, but also developed high self-confidence and overcame other fears in my life.

I might not have been born with the talent to be a "people person" — I still prefer solitude to crowds — but with self-discipline and consistent work, I still achieved astounding results.

Next time, before you complain that you don't have a talent for something or weren't "born this way," remind yourself that self-discipline, in many situations, can more than make up for a lack of inborn traits.

# Day 12: On Calmness of Mind

> *Calmness of mind is one of the beautiful jewels of wisdom. It is the result of long and patient effort in self-control. Its presence is an indication of ripened experience, and of a more than ordinary knowledge of the laws and operations of thought.*
>
> —*James Allen*[12]

If I asked you to show me a symbol of self-discipline, you might think of a Buddhist monk, capable of sitting still for hours on end with an empty mind and only a hint of a smile on his face, content simply to *be*.

Such self-control feels like a superpower in today's busy and fast-moving world, in which distractions lurk at every corner and buzz in every pocket. A person who's capable of maintaining calmness of mind is a rare individual — but fortunately you can also become one, if you're only willing to put in some effort.

Implementing some kind of a meditative practice in your weekly schedule will not only help you increase your self-control and develop more patience, but also reduce your stress and make you feel happier.

The most common practice to learn how to calm your mind is to meditate. However, meditation isn't the only habit that puts you in a meditative state.

The key to developing everyday calmness is focusing your attention on the present moment or on a single activity that you're performing. Engaging in a high-focus sport like yoga, rock climbing, or boxing can be a good way to tap into this state — and so can be something as mundane as gardening, dancing, or knitting.

The more often you put yourself in a meditative state, the calmer you'll become in everyday situations. Cultivating calmness will lead to even more self-control, and that will lead to an ever-heightening ability to control your state of mind and prevent emotions from clouding your judgment.

# Day 13: On What You Want Now and What You Want Most

> Discipline *is* choosing between what you want now and what you want most.
>
> *—Unknown*

If you're on a diet and decide to eat a piece of chocolate, you're deciding that the instant fleeting pleasure is worth it more than your long-term goals.

Obviously, one piece of chocolate doesn't immediately translate to gaining weight, but it sets a precedent that (over the long term) *does* change your body in such a way that it reflects your preference for "what you want now," not "what you want most."

Each time you make a choice that favors instant gratification, your behavior signals that you have weak motivators. If your "reasons why" were strong enough, you'd be less likely to go with what you want *now*.

Imagine a straight line. On one end, there's the satisfaction you get from what you want *now*, and on the other end, there's the satisfaction you'll get from what you want *most*. If the two ends are close to each other — meaning you only want what you want most *a little bit* more than what you want now — you'll have a problem delaying gratification. If, on the other hand, the thing you want most is so much more rewarding than what you want now, you'll have an easier time resisting the temptation.

To achieve your long-term goals, make sure that the satisfaction you get from what you want most is always much stronger than the satisfaction you can get from what you want now.

# Day 14: On Long-Term Focus

*In order to succeed, you must have a long-term focus. Most of the challenges in our lives come from a short-term focus.*

—*Tony Robbins*[13]

I spent several long years starting one business after another, deluding myself that it was possible to build a six-figure business in a few months. Each time I failed to reach this goal, I closed one business and started working on another. Sometimes I worked on two or three ideas at the same time, thinking that one of them would surely succeed.

I would have saved myself a lot of time if I had realized that I had a short-term focus and this attitude had been the very reason why I couldn't accomplish my goals. The moment I switched my mindset to that of being in it for the long haul, things started falling into place.

When I look back at my other goals, I struggled in a similar way due to the same reason.

In fitness, I wanted to build a well-defined physique as quickly as possible. I frequently reduced my daily caloric intake to levels that were impossible to maintain over the long term. In the end, I would have accomplished my goals more quickly by taking a more sustainable approach that would take me a year or two to reach my goal than fooling myself I could reach it in two or three months.

In learning languages, I wanted to learn new words as quickly as possible and soon found myself discouraged from looking at even one more word. I wanted to learn a few dozen words a day, but in the end I would have accomplished more with a routine of learning just 5-10 words a day but maintained and used over years, not just weeks or months.

Analyze your goals and how you approach them. Replace short-term-oriented behaviors with those that show that you're in it for the long haul. Self-discipline isn't limited to rejecting a cake or sticking to an exercise habit; you also need self-discipline to maintain a long-term focus in all of your endeavors.

# WEEK 3

# Day 15: On Constant Improvement

*Knowledge has to be improved, challenged, and increased constantly, or it vanishes.*

—*Peter Drucker[14]*

Just like knowledge, you can't take self-discipline for granted. Unfortunately, being a self-disciplined person isn't a "one and done" kind of thing. Once you have learned how to live that way, you can still lose it if you don't consistently strengthen it by setting new challenges and rejecting instant gratification in favor of bigger future rewards.

Never assume that you're "disciplined enough." There's always a new area in which you can improve your self-control and further expand your comfort zone.

For example, regular exercise poses no challenge for my self-discipline. In order to strengthen it, I need to set bigger and bigger exercise-related challenges for myself.

Instead of focusing on fitness, I can also find a new area in which my discipline is lacking (such as developing more patience when dealing with other people) and focus on improving it until it's no longer a test for my resolve.

Such consistent practice ensures that you're at least *maintaining* your level of self-control, and ideally always getting better at it.

# Day 16: On Self-Reliance

*A man then must stand erect, not be kept erect by others.*

—*Marcus Aurelius*[15]

There's no doubt that surrounding yourself with people who support your goals is helpful. It's easier to exercise with a friend, diet along with your spouse, or belong to a community of frugal people.

However, as Marcus Aurelius says, you need to beware of relying too much on others.

If the only reason why you exercise is because you're doing it with a friend, the moment they drop it, you'll likely revert to the old ways, too.

If you're on a diet only because you want to lose weight to attract this beautiful friend of a friend, the moment you learn they're in a relationship or aren't interested in you, your self-control will be gone.

If you're productive at work only because you're afraid of your boss, how likely will you be to exhibit productivity when they aren't around?

Your motivators should always start with you and your own resolve to make changes. External support can be valuable, but just like a person recovering from an injury isn't fully recovered if they can't stand without a crutch, you aren't self-disciplined enough unless you can still stick to your resolutions even without the help of other people.

# Day 17: On Rising from the Ashes of Failure

> *A setback has often cleared the way for greater prosperity. Many things have fallen only to rise to more exalted heights.*
>
> —*Seneca the Younger*[16]

No matter how self-disciplined you are, there's no escaping the fact that sometimes you'll stumble. Perhaps you'll eat a piece of a cake instead of a salad. Maybe you'll skip a workout out of laziness. It's possible that when your efforts result in a failure, you'll lose the self-discipline to continue and revert back to your old undesirable habits.

It's all par for the course, and the sooner you accept, it, the easier it will be to handle the setbacks once they occur. However, don't consider your failures a useless waste of time and energy; a failure can often present new opportunities or lead to important realizations.

I failed to learn how to play tennis despite putting considerable amount of time, energy, and money into it. However, this made me realize that I wanted to concentrate on rock climbing, and the failure with tennis cleared the way for dramatic improvements in my climbing performance.

When discouraged, remember that all struggles present opportunities that, given enough time, you can convert into successes or lessons that will aid you in other areas of life.

# Day 18: On Higher Standards

> *Hold yourself responsible for a higher standard than anybody else expects of you. Never excuse yourself. Never pity yourself. Be a hard master to yourself — and be lenient to everybody else.*
>
> —*Henry Ward Beecher*[17]

The only standards that should concern you are your own standards. If you act in accordance with the standards of the majority of people, you'll be overweight, unfit, unhealthy, lazy, hating your job, not having enough time for your family, and in debt.

I sometimes get flak for my goals. "You're already slim. Why do you still watch your diet?" "Why do you save so much money? You should live it up!" "Can't you live like a normal person, instead of waking up at 5 a.m. and going to sleep as early as 8 p.m.?"

By the standards of the person criticizing me, I should have stopped improving myself a long time ago. According to *my* standards, the growth should never end. I always hold myself responsible for a higher standard, and this allows me to maintain success-friendly habits in my life and achieve even more success.

If you allow yourself to have low standards, how are you supposed to ever achieve excellence? Exhibiting self-control is one of the most powerful demonstrations of having high standards; letting fleeting emotions and urges control your life — as most people do — is a sure-fire path to mediocrity.

# Day 19: On Fighting Well

> *The important thing in the Olympic Games is not to win, but to take part; the important thing in life is not triumph, but the struggle; the essential thing is not to have conquered but to have fought well.*
>
> —*Pierre de Coubertin*[18]

Nobody will ever give you any grades for your level of self-discipline. There's no finish line and there's no podium for the winners. The only purpose of building self-discipline is to conquer yourself — your own urges, your own weaknesses, and your own self-sabotaging behaviors.

It's easy to forget this fact and assume that when you reach your goals you're done. In fact, the moment you make your dreams come true isn't the most important moment. It's important, no doubt, but without the process leading to it, in itself it means little.

The most important moments are the moments of struggle, when you're striving to fight even when you can barely stand and the whole world is spinning around you. It's this very act that proves your mettle and showers you with life-encompassing benefits, not the act of winning in itself.

Whenever you find yourself frustrated that you're still a long way from the finish line, remember that it's right now, at this very moment, that you're collecting the biggest rewards. It's the struggle in itself that improves you and makes you a more successful person.

# Day 20: On Taking Small Steps

*We should discipline ourselves in small things, and from there progress to things of greater value. If you have a headache, practise not cursing. Don't curse every time you have an earache. And I'm not saying that you can't complain, only don't complain with your whole being.*

—*Epictetus*[19]

Rome wasn't built in a day, and you won't build self-discipline overnight. If you've never been particularly disciplined, start small with easy challenges and then build on top of them.

Epictetus suggests a simple exercise of not complaining when you feel unwell. To make the first step even easier, he says that you don't even have to immediately stop complaining at all — just stop complaining "with your whole being."

Could you do it just for today? Once you successfully go one day without complaining with your whole being, how about two days? Three days? A week? A month? Could you then add other little challenges and consistently strengthen your willpower?

Other simple practices you can implement to begin building more self-discipline include:

- Resisting the temptation to yell in anger when another driver does something that irks you.

- Eating just slightly less than you'd like to eat, like one square of a chocolate or one potato chip less.

- Working for just one minute longer when you're ready to call it a day.

Work on several such little challenges and soon you'll gain more self-control and be able to progress to bigger changes.

# Day 21: On the Importance of Habits

*Success is actually a short race — a sprint fueled by discipline just long enough for habit to kick in and take over.*

—*Gary Keller*[20]

Habits are like magical powers. The moment they kick in, you no longer need more than perhaps a modicum of self-discipline every now and then to continue performing the same action on a regular basis. What originally was extremely difficult to do is now something you largely do automatically, with little thought or willpower.

When something becomes a part of your routine, resistance drops to nearly zero. The challenging part is forming a new habit. Research suggests that it takes anywhere from 18 to 254 days[21] to form a new habit, with 66 days being the average time (not 21 days, as the common knowledge goes).

When working on your goals, remind yourself that it's the first months that will be the hardest. Once the proper habits kick in, things will get easier.

Remember that in the long term, only habits — and their subsequent permanent changes in lifestyle and identity— can ensure lasting success. Consequently, it's key to think in terms of lifelong routines.

As long as you're jumping from one two-week diet to another instead of establishing new nutritional habits, you're destined to regain weight. As long as you're switching between different six-week workout programs to lose some weight — and not thinking of exercise as a permanent part of your weekly routine — sooner or later, you'll revert to inactivity.

Analyze your goals and assess whether your plans employ self-discipline to help you build a habit or if you're using self-control as a means of *temporarily* sustaining an impermanent change.

# WEEK 4

# Day 22: On Self-Discipline as Freedom

*Self-discipline is a form of freedom. Freedom from laziness and lethargy, freedom from the expectations and demands of others, freedom from weakness and fear or doubt. Self-discipline allows a pitcher to feel his individuality, his inner strength, his talent. He is master of, rather than a slave to, his thoughts and emotions.*

—*H. A. Dorfman*[22]

Changing the way you think about self-discipline can help you become more self-disciplined. If you think about it in terms of deprivation and suffering, guess what! You'll never find enjoyment in personal growth, and most likely will soon give up on your endeavors.

On the other hand, a person who thinks of self-discipline as a form of freedom will welcome opportunities to practice his or her self-control.

When facing temptations and fighting hard to not let them enslave you, remember that through letting go of them, you aren't losing anything substantial; the freedom to be a master of your thoughts and emotions is ultimately worth more than any temporary gratification, of which you're depriving yourself.

# Day 23: On Disciplined Education

*To read a newspaper is to refrain from reading something worthwhile. The natural laziness of the mind tempts one to eschew authors who demand a continuous effort of intelligence. The first discipline of education must therefore be to refuse resolutely to feed the mind with canned chatter.*

—*Aleister Crowley*[23]

The way you get information can affect your self-discipline. By getting your news from just one source and blindly believing it, you run the risk of mental laziness. After all, why think about what the provided news really means or whether it's even true in the first place? It's the job of the newspaper or news site, isn't it?

Take advantage of the opportunity to improve your self-discipline by exposing yourself to other points of view and thinking for yourself. It takes work and questioning your beliefs is uncomfortable, which results in a great exercise for your self-discipline.

Another risk lies in defaulting to easy entertainment or avoiding difficult topics. While there's nothing wrong in reading easy books to relax, you miss out if you stay away from more demanding and complex works.

Reading thought-provoking and/or long titles conditions your brain to eschew mental laziness. When a book provides an intellectual challenge and you keep going, you train yourself to stay with problems for as long as necessary to figure them out instead of giving up — and that's a habit that will surely help you in other endeavors, too.

# Day 24: On Happiness Through Self-Discipline

> *It is one of the strange ironies of this strange life that those who work the hardest, who subject themselves to the strictest discipline, who give up certain pleasurable things in order to achieve a goal, are the happiest. When you see 20 or 30 people line up for a distance race in some meet, don't pity them, don't feel sorry for them. Better envy them instead.*
>
> *—Bruce Hamilton*

For a person who has never tested their self-discipline over a long period of time, it's hard to believe that giving up pleasure can lead to immense happiness. Most certainly, it doesn't feel that way when you're fighting against the craving for chocolate, compare exercise to torture, or feel sad that you have to set money aside and can't spend it on this new cool gadget.

However, in the long haul, based on my personal experience, subjecting yourself to a strict discipline *does* lead to a happier life — and it can be a powerful motivator in the moments of doubt.

Let me explain why…

Firstly, as we talked about in Day 1, living your life the hard way makes it easier. People who voluntarily expose themselves to challenges are more capable of handling unforeseen hardships.

Moreover, giving up certain pleasures (such as unhealthy food and sitting all day in front of the TV) can lead to immense improvements in one's well-being. Maintaining a healthy weight and beneficial nutritional habits doesn't just lead to physical improvements; it also affects self-esteem, reduces the risk for depression, and improves your body image[24].

Giving up on pleasurable things (such as spending money without control) can also help you avoid crushing problems in the future. Today it might be inconvenient that you can't spend your entire salary, but tomorrow your savings can save you from bankruptcy or pay for an urgent medical intervention.

Lastly, self-discipline is in itself a manifestation of your higher being, and is connected with nobler strivings. A human being, reduced to its primal form, has little ability for self-control. Operating in "scarcity mode" and left to its own devices, your primal brain will stuff your body until you won't be able to walk. It will make you cheat on your partner with every passing stranger. It will assume that every step outside the comfort zone is a danger, and so you'll never grow.

Exerting self-control is working against the dominance of your primal brain. You forego primal urges in order to reach bigger and more important goals or to cultivate values that are important to you. You can live your life in a way that is congruent with who you are as a deeply complex human being, not a mere animal with the ability to reason. This leads to experiencing a wide variety of experiences that life has to offer; many of them are immensely more gratifying than merely satisfying the most basic human needs.

# Day 25: On Starting Today

*Don't wait for tomorrow to do something you can do today.*

—*Spanish proverb*

Have you been pondering starting on a new goal but are still procrastinating on it? Come up with the easiest, simplest, and quickest action you can take today to initiate momentum.

If you want to stop eating sugar, eliminate all chocolate bars from your house or choose one day a week during which you won't eat sugar in any form. Take it from there, step by step.

If you want to start exercising on a regular basis, do three push-ups and three squats now or any other super quick exercise. Tomorrow, do one more repetition. Find a more suitable workout once you establish the basic habit of *some* exercise — even if it's just a few push-ups a day.

If you want to start saving money, take just one dollar out of your wallet and put it in a jar. Yes, it won't change anything today, but if you add one dollar for the next three months, you'll have saved 100 bucks and established a habit of saving.

There's no excuse to *not* take any of those simple actions now and finally break the chain of procrastination. Don't overthink it and don't obsess over the future; take care of establishing a tiny habit today, and take it from there.

# Day 26: On the Long-Term Consequences of Your Choices

> *Whenever you are presented with a choice, ask yourself which option you would prefer to have taken in ten years.*
>
> —*Erik D. Kennedy*[25]

Self-discipline is largely dependent on your ability to look into the future and imagine yourself not having taken the difficult choice today. If you paint the mental picture with enough detail, you won't be able to bear the thought of letting the situation remain the same or getting worse.

A simple exercise of asking yourself which option you would prefer to have taken in ten years can help you avoid succumbing to temptations. And let's not fool ourselves — it probably won't work every time, but even if it doesn't work every time, at least it will make you pause *sometimes*.

Let's imagine that you're torn between buying a new piece of furniture you don't really need but like a lot, or saving that money for your retirement. In ten years, would you rather have a crumbling piece of furniture you rarely use or — thanks to the power of compounding — twice the amount you're now pondering on spending?

For this technique to work, you need to consider your failure to stick to your resolutions not as a once-off event, but a precedent that can ruin your long-term progress. Otherwise this technique won't work.

For example, if you're on a diet and are tempted to eat this awesome chocolate chip cookie, if you tell yourself that it's simply this one time, obviously in a ten-year timeframe it means nothing. And it's true — one cookie eaten today won't ruin your diet for the next decade.

However, it's not about eating this specific cookie. It's about the precedent it sets and a possible pattern of cheating during a diet that might develop from making this decision. In ten years, would you prefer to have developed a habit of eating cookies while on a diet or established a habit of *not* eating cookies at all, or only on special occasions?

# Day 27: On Following the Wrong Path

> *If something scares you in an excited way, (something that \*gives\* you energy) — that's a good sign.*
>
> BUT IF SOMETHING IS MAKING YOU MISERABLE AND DRAINING YOUR ENERGY, PLEASE STOP.
>
> *Life is telling you that is not the path for you.*
>
> —*Derek Sivers*[26]

When you think about pursuing your goals, you might be tempted to think that the process will be long, arduous, and painful. While it's good to assume that it won't be a walk in the park, there's a danger in equating the journey with being miserable.

Self-discipline is powerful as long as you apply it to the goals you care about— the ones that, even when they are difficult to accomplish, energize you. If, as Derek Sivers points out, your goal is draining your energy, chances are it's better to stop.

For example, I was working on building a company in the Software as a Service industry. I know nothing about programming, and this business not only required some technical knowledge, but also relied heavily on phone sales — something I hate to the core.

My goal to build a successful company was of immense importance to me, but the path I chose was making me so miserable that I hated waking up every morning. I could have pressed on, tapping into the deepest reservoirs of my willpower, but ultimately life was telling me that this path wasn't for me; I made the right decision to cut my losses and sell the business.

# Day 28: On Living in Offensive Mode

> *Life is an ongoing process of choosing between safety (out of fear and need for defense) and risk (for the sake of progress and growth): Make the growth choice a dozen times a day.*
>
> —*Abraham Maslow*[27]

If you're reading this book, you're most likely living in relative abundance, whether you agree with that perception or not.

You have access to some kind of an electronical device for reading, which means you have some disposable income, which means you don't live in extreme poverty. You also most likely don't live in a native tribe somewhere in the jungle or in a small village in the warzone, where survival is a daily challenge.

Consequently, you don't have to live in defense. The negative consequences of your acts, when compared to people who aren't as lucky as you, are in most cases negligible.

You can afford to venture out into the world without the risk that the enemy tribe will kill you. You can risk launching a side business because even if it fails, you'll still have a secure job and perhaps even some savings. You can go on a diet and temporarily restrict caloric intake — I assure you that you won't starve to death.

Analyze the decisions you've taken during the past week and ask yourself whether they were motivated by the need for defense and safety or by the prospect of progress and growth. Make sure that the great majority of your decisions favors some *smart* risk-taking instead of letting the fear stop you dead in your tracks.

# WEEK 5

# Day 29: On Avoiding Effort

> *There is just something wrong with getting up every day and moving through your existence with the least possible effort. If your expectations are always those of someone content to live without physical challenge, then when it comes time for mental, moral, or emotional challenge, you fail to meet it because you are out of practice.*
>
> —*Mark Rippetoe*[28]

I consider physical exercise a fundamental habit for every person who wants to build self-discipline and achieve their goals. Granted, not everyone has the health required for strenuous physical activity, but there's always some kind of effort you can undertake to move your body in a beneficial way.

In addition to obvious health benefits, physical activity provides another immense benefit: it's an exercise in exposing yourself to effort and challenge for the sake of bettering yourself. As Mark Rippetoe states in the quote, living your life without physical challenges makes you rusty when it comes to dealing with other types of challenges — including mental, moral, or emotional challenges that sometimes require more strength than a fitness workout does.

How often do you avoid effort when it would have been beneficial to face it? If you're content to live an easy, effortless life, are you also content to live your life without ever realizing your full potential as a human being that has evolved to thrive in a challenging environment?

# Day 30: On Looking Like a Fool

*You have to look like a fool while you're looking for answers you don't have.*

—*Dan Waldschmidt*[29]

A frequently overlooked aspect of building self-discipline is the fact that if you want to rise above mediocrity, you need to be fine with the fact that you'll undoubtedly make a fool of yourself every now and then.

Perhaps you tell all of your friends that you're going to build a business, but the business goes bankrupt and you lose all of your savings.

Maybe you set a goal to harness the power of your self-discipline to learn public speaking (even though you're terrified of standing in front of the crowds), and then deliver a less than stellar performance.

This is normal — you have to fail your way to the success — but for many people, it's a blow they can't withstand. They might be so harmed by it that they'll do *anything* to avoid future humiliation — including giving up on their goals.

Failure, rejection, and humiliation are anything but pleasant. However, the ability to withstand it and keep going is one of the key differences between successful individuals and those who fail to make their dreams come true.

As disagreeable as it can be, accept that occasionally looking like a fool as a part of the process of becoming a successful person.

Fortunately, the more often you voluntarily expose yourself to rejection, humiliation or failure, the easier it will be to handle the feelings they generate.

# Day 31: On Being "Normal"

*To be "normal" is the ideal aim for the unsuccessful, for all those who are still below the general level of adaptation. But for people of more than average ability, people who never found it difficult to gain successes and to accomplish their share of the world's work — for them the moral compulsion to be nothing but normal signifies the bed of Procrustes — deadly and insupportable boredom, a hell of sterility and hopelessness.*

—Carl Jung[30]

There's nothing "normal" in building self-discipline. Most people avoid all kinds of discomfort and effort. They don't want to experience personal growth because it interferes with them stuffing themselves with French fries, wasting countless hours in front of TV, spending money they don't have on things they don't need, lollygagging at work, and cutting corners whenever they can.

If you want to join the minority of people who *do* possess self-control and strive to strengthen it even further, you'll be considered weird. This means that you need to prepare yourself for potential ridicule, being frowned upon, and not being understood.

It might be hard at first to face so much adversity when all you want to do is to improve yourself. To overcome this situation, get the following fact at the forefront of your mind: "normal" is the ideal for the mediocre, "exceptional" (or, in the words of the unsuccessful, "weird") is the ideal for the high-achievers and trailblazers.

Every time you feel out of sync with the rest of the world, remember that there *are* other people like you. During the challenging times, when're you're stumbling, remind yourself that even when you're failing, you're still forging your own path, something that the vast majority of people will never do. You can enjoy the fruits of your success in a way that they will never experience, and that's why it's worth it to be exceptional. Be exceptional.

# Day 32: On Cultivating Self-Discipline Like a Plant

> *Virtue is not a mushroom, that springeth up of itself in one night when we are asleep, or regard it not; but a delicate plant, that groweth slowly and tenderly, needing much pains to cultivate it, much care to guard it, much time to mature it, in our untoward soil, in this world's unkindly weather.*
>
> —*Isaac Barrow*[31]

If self-discipline were like a mushroom that springs up of itself without the need for a gardener, everybody would possess it. Unfortunately — or fortunately, depending on how you look at it — it's more like a plant that you need to constantly cultivate, or else it withers.

Some people believe that one either possesses a "green thumb" or not — as if one person were born with an inborn talent to care for plants and another not.

In reality, the person with the supposed green thumb is simply more attentive to their plants. They make sure their plants have everything they need to thrive and regularly check up on them to make sure they stay healthy.

Think of self-discipline in the same way. You plant its seeds the moment you decide it's time to stop coasting through life and prioritize long-term rewards over instant gratification. However, this moment is just the very beginning; as in the case of planting the seed for a new flowering plant, there's a lot of time and energy you'll still need to invest to make it bloom. If you want to have a beautiful plant, you can't water it occasionally or move it from one place to another every other week.

Ask yourself: what kind of a gardener am I for my own self-discipline? If your self-control were a plant, how would it look based on how you've been cultivating it the past years?

# Day 33: On Things You Can't Rush

*The bearing of a child takes nine months, no matter how many women are assigned.*

—*Fred Brooks*[32]

Patience and self-discipline are close cousins. If you want to reject instant gratification for the sake of accomplishing your long-term goals, it might take months or years before you receive your big compensation. Without patience, you'll get nowhere.

While sometimes you can force results to come more quickly — by pushing yourself harder and being as diligent as you can during the process— oftentimes things take time and there's no way to rush them, no matter how many resources you apply.

Like pregnancy, some things follow a natural schedule you can't control. If you fail to identify which things cannot be rushed, you might misapply the power of self-discipline and instead of achieving them more quickly, fail to achieve them at all.

For example, a body has a natural limit of how much body fat it can burn during a week without breaking down your muscle. If you try to rush the process by starving yourself, the most likely end result is an unplanned cheat week that will not only take you back to square one, but most likely add some additional body fat to your frame.

Even with things that are difficult to measure, such as learning to control your mind so that you can eventually radiate optimism, you can't force yourself to change overnight. Rewiring your brain takes time, and it doesn't matter how much time you spend meditating or reading books about emotional control; a process that is so profound takes time.

Generally speaking, if it has taken you years or decades to develop a negative trait, don't expect that you can reverse it within weeks or months. Approach such undertakings with the belief that you'll do your best, but that you won't get discouraged or frustrated if the process is slow. It would be as futile as a woman complaining that pregnancy lasts nine months.

# Day 34: On Enlightenment

*Before enlightenment, chopping wood and carrying water. After enlightenment, chopping wood and carrying water.*

—*A Zen saying, attributed to Xinxin Ming*

It's tempting to believe that, after enough time passes, suddenly you'll attain enlightenment and acquire permanent, unbreakable self-control.

In reality, there's no sudden awakening that will happen if you deny temptations for long enough. Just like today you're consciously choosing to reject a chocolate bar so you can enjoy an attractive physique a year from now, a year from now you will still need to reject a chocolate bar to maintain the body you attained.

There are no secret powers that self-disciplined people have somehow attained that give them magical powers to resist temptations.

Despite having built a healthy, fit physique, I still fight — and sometimes fail — to overcome temptations. I still need to make sure my plates are full of satiating, healthy foods so that I don't fill them later on with something less than healthy, yet again. I still need to monitor how much I eat and avoid places where I'm likely to overeat. I still do full-day fasts every now and then to practice self-control that is associated with hunger.

No matter the challenge, I still mostly use the same strategies I'd been using prior to accomplishing my goals. The actions don't change. What changes is the person performing them.

For example, rejecting chocolate today may feel like the greatest punishment in the world. A year from now, rejecting chocolate is simply a fact of life: you want to stay in top shape, so you don't stuff yourself with chocolate on a daily basis.

It will still require self-control, but as long as you diligently exercise your willpower muscle, the temptation will most likely be easier to overcome. And in the end, that's what building self-discipline gives you: an easier life, through voluntarily choosing to live it the hard way.

# Day 35: On the Value of Difficulty

*What we obtain too cheap, we esteem too lightly.*

—*Thomas Paine*[33]

Easy successes may be pleasant, but if they're the only successes you achieve, you'll come to expect quick, effortless results. Then, when life hits you hard with a difficult challenge, you'll lack the mental toughness to overcome it.

Moreover, you'll never appreciate the easy successes as much as the ones that required blood, sweat, and tears.

Does it mean that you should reject easy successes and seek the most difficult ways to accomplish your goals? Of course not.

However, you should make sure that you don't deliberately avoid hardships. Resist the temptation to set your aims low. Scoring exclusively easy wins might feel good, but you're limiting your potential that way.

Over the long term, make sure that you always have at least one big, ambitious and demanding goal in life, as that's where the power of self-discipline shines, where most personal growth happens, and which delivers the greatest feeling of having accomplished something worth doing.

# WEEK 6

# Day 36: On Pushing Your Limits Step by Step

*That day, for no particular reason, I decided to go for a little run. So I ran to the end of the road. And when I got there, I thought maybe I'd run to the end of town. And when I got there, I thought maybe I'd just run across Greenbow County. And I figured, since I run this far, maybe I'd just run across the great state of Alabama. And that's what I did. I ran clear across Alabama. For no particular reason I just kept on going. I ran clear to the ocean. And when I got there, I figured, since I'd gone this far, I might as well turn around, just keep on going. When I got to another ocean, I figured, since I'd gone this far, I might as well just turn back, keep right on going.*

—***Forrest Gump**[34]*

There's no law stating that if you want to build self-discipline, you need to immediately wake up at four in the morning, eat nothing but vegetables and fruits, work productively for 12 hours, seven days a week, and abstain from every pleasure, trying to mimic the life of a medieval ascetic.

Setting aside the fact that most of these habits are not necessary to become self-disciplined, self-control isn't built in one day. You're building it step by step — starting from an easy challenge, and then building on top of it.

Don't feel anxious or guilty that you begin your exercise plan with a 5-minute walk or that you commence your new nutrition plan with a resolution that you'll add one vegetable and subtract one candy bar a day. Try it, see what happens, and if it works out, set a bigger challenge. Nothing else is needed to begin the journey to a new you.

# Day 37: On Initial Resistance

*It is easier to resist at the beginning than at the end.*

—*Leonardo da Vinci*[35]

To avoid procrastination at work, I use a rule I like to call "the zero-second rule": the moment I realize that I'm wasting my time to avoid work, I *immediately* stop whatever unproductive thing I'm doing and start working.

If I let myself ponder whether I want to start working or not, my resistance will only grow, and soon, it will be so difficult to overcome that I may fail to accomplish anything productive for the rest of the day.

This trick works because (like Leonardo da Vinci said) resistance is greatest at the beginning. Once you start performing an unpleasant task and gain some momentum, it's easier to stick to the task than to give up and return to procrastination.

Whenever you catch yourself putting off something unpleasant, act right away and deal with it now. The sooner you act, the sooner you'll be done with it.

For example, I always wash the cookware I used to cook my dinner before I eat my meal. This way I can eat my dinner without the unpleasant thought in the back of my mind that I'll not only have to wash the dishes, but also the pots and pans I used for cooking.

Small habits like that can help establish a habit of choosing to do the hard things now instead of letting all the hard tasks accumulate like a backlog at work. When you adopt this habit, you'll greatly reduce the impact of procrastination on your life — and enjoy more tranquility to boot!

# Day 38: On Moderation as a Good Thing

> *Monks, these two extremes ought not to be practiced by one who has gone forth from the household life. What are the two? There is addiction to indulgence of sense-pleasures, which is low, coarse, the way of ordinary people, unworthy, and unprofitable; and there is addiction to self-mortification, which is painful, unworthy, and unprofitable. Avoiding both these extremes, the Tathagata has realized the Middle Path; it gives vision, gives knowledge, and leads to calm, to insight, to enlightenment and to Nibbana.*
>
> —*Gautama Buddha*[36]

When you set firm resolutions to improve yourself, you might be tempted to push your limits well outside of what you're capable of doing. Ambitiousness is a virtue, but there's danger involved in going from one extreme to another.

If you're currently struggling to be productive, don't force yourself to work sixteen hours a day. If you're struggling to control your appetite, don't impose a week-long fast. If you can't find it in you to choose the stairs over the elevator, don't expect that you'll maintain a workout plan that requires you to work out every single day.

Find the middle path, stick to it for at least several weeks, and then, based on the results you get, decide whether you can further stretch your limits or require more time before advancing.

As much as I believe in pushing your boundaries and exploring the extremes, you don't need to put yourself through mortification to achieve good results. Subjecting yourself to extreme hardships has some merits, but over the long term it's unsustainable, if not downright dangerous.

Remember that there should be moderation in all things, including moderation itself. Sometimes a more extreme approach is needed for a short period of time, and sometimes it's beneficial to set your goals lower. In whatever you do, seek to not spend too much time loafing around, but also make sure that your life hasn't turned into the life of a self-flagellating ascetic.

# Day 39: On Moderation as a Bad Thing

*Sometimes moderation is a bad counselor.*

—*Fausto Cercignani*[37]

In yesterday's entry, we talked about moderation being a good thing. Today we'll approach the topic from a different perspective.

Some people use moderation as an excuse to not do their best, often mistaking mediocrity for moderation.

"Let's call it a day. I've already worked five minutes more than yesterday. You gotta stay in balance."

"Let's stick with the same weight for the next five workouts, even though I can easily lift it. Moderation is key."

"I've already gone down two sizes. I guess I'm still a bit overweight, but let's not forget that going to the extreme is a bad thing."

If you use moderation as an excuse not to push your limits, you're mistaking moderation with mediocrity. If you're trying to lift a weight that you can barely lift off the floor, some moderation will be good for you. If you're lifting it like it's a feather and telling yourself you're still doing great because at least you're exercising, you're letting mediocrity limit your growth.

Sticking to easy things that are well within your grasp isn't moderation.

Equating mediocrity with moderation largely comes down to having low standards. A person who thinks that exercising once a week is incredible because most of his friends only exercise with a TV remote will most likely stop challenging themselves well before it would be wise to remember about moderation.

That's not to say that you should compare yourself to other people; compare yourself to yourself from the past. If today (a year since you started to exercise) you're still performing the same exercises with little to no improvement, perhaps you've confused moderation with self-congratulation.

Moreover (as we've already covered when talking about moderation as a good thing), you should also apply moderation to moderation itself. It's impossible to always follow the middle path.

Sometimes you'll zig and sometimes you'll zag. One day might spend 12 hours working on an important project so that you can spend the entire next day with your family. There's nothing unbalanced in it, as long as you move from an extreme in one thing (like work) to an extreme in another (like family), without staying too long in either one.

# Day 40: On Talking vs. Doing

*It is better to practice a little than talk a lot.*

—*A Zen saying, attributed to Muso Soseki*

Announcing to all of your friends, family members, and colleagues that you're going to change and going deep into details how you're going to do it is useless at best and sabotaging at worst.

Firstly, not everyone will be happy to hear that you want to improve yourself because it will make it painfully obvious that they're lazy or don't have as much courage as you do. Instead of support, you can receive criticism that might make you less likely to act upon your dreams.

Secondly, research suggests that announcing your plans makes you less motivated to accomplish them.[38] By talking about your plans, you get the erroneous satisfaction that you've already taken action to change yourself and consequently, you're less likely to take real action.

If you want to tell your friends about your new goal, choose a person whom you know will support you. In addition, instead of telling them in a self-congratulatory way that you're finally going to achieve your dreams, ask them to hold you accountable if you don't honor your resolution.

# Day 41: On Arrogance

*Receive wealth or prosperity without arrogance; and be ready to let it go.*

—*Marcus Aurelius*[39]

Never take self-discipline for granted or assume that if you can control your urges, you're now invincible.

Humility plays an important role in helping you maintain self-control. An arrogant person will be more likely to unnecessarily test their willpower, which will eventually lead to their downfall. This happens because of the restraint bias — the tendency for people to overestimate how capable they are of controlling impulsive behaviors.

Research shows that people who had an inflated belief in their self-control overexposed themselves to temptations, such as recovering smokers putting themselves in situations tempting them to smoke, which increased the risk of a relapse.[40]

Assume that your self-discipline is like prosperity. It's possible that it will stay with you for a long time, but it's also possible that it will disappear. Consequently, you'll work harder to keep it in your life. If it does go away when you make some mistakes, you'll accept it with more tranquility and be more likely to regain it quickly.

# Day 42: On Diligent Practice

*You can know how to win through strategy with the long sword, but it cannot be clearly explained in writing. You must practise diligently in order to understand how to win.*

—*Miyamoto Musashi*[41]

Reading hundreds of books, blog posts, articles, and watching countless videos on self-discipline isn't going to automatically reprogram your brain so that one day you'll wake up with the self-control of a samurai.

The intention behind this book is to offer you quick, interesting tidbits related to self-discipline that you can easily act upon. No matter how detailed my writings are, you'll always learn more by taking one little action than by reading ten of my books or re-reading the same book over and over again.

For example, I can *tell* you that the greatest amount of willpower is needed during the first few minutes of an uncomfortable task, such as taking a cold shower. Once a couple of minutes pass, your body will adapt to the challenge and it gets easier to handle.

But that's just me talking. Go and actually take an ice-cold shower. *Experience* the wild emotions, start shivering, *feel* the overpowering temptation to turn on hot water, and wonder if you can last even a second longer, and then — two or three minutes later — feel your body start to relax, with the ice-cold water no longer feeling like the worst torture in the world. Then step out the shower feeling, elated that you managed to overcome your weakness of will.

The next time you face an uncomfortable situation, tap into your real-world experience — not mere words read in a book — to realize that, just like with an ice-cold shower, you can adapt to this situation, as well.

# WEEK 7

# Day 43: On Making Continuous Efforts

*Genius is often only the power of making continuous efforts. The line between failure and success is so fine that we scarcely know when we pass it — so fine that we are often on the line and do not know it. How many a man has thrown up his hands at a time when a little more effort, a little more patience, would have achieved success. As the tide goes clear out, so it comes clear in. In business sometimes prospects may seem darkest when really they are on the turn. A little more persistence, a little more effort, and what seemed hopeless failure may turn to glorious success. There is no failure except in no longer trying. There is no defeat except from within, no really insurmountable barrier save our own inherent weakness of purpose.*

—*Elbert Hubbard*[42]

I'm an avid rock climber. In rock climbing, particularly when climbing long routes, your forearms can get pumped to such an extent that you can no longer hold onto the rock. Climbers afraid of failing will often ask their belayer to take in the rope so that they can rest and try again with renewed strength.

While this strategy is good for learning how to climb a difficult route, sometimes it costs a climber an on-sight (a clean ascent with no prior practice of the route) or a redpoint (completing a route without resting on the rope) because they give up too quickly, right after they start feeling overpowering discomfort.

Even when you can barely hold onto the wall, often you can still perform one or two moves more — and those moves may be enough to upgrade your position to a rest stance where you can safely recharge and continue climbing without resting on the rope.

It's the same with many other areas of life. You believe that you can't go on any longer, that your self-discipline has run out and it's time to throw up your hands in defeat, while in reality, persisting just a little bit longer is all that separates you from success.

The next time you feel like giving up, persuade yourself to push a little bit longer. Chances are, success is right around the corner.

# Day 44: On Optimism

*Optimism is the faith that leads to achievement; nothing can be done without hope.*

*—Helen Keller[43]*

A positive attitude is essential if you want to build self-discipline. What's the point of denying yourself instant gratification if you don't believe that you'll get a greater compensation for it in the future?

If you suffer from pessimism, realize that along with improving your self-control, you'll need to improve your ability to see the world in brighter colors. Three easy steps you can take today to become more optimistic include:

1. Express gratitude for what you already have. If you can't be happy with what you have today, you won't be happy with what you have tomorrow.

2. Reframe negative events into opportunities and lessons. An event is bad for you only if you decide it is. Think of it as a lesson or an opportunity to change your life, in order to give it a positive meaning.

3. Surround yourself with positive input. If you only read fear-mongering news and hang out with pessimistic grumblers, you'll have a hard time exhibiting optimism.

# Day 45: On Honesty

*I hope I shall possess firmness and virtue enough to maintain what I consider the most enviable of all titles, the character of an honest man.*

—*George Washington*[44]

For many people, one of the hardest challenges for their self-discipline is the resolution to stop lying. We constantly encounter opportunities to lie, wherever we go and whatever we do. It seems it's even socially permissible to lie a little, whether by telling a white lie, making yourself look better on a resume, or tweaking your height, weight, and financial situation on online dating sites.

As the old saying goes, honesty is the best policy — and it's also one of the best ways to strengthen your character. It's one thing to deny yourself a piece of cake, and it's a completely different thing to tell the truth when you think it will make you look bad or threaten the relationship you have with someone. Yet, over the long-term, the truth always emerges — and if not, it still eats away at your conscience, so why postpone the discomfort you'll eventually feel anyway?

Vow to tell the truth no matter the circumstances (except for extreme situations, such as your life being in danger).

Please note that being honest doesn't mean that you need to share everything about yourself with other people. that Telling them, "I don't feel like answering that question" (without giving any justifications — it's your right to not explain any of your decisions) is a simple way to remain honest when a person asks you a question you'd normally answer with a lie.

# Day 46: On Looking Fear in the Face

*You gain strength, courage and confidence by every experience in which you really stop to look fear in the face. You are able to say to yourself, "I lived through this horror. I can take the next thing that comes along." (...) You must do the thing you think you cannot do.*

—*Eleanor Roosevelt*[45]

Self-discipline is a lot like dealing with fear. When you face temptations, look them straight in the eye and send them packing, the next time they appear in your life, you'll be able to say to yourself, "I managed to overcome them once. I can handle them this time as well."

The more times you successfully overcome the temptations, the easier it will be to handle them again. Regular practice will make you less susceptible to temptations and even more likely to ignore them, just like looking fear in the face will make you more likely to act in spite of it.

Granted, it's not that with enough experience, you'll become unconditionally self-disciplined, just like you won't one day stop being afraid of anything. Just remember that each situation that tests your resolve is another experience from which you can draw inspiration to overcome future challenging circumstances when they occur.

# Day 47: On the Folly of Loafing Around

*The loafer believes he is enjoying life, but sooner or later he must face disillusion.*

—*Fausto Cercignani*[46]

Since self-discipline shines in the long term, and often doesn't seem to provide any benefits in the short term, you may be tempted to believe that people who are loafing around have it better.

While you're watching your finances like a hawk, they spend money they don't have and show off with all the new cool gadgets.

While you're eating a salad and washing it down with a cup of green tea, they're eating a bag of delicious potato chips and gulping down sugary cans of Coke.

While you feel like throwing up during your workout from trying to to squeeze out one more rep, they squeeze more mayo out of the bottle to put it on the French fries they gorge on while watching their favorite TV shows.

It might seem they have it better, but sooner or later the person exposing himself or herself to discomfort for the sake of achieving their long-term goals will come out on top, while the people loafing around will get to feel the negative consequences of their laziness.

Irresponsible spenders will realize they're on the brink of bankruptcy. Potato chip addicts will be diagnosed with diabetes. The inactive TV fans will start taking hypertension medication.

You, on the other hand, will look back at your past sacrifices and smile, happy that you've never succumbed to the temptation to take it easy and loaf around.

# Day 48: On the Deadening of the Soul

> *Most of us dread the deadening of the body and will do anything to avoid it. About the deadening of the soul, however, we don't care one iota.*
>
> —*Epictetus*[47]

It's curious that millions of people all over the world spend countless amounts of money and time to improve their appearance through the use of cosmetics, plastic surgery, expensive clothes, supplements, and other treatments, but spend little to nothing on improving themselves on the inside.

It's more important to avoid wrinkles than to prevent negative habits from forming. It's a better investment to fix your sagging cheeks than to learn how to exercise restraint in unnecessary spending. Nobody will comment or even notice your deterioration of mental toughness and a growing preference for complacency over growth, but everybody will praise you for your new clothes. $10 for a book that can change your life is too expensive. $100 for another pair of jeans is a screaming deal.

Your spending habits — including spending in the monetary sense and the investment of energy or time — reveal your true priorities.

How much do you spend on your external appearance, and how much do you expend on developing your inner world? Is the proportion healthy, or do you find it hard to justify spending for personal growth, but never fail to invest in your superficial appearance?

# Day 49: On Obeying Lusts

*Bad men obey their lusts as servants obey their masters.*

—*Diogenes Laertius*[48]

A forbidden fruit is the sweetest. If it weren't so pleasant to submit to your urges, nobody would ever struggle with self-discipline.

However, notwithstanding how much pleasure it can bring, it's important to see the temptation for what it is — your enemy on the path toward freedom.

Obeying your lusts enslaves you, while rejecting them increases your freedom. The reward you'll get for not succumbing to your temptations will more than make up for the price you pay today for missing out on the instant gratification.

Self-disciplined people may appear to some as if they were the ones being enslaved. After all, they're the ones whose lives are so limited: they don't get to eat junk food, they follow a strict routine, deliberately expose themselves to discomfort, and reject what society considers the spice of life — gluttony, laziness, and engaging in other vices.

What the critics fail to see is that, through the rejection of those temptations, the self-disciplined become the masters of their lives. They serve the goals chosen by themselves instead of fleeting, spontaneous temptations. They choose to forego temporary satisfactions for deeper, more lasting ones later on.

In the meantime, in the long haul, the people who fail to control their urges — or rather, don't even try to control them — fail to control their lives, manipulated by the temptations like a marionette.

# WEEK 8

# Day 50: On Not Resting on Your Laurels

*I think if you do something and it turns out pretty good, then you should go do something else wonderful, not dwell on it for too long. Just figure out what's next.*

—*Steve Jobs*[49]

To be human is to grow, challenge yourself, and strive to always become better. It's important to celebrate your triumphs, but dwelling on them for too long can lead to resting on your laurels and jeopardizing your future growth.

After you're done celebrating your success, figure out what your next challenge is. How can you take your life to an even higher level?

For example, if you've successfully lost weight, now is a good time to gain some muscle or improve your nutritional habits. If you've put your financial life in order by building a small nest egg, it's a good opportunity to take it one step further and work on achieving financial independence.

Treat wonderful accomplishments as opportunities to accomplish even more wonderful things, and not as permission to become lazy.

# Day 51: On Taking Action, in Spite of Potential Criticism

*People who say it cannot be done should not interrupt those who are doing it.*

—*Unknown*

Some people don't want to start exercising because they're afraid that others will laugh at their inability to perform a pushup or run for more than sixty seconds without losing their breath. They might be afraid that their friends will talk behind their backs, taking bets when they're going to fail.

Thousands of people all over the world dream of entrepreneurship, but are afraid to take the first step because if their business fails, their ego will suffer too hard of a blow.

Self-discipline isn't only about forcing yourself to do things that are unpleasant for the sake of long-term goals. It's also about resisting the temptation to stay mediocre in order to avoid criticism. True, staying in your comfort zone is safe and there's little criticism you'll encounter along the way. However, there's a high price associated with this choice: you won't ever get to change your current situation.

Over the long term, how important is it really that some unintelligent meathead smirks at you at the gym when you're struggling to complete a set of pushups? Is the momentary pain of that really greater than the pain of regret when you realize that another year has passed without you acting on your goals?

# Day 52: On Thinking for Yourself

*When I meet someone, I consider how normal their life is. I do this not because it's a one hundred percent accurate heuristic on how much I'll respect someone, but because it's damn close. If you have a totally normal life, then there are only two possibilities: you've thought through every aspect of your life and miraculously agree with society on each one, or you don't think at all. I try not to associate with people who don't think.*

—*Tynan*[50]

Self-discipline is hard to attain, and because it's not common, sooner or later somebody will deem your behaviors abnormal.

I maintain a healthy weight and physique, but I still fast for 16 to 20 hours daily, and abstain from food for 36 hours or more every several weeks.

My relationship with food is often criticized by other people. If I don't stuff my face with food every three hours, then surely I've developed an eating disorder. The norm is to eat often, and if your behavior differs from it, you're weird. However, I do what I consider to be best for me, and I refuse to follow different eating habits merely because it's the most common way of doing things.

It's difficult to trust your own judgment when everybody around you is doing something different, but if everything you do is in accordance with society's norms, then what you're going to get is the same results as everybody else does who follows those norms.

So what if others think it's weird that you'd rather save money instead of buying a new car every two years? You're the one who has less financial stress, even if it costs you a little to reject the temptation to spend money unnecessarily.

So what if you're not partying every weekend like everybody else and instead work hard to grow your business? You're the one who will eventually enjoy wealth, while those others will complain about their finances for the rest of their lives.

So what if people consider you weird because you go to sleep at nine and wake up at five in the morning, while they stay up until two in the morning watching TV shows? It's you who's going to get more done by ten in the morning than they'll accomplish in the entire week!

Trust your own judgment and think for yourself. It's better to suffer from your own choices than waste your life away because you were mindlessly following the herd.

# Day 53: On Having a Burning "Yes" Inside

> *You have to decide what your highest priorities are and have the courage — pleasantly, smilingly, non-apologetically — to say "no" to other things. And the way to do that is by having a bigger "yes" burning inside.*
>
> <div align="right">—<i>Stephen Covey</i></div>

Without the bigger "yes" burning inside of you, there's no way you'll continue making the uncomfortable choices over the long term for the sake of your goal.

The primary reason why I stuck to entrepreneurship, despite countless failures, was my intention to help my parents build a house in the countryside. It was their dream, and by extension, *my* dream.

This big "yes" had been burning inside me no matter what was happening with my business. Even after another big defeat, I still knew that I would never "lay down my arms" in the fight to become able to give them their dream. If you have such a strong "yes" inside you, you'll also refuse to surrender the fight to achieve *your* dream.

Your burning "yes" will also help you pinpoint your priorities and disregard distractions. For example, if you decided to save money for the future education of your child, saying "no" to spending money on things you'd like to have (but don't need) would be much easier than without such a powerful motivator. You would be focused on the long-view of where you wanted to be when your child was older.

If your biggest dream in life is to become a surgeon, you won't feel apprehensive about declining an invitation for a party because you want to prepare yourself for an important exam. The "yes" burning inside you would be stronger than the fear of missing out on a few hours spent drinking with your friends.

Granted, as we've already discussed, there should be some balance in everything, but generally speaking, you'll do well if you can discover a burning reason why you want to accomplish a given dream and unapologetically say no to anything that might threaten your chances of making it come true.

# Day 54: On Underestimating the Long-Term Approach

*We always overestimate the change that will occur in the next two years and underestimate the change that will occur in the next ten. Don't let yourself be lulled into inaction.*

—*Bill Gates*[51]

Bill Gates' quote refers to the evolution of personal computing, but the world of self-discipline isn't any different.

A staggering number of people give up on their goals just weeks or months into them, discouraged that they *still* haven't reached their goals or that their results are lackluster.

Sorry to have to break it to you, but the world doesn't work that way. With few exceptions, nobody can build a successful business in six months, achieve a perfect physique in three months, learn a new language in four weeks, or become a self-disciplined person overnight.

However, the sky is the limit for those who are in it for the long haul. Ten years of dedicated practice can turn anyone into a world-class expert. When you gain momentum, you'll get exponential results. The trick is to stick to your goals long enough for the velocity to accrue.

For example, in the first year you might only get your business off the ground, but in its third or fourth year it can explode virtually overnight. What actually happens is not an overnight success, but a process that took place over several years, during which it built upon itself in an exponential way.

When you look at my catalog of books, you might be tempted to say that I succeeded right away. "Martin's first book became a bestseller, so it's possible to become a bestselling author in a few months."

That would be a great example of overestimating what you can achieve in a short period of time. My first book wasn't actually my first book. I'd been writing — articles, blog posts, books, etc. — for a long time before I started writing about self-discipline. It was a process of well over ten years that resulted in my becoming a bestselling author.

Whenever setting a new goal, take the long-term approach. Unlike the person who assumes that their world can change overnight, be in it for the long haul, and the short-term fluctuations won't make you give up.

# Day 55: On Bearing Misfortunes Nobly

*Remember too on every occasion which leads thee to vexation to apply this principle: not that this is a misfortune, but that to bear it nobly is good fortune.*

—*Marcus Aurelius*[52]

Hardships are a part of life and while nobody (with the exception of masochists) enjoys pain, they can be valuable because they present an opportunity for personal growth.

I like to say that you discover how deep your self-discipline goes when you struggle, and not when everything goes well.

You aren't self-disciplined because you worked hard when you were fired up to work. You're self-disciplined when you *continue* to work hard when the last thing you want to do is work.

You aren't self-disciplined because you can't afford candy, so you don't eat it. You exhibit self-control when you deny the treats that are offered freely to you, for example when you're at a party with a buffet selection of high-calorie snacks.

You aren't self-disciplined when you wake up early in the morning to work on your new business. You're self-disciplined when you *still* wake up early in the morning when it seems that your business is going nowhere.

Misfortunes aren't fun to deal with, but bearing them nobly strengthens your ability to handle even worse circumstances in the future. In a sense, trials and tribulations are like training. You may not enjoy it, but you know that eventually it will pay off and more than recoup for any suffering you're going through at the moment.

# Day 56: On Thinking You Can

*If you think you are beaten, you are;*
*If you think you dare not, you don't.*
*If you'd like to win, but think you can't,*
*It's almost certain you won't.*
*If you think you'll lose, you're lost,*
*For out in the world we find*
*Success begins with a fellow's will.*
*It's all in the state of mind.*
*If you think you're outclassed, you are;*
*You've got to think high to rise.*
*You've got to be sure of yourself before*
*You can ever win a prize.*
*Life's battles don't always go*
*To the stronger or faster man.*
*But soon or late the man who wins*
*Is the one who thinks he can.*

—*Walter D. Wintle*[53]

We often limit ourselves because we don't think we can achieve something. Today it may be hard for you to imagine that you can live without dessert or that you can live below your means. It doesn't mean it's impossible, though; it's only your subjective *opinion*, not a fact of life.

Moreover, thinking that you're unlikely to win means that you'll put in less effort than you could. Why would you work your fingers to the bone if you were uncertain of success?

Rock climbing has made it particularly clear to me. When you approach the route thinking that it's beyond your abilities, you won't do your best. After all, why try your best if you know that you aren't going to climb it anyway?

You'll most likely give up when you encounter the first obstacle, while a person thinking they *can* climb it will fight as hard as they can to keep climbing. In the end, the person that doesn't believe in their abilities will give up along the way while the person that is certain of their abilities will reach the top.

Periodically try things that you think are outside of your ability with a positive attitude and the belief that you can succeed. Chances are you'll get a positive surprise and achieve something you thought was beyond your reach.

# WEEK 9

# Day 57: On Two Types of Happiness

> *People who have high levels of what is known as eudaimonic well-being — the kind of happiness that comes from having a deep sense of purpose and meaning in life (think Mother Teresa) — showed very favorable gene-expression profiles in their immune cells. They had low levels of inflammatory gene expression and strong expression of antiviral and antibody genes.*
>
> *However, people who had relatively high levels of hedonic well-being — the type of happiness that comes from consummatory self-gratification (think most celebrities) — actually showed just the opposite. They had an adverse expression profile involving high inflammation and low antiviral and antibody gene expression.*
>
> —*Mark Wheeler*[54]

Science suggests that the fleeting happiness you get from succumbing to a temptation is inferior — at least when it comes to its effect on how your genes express — to the type of happiness you can draw out of a sense of purpose and meaning in life.

According to the study, a person guided by a deep sense of purpose is less likely to suffer from inflammation and more likely to have a stronger immune system. While both types of happiness can generate the same positive emotions, it's those with high levels of eudaimonic well-being that benefit more.

Since the results come from a study on just 80 participants, we shouldn't treat the conclusions as a broadly-applicable scientific fact. However, there's definitely immense power in having a mission in your life.

When all of your decisions are aligned toward a better future (even if you're suffering at times because things don't go as planned or it's hard to maintain self-discipline), you wake up fired up, with vigor and a sense of purpose you'd never get if you were to prioritize hedonic well-being.

# Day 58: On Cultivating Physical Excellence

*For in everything that men do the body is useful; and in all uses of the body it is of great importance to be in as high a state of physical efficiency as possible.*

*Why, even in the process of thinking, in which the use of the body seems to be reduced to a minimum, it is matter of common knowledge that grave mistakes may often be traced to bad health. And because the body is in a bad condition, loss of memory, depression, discontent, insanity often assail the mind so violently as to drive whatever knowledge it contains clean out of it.*

*But a sound and healthy body is a strong protection to a man, and at least there is no danger then of such a calamity happening to him through physical weakness: on the contrary, it is likely that his sound condition will serve to produce effects the opposite of those that arise from bad condition. And surely a man of sense would submit to anything to obtain the effects that are the opposite of those mentioned in my list.*

*Besides, it is a disgrace to grow old through sheer carelessness before seeing what manner of man you may become by developing your bodily strength and beauty to their highest limit.*

—*Socrates*[55]

Socrates points out that there are several dangers in not cultivating physical excellence.

First, an unhealthy body leads to an unhealthy mind. Can a person suffering from preventable health disorders dedicate all of their resources toward personal growth? Physical debilitations that you can overcome with your own efforts (such as obesity or a weak immune system due to bad nutritional habits) sap your energy and limit your potential.

If you're constantly getting sick, how likely are you to maintain self-discipline? I don't know about you, but whenever I get so sick that I can barely walk around the house, my routine is out of the window and it takes a considerable amount of time to return to it. The more often you get sick, the more difficult it is to build new habits and maintain successful routines.

Second, a strong body is better prepared — both physically and mentally — to deal with any health problems that you can't prevent. Consequently, you can more quickly recover from those hardships (or accept them with more ease) and refocus your efforts on your most important long-term goals.

Last but most definitely not least, developing your body to your own highest limit (which doesn't mean becoming a muscle head or having a perfectly sculpted body) is a valuable goal in itself. It shows you how much you can push your limits, teaches you how powerful long-term dedication can be, and can transform your entire mindset. In fact, just cultivating physical excellence on its own can develop powerful self-discipline.

I can attest to these benefits. When I started exercising and my body began to change, I soon saw my mental state reflect the positive external changes. A great amount of the experience I have had with overcoming temptations and sticking to my resolutions comes from physical activity and my resolve to become the strongest person I can.

If you aren't putting your health and fitness first, it's high time you change that.

# Day 59: On Your Vices Masquerading as Virtues

> *No vice exists which does not pretend to be more or less like some virtue, and which does not take advantage of this assumed resemblance.*
>
> Jean de La Bruyère[56]

Bad habits are so difficult to give up not only because they're pleasant, but also because they often masquerade as virtues. When you think of your vice as a friend rather than your enemy, it's even harder to eliminate it from your life.

For example, people who sleep in and suffer from low productivity might claim that, thanks to staying up late, they have a great social life. They fail to notice they're paying too high a price for a benefit they could obtain in a different way without jeopardizing their long-term goals.

I used to believe that it was good to jump from one business idea to another. I thought that by trying different things, I would eventually find the perfect idea that would magically grow into a successful business.

In reality, I lacked the self-discipline to focus and wasted several years on endeavors that were destined to fail. Were there some benefits in spreading my attention so thin? Certainly. They weren't more valuable than what I was losing, though, and what I considered a virtue was actually a vice that was sabotaging my goals.

Are there any vices of yours that might masquerade as virtues? Question your deeply-held beliefs and ask yourself if your supposed virtues are indeed helpful, or perhaps they're like a friend that gives you one dollar with one hand while stealing five dollars from your wallet with the other.

# Day 60: On Pressing On

*Nothing in the world can take the place of persistence. Talent will not; nothing is more common than unsuccessful men with talent. Genius will not; unrewarded genius is almost a proverb. Education will not; the world is full of educated derelicts. Persistence and determination are omnipotent. The slogan "press on" has solved and always will solve the problems of the human race.*

—*Calvin Coolidge*

When in doubt, press on. It sounds obvious and trite, yet the simple fact of life that people who are persistent are usually more successful than less-determined geniuses often escapes us. Time heals all wounds, and time — or rather, persistence that is exercised over a long period of time — also leads to success.

In the world of self-publishing, many authors are extremely talented, but they fail to achieve success because they give up after releasing one or two flops. Meanwhile, the ones who initially lack writing skills or formal education but keep on going, writing one book after another until one finally succeeds, are the ones who occupy the bestseller lists.

People who can speak foreign languages aren't born with a gene that allows them to acquire them quickly. Most of them aren't smarter than you or me, yet they manage to master several languages, including the ones that are thought to be almost impossible to learn by a foreigner. Their secret lies in persistence. If you learn 10 new words a day, you learn 3650 words a year. Consequently, within a few years you'll possess an extensive vocabulary — all thanks to a small, daily time investment that doesn't require any special talents or being a genius.

If you're currently struggling with your goal, remind yourself that even if you feel like you're lost in a maze, pressing on will eventually help you reach your destination and in many cases, it's the only thing that separates the winners from the losers.

# Day 61: On Extreme Actions

*You don't get extreme talent, fame, or success without extreme actions.*

—*Derek Sivers*[57]

It's important to approach your goals in a sustainable way, thinking in terms of months, years, or decades instead of mere days or weeks. However, at the same time, taking extreme actions can pay handsome dividends, too.

Balancing between the extreme and more sustainable approach is a difficult art, but in essence it comes down to taking extreme actions during a relatively brief period of time, while ensuring that your actions are sustainable over the long term.

For example, when my first book became a bestseller, I stuck to a strict publication schedule to benefit from the gained momentum. I launched my second book (on which I had been working since I finished the first draft of my first book) a mere three weeks later. My third book went live in another two weeks, and my fourth was released three weeks after the previous one.

From there, I slowed down my pace, but I still managed to release at least four new books each year. In the short term, my actions were extreme. And precisely because of that, I was able to build a large following quickly. However, after an initial sprint, you need to slow down to go the distance— and that's when I transitioned to a little less extreme approach, but one still exhibited by few authors.

Are you taking extreme actions to gain momentum and separate yourself from the ones who don't have the self-discipline needed to push themselves hard for a short period of time? How can you intensify your efforts for a couple of weeks or months to maximize your results before transitioning to a more sustainable and less extreme approach?

# Day 62: On Moonshot Projects

*We choose to go to the Moon in this decade and do the other things, not because they are easy, but because they are hard.*

—*John F. Kennedy*[58]

As we've already discussed several times, living your life the hard way makes it paradoxically easier, while avoiding the hard things makes your life more difficult.

When it comes to accomplishing your goals, the hard truth is that easy accomplishments often go away quickly, while larger projects produce more lasting results.

For one, setting close to impossible goals requires you to think in categories producing pivotal differences, and not mere tweaks.

For example, losing 5 pounds (or 2 kilos) requires a small tweak. You can eat less for two weeks and you'll accomplish your goal. However, you won't fix the underlying issue of being overweight, and probably soon regain the weight.

How about losing 50 pounds (or 20 kilos) this year? You can no longer afford to think in terms of small tweaks. You need a permanent change — a change in your habits and identity that will address the *cause* of the problem and lead to a permanent solution.

Audacious goals can also transform your life, while reaching safe, easy objectives won't change much in the grand scheme of things.

If you want to save a million dollars for retirement, you'll need a different strategy than if you only want to save enough for a rainy-day fund. A moonshot project of building a $1 million nest egg might lead you to building a business that will not only generate a million dollars for retirement, but also help you retire early — a pleasant side effect you initially didn't anticipate at all.

As an additional benefit, big goals are more motivating, which means you'll be less likely to give up when you encounter obstacles. Granted, you need to pursue the hard things in a smart way so that you won't find yourself walking with your head in the clouds. Set an audacious goal, but accompany it with a realistic deadline. An ambitious goal is still a big accomplishment, even if it takes you years to achieve it.

# Day 63: On the Will Being Stronger Than the Skill

*Champions aren't made in gyms, champions are made from something they have deep inside them — a desire, a dream, a vision. They have to have last-minute stamina, they have to be a little faster, they have to have the skill and the will. But the will must be stronger than the skill.*

—*Muhammad Ali*[59]

When you switch your focus from instant gratification toward long-term accomplishment, create a mental image of why you should reject the instant rewards and keep going — despite hardships, failures, sacrifices, and lack of compensation.

A detailed vision of your wished-for future will fuel your resolve, compensating for any weaknesses you might have or difficulties that might stand on your way toward success.

For example, I struggled with extreme shyness as a teenager. I set a goal to develop self-confidence and feel relaxed in all kinds of social settings. I was, and still am, an introverted lone wolf who needs solitude more than I need other people.

However, my will was strong. I knew I needed to make this change in order to stop limiting my personal growth, something I found and still find is one of my most important values. This deep desire kept me going, despite my personality being extremely unsuited to social settings.

Note that your deep desire doesn't have to be about you. You've surely heard stories about people performing incredible feats of strength to rescue a victim of an accident. For example, in 2013 in Oregon, teenage sisters Hanna (age 16) and Haylee (age 14) lifted a 3,000-pound (1360 kg) tractor to save their father, who was pinned underneath it.[60]

The mechanism that supports such impossible actions still baffles scientists. We only know one thing for sure: under normal circumstances, Hanna and Haylee wouldn't be able to lift a tractor. It was their will — their immense desire to save their father — that gave them superhuman strength.

If you're struggling with a certain goal, think who could benefit from you achieving it. How could you improve somebody's life — or perhaps even save a life — thanks to persevering and accomplishing your objective?

# WEEK 10

# Day 64: On Seeing Obstacles as Hurdles

> *If we choose to see the obstacles in our path as barriers, we stop trying. If we choose to see the obstacles as hurdles, we can leap over them. Successful people don't have fewer problems. They have determined that nothing will stop them from going forward.*
>
> —*Ben Carson*[61]

One might argue that it's mere semantics — barriers or hurdles; both make it difficult to reach success. However, thinking of a problem as a *hurdle* means approaching it as something that you can possibly walk around or leap over, but a *barrier* sounds like something that is impermeable and a fixed limitation.

Nobody likes to face obstacles, but it's thanks to the obstacles you face today that you gain the ability to overcome other hardships in the future — ones that would possibly crush you if it weren't for the experience you're having today.

Problem-solving skills are exactly that — skills. The more often you encounter problems and resolve them, the better you'll get at dealing with them.

For this reason, as a great exercise for building self-discipline and mental resilience, I strongly suggest exposing yourself to difficult tasks. Embrace problems in your life and look at dealing with difficulties as training yourself to see problems as hurdles instead of barriers.

Exert willpower to deal with the hard problems, instead of looking for the easiest way out. Consider several ways to tackle the issue and try to visualize how each solution can help you leap over the hurdle. You don't necessarily have to throw problems at yourself from every direction; you can also practice by helping your friends solve their problems or by imagining you're facing the problems you're reading about in a book or seeing in a TV show.

Just for practice, imagine that you were about to launch your business when a key investor backed out, leaving you $20,000 short of the budget necessary to produce the first line of your product. To make matters worse, you've already accepted payments from your first clients and need to deliver within two months. Most people would consider it an impermeable barrier. Game over, say goodbye to your dreams. You, as a mentally resilient and self-disciplined person will look at it as a hurdle. What can you do to leap over it and keep going, despite such a difficulty being thrown in your way?

# Day 65: On Self-Discipline with Money

*Try to save something while your salary is small; it's impossible to save after you begin to earn more.*

—*Jack Benny*

Whenever the topic of winning the lottery comes up in a conversation, I always say that what so many people consider the biggest blessing in their entire lives is actually the biggest curse for most people. Let me explain why, but first, some curious facts…

The numbers are terrifying. According to 2015 research from The Pew Charitable Trusts, 41 percent of respondents don't have enough liquid savings to cover an unexpected $2,000 cost (such as a medical emergency) and a typical household can't replace even one month of income with liquid savings.[62]

It's important to note we aren't talking about people living in poverty; the same respondents are the ones buying new homes, cars, TVs, smartphones, and other gadgets. The reason for their lack of savings isn't lack of income; it's lack of self-discipline.

While a small percentage of respondents probably do exercise some kind of financial self-control, a great majority doesn't. What do you think? How likely would they be to exercise self-discipline with money upon winning the lottery if they can't manage their finances now? Even if they won millions of dollars, later on they would be in the same spot as they are today — if not in an even worse situation. That's why winning the lottery — the dream of so many — can actually be the biggest curse.

For this reason, no matter how well off you are today, it's of crucial importance to start saving your money now if you aren't doing so already. It doesn't matter if you're saving ten dollars or ten thousand dollars a month; it's the habit that counts. When your financial situation improves (and as a person interested in building self-discipline, it most likely will), it will ensure that you continue exerting self-control with money.

If you're lacking such a habit today, don't fool yourself into thinking you'll control your finances when you start making more. Build healthy financial habits when you have little disposable income, and saving money will be easier when you'll have more money to save. And if you *do* win the lottery, you'll thank me for encouraging you to instill financial discipline today!

# Day 66: On Pointless Complaints

*"But my nose is running!" What do you have hands for, idiot, if not to wipe it? "But how is it right that there be running noses in the first place?" Instead of thinking up protests, wouldn't it be easier just to wipe your nose?*

—*Epictetus*[63]

Grumbling about everything is a favorite pastime of countless individuals, all over the world. It's incredible how much time and energy people waste on something as pointless as complaining, particularly when they can do nothing about their source of protests.

It takes self-discipline to stop complaining — and a great deal of it if you're like most people, who can't go even one day without voicing their dissatisfaction with the world. Consequently, managing your complaints is a great exercise to improve your self-control.

Starting today, try to go without complaining for as long as you can. Whenever you catch yourself complaining, turn it into a solution, try to find something good about whatever dissatisfies you, or let it go if the solution is beyond your control or the problem isn't worth your energy.

For example, if you're at a restaurant and your meal isn't as warm as you'd like it to be, you can ask the waiter to heat it (turning a complaint into a solution), consider it an exercise in voluntary discomfort (finding something good about the source of the complaint), or simply eat it, having decided that complaining about it isn't worth your energy.

Such mental training will not only improve your impulse self-control, but also make you a more positive person. In contrast, what do you get out of complaining besides ruining your mood?

# Day 67: On Borrowing Money

*Every time you borrow money, you're robbing your future self.*

—*Nathan W. Morris*

Borrowing money for consumption is a widespread disease in today's world, fueled by excess and materialism. Unlike taking on a business loan to achieve a return on investment that is higher than the interest rate — a practice that, when done wisely, can enrich your future self — consumer loans only serve to satisfy the desire for instant gratification, while robbing (sometimes spectacularly) your future self.

Each time you're thinking about getting a loan to satisfy a desire to own an item that belongs in the "want" category, imagine that you have the power to stop your past self from getting all the consumer loans you have today (if you don't have any, pretend that you do). Just like that, you can erase all of them and finally gain peace of mind. Would you still go into debt to finance your toys?

Five years from now, you'll look back at your past self, puzzled at how short-sighted you were to gift yourself with such a bad future for the fleeting gratification of getting a new car or TV.

"But I can get such great terms, it's almost a free loan!" you're saying? The terms don't matter; the habit of prioritizing your present self over your future self eventually affects not only your finances, but every other area of your life.

Developing discipline to do without unnecessary feel-good purchases you can't afford is one of the most important things you can do to gain more self-control and ensure that your future is better than the present.

# Day 68: On Choosing the Right Motivator

*For me success was always going to be a Lamborghini. But now I've got it, it just sits on my drive.*

—*50 Cent*[64]

External rewards like a Lamborghini are poor motivators.

For one, I've heard countless times about people willing to endure immense torture to stay true to their values or save their loved ones, but I've yet to hear a story of a person willing to die for their new Lexus.

Second, materialistic rewards give fleeting happiness and often come with more problems than benefits. Just ask any owner of a Lamborghini how much fun it is to see people constantly taking pictures of their car, how fun it is to spend thousands of dollars for a simple check-up, or how stressed-out they are in the parking lot, afraid of an envious driver of a beat-up car dinging their shiny vehicle.

Last but most definitely not least, a powerful motivator should feel like a necessity, a thing you can't live without, and not a mere toy that displays your high status, which ultimately nobody cares about.

If you're struggling to stick to your resolution, perhaps the only motivation you have is the extrinsic type, driven by money, fame, or prizes. This type of motivation isn't bad per se; what's bad is when it's the only thing that keeps you going.

Whenever you're setting new goals, go beyond mere external rewards. Instead, support your self-discipline with intrinsic motivators — internal rewards, such as doing something out of a need to grow as a person, achieve more independence, realize your full potential, enjoy yourself, learn, or explore.

Combine this motivation with a need to make the world a better place, and you'll have a powerful source of inspiration that will enable you to grin and bear the difficulties that you'll undoubtedly encounter along the way.

# Day 69: On Climbing Steep Hills

*To climb steep hills*
*Requires slow pace at first.*

—*William Shakespeare*[65]

If you think of your goal as a steep hill, imagine how ridiculous it would be to stop midway just because you're slowly scrambling up instead of sprinting all the way to the top. That's precisely what many people do when they start working on a new goal and realize that the journey will take longer than they expected.

What difference does it make that reaching a goal takes you longer than you planned? If you want to climb a steep hill, will you stop climbing it because you can't climb it in two hours, but can in three? Will you retreat to the bottom of the hill and forever stare at its peak, frustrated by the dissatisfying pace of the climb?

Another mistake is the assumption that if something is slow in the beginning, it will stay that way.

When I started my career as a self-published author, I tried several different genres. Things were going slow at the beginning because I needed to figure out which genre and style fitted me best. Once I established the proper direction, I released my first bestseller, then the second, and soon there was a snowball effect. How wise would it have been to give up during the first several months, frustrated by the slow pace?

# Day 70: On Parkinson's Law

> *It is a commonplace observation that work expands so as to fill the time available for its completion.*
>
> —*Cyril Northcote Parkinson*[66]

Limiting the time available to complete a given task is one of the most powerful secrets of productive people and a powerful way to overcome procrastination.

If you lack the self-control needed to work in a focused way, give yourself a challenging deadline to enforce concentration. Suddenly, what normally takes two hours to accomplish (or rather, two hours of intermittent work and distractions) will only take thirty minutes (or less) of 100% focused work at your highest potential.

At the moment I'm writing these words, I have a goal to write four entries in 50 minutes. Because of my self-imposed time pressure, I'm 100% focused on the task at hand. I can't distract or second-guess myself, two things that interrupt the creative process and slow down my writing pace.

Since I have given myself little time to get the task done, procrastination is a non-issue — I can't afford to dilly-dally because I'll miss my deadline. To further motivate myself to work quickly, I established a reward for performing the task on time: reading the new autobiography of Richard Branson, one of my business idols.

This simple trick can become one of your most powerful allies toward increasing your productivity. If you've been putting off a

152

certain unpleasant task, get to it now, but instead of giving yourself plenty of time to finish it, do it in 25% of your usual timeframe.

The new, greatly shortened period of work should reduce your resistance to getting started, and the challenge of doing it more quickly should bring out some excitement that will additionally fuel your resolve to get it done.

# WEEK 11

# Day 71: On Taking a Step Forward

*If you don't ask, the answer's always no. If you don't step forward, you're always in the same place.*

—*Nora Roberts*[67]

When I was battling against my shyness, I set a goal to approach attractive women in the street. I knew that if I did it several dozen times, I would most likely overcome my social fears and transform into a new person.

What helped me act (in spite of immense anxiety) was the realization that talking myself out of approaching a woman would certainly equate to a "no." Approaching her and getting rejected couldn't worsen my situation. In fact, I could only gain, because even a rejection was still a valuable lesson I wouldn't learn if I chose inaction.

Likewise, many people hesitate to start working on their goals out of a fear of failure or self-doubt. They fail to realize that if they don't a take a step forward, they'll be in the same place. Even if they take an unsuccessful step forward and need to backtrack, they'd still gain some experience. There's nothing to lose, and potentially a lot to gain.

Are there any goals you'd like to pursue, but are afraid that you'll embarrass yourself or fail? Have you ever considered that not acting on them leads to sure-fire failure, while an attempt gives you at least a small chance of success and a 100% chance of learning something new?

# Day 72: On the Value of the Struggle

*To have striven, to have made the effort, to have been true to certain ideals — this alone is worth the struggle.*

—*William Osler*[68]

We fantasize about the day we receive a trophy, cash out, step on the scales and see the perfect weight, travel to this beautiful place, step into this new spacious house, or marry that beautiful girl or guy.

The focus is on the success, not the struggle. And it's understandable — success is glamorous, memorable, and marketable, while the struggle is drab, disagreeable, and unattractive for the general public.

Yet, it's making the effort, struggling, and sticking to your resolutions that shapes you as a person. Success is a reward for having given it your best, but it's not always within your control whether and when you get to enjoy it.

Whenever you find yourself discouraged by your lack of success, remind yourself that the process alone is your reward. It's in your hands whether you allow yourself to see the rewards the struggle generates or ignore them, mindlessly pursing the end result as the sole indicator of success.

I failed numerous times in business. I could have despaired that I had lost so much time and money, but I hadn't really failed. I had been true to my values of pursuing the entrepreneurial life. I kept going, despite the obstacles I constantly encountered along the way. Over and over again, I beat entrepreneurial depression and found it in myself yet again to get back up and try again.

Eventually my efforts paid off, but even if it had taken longer to get the results — or if I had died before reaching them — the struggle would still have been worth it for the immense changes I underwent on the journey to pursue my dreams.

# Day 73: On Having Fun

*Fun is at the core of the way I like to do business and it has been key to everything I've done from the outset. More than any other element, fun is the secret of Virgin's success. I am aware that the idea of business as being fun and creative goes right against the grain of convention, and it's certainly not how they teach it at some of those business schools, where business means hard grind and lots of "discounted cash flows" and "net present values".*

—*Richard Branson*[69]

Building self-discipline and working on your long-term goals doesn't have to be a chore. In fact, if it is, you'll have a hard time reaching success because if something bores you to tears or doesn't produce much excitement, it's difficult to stick to it in the long term.

Probably the most common area in which I see most people struggling because of lack of fun is exercise. If you succumb to the popular notion that exercise has to be repetitive, painful, and boring, guess what… A few weeks from now, you'll be back in front of your TV, wondering what motivated you to do such a stupid thing as attending those torturous fitness classes.

The only way to develop a permanent habit of regular physical activity is to find an exercise you enjoy. Without the fun factor, exercise will always feel like a chore, and you probably already have enough obligations in your life.

The same applies to virtually any other endeavor. I treat my business seriously, but at the same time I'm trying to make it a bit more fun, either by throwing in a joke here and there while writing a book, coming up with a fun writing challenge, or testing new exciting ideas.

Do you consider working on your goals enjoyable and fun or is it mostly a chore? If it's the latter, time to grab a notepad and make a list of things you can do to introduce more fun and excitement.

# Day 74: On Acting Less and Thinking More

*Act less, think more. Reflect on what really matters to you. Stop doing anything that isn't valuable, that doesn't make you happy. Savor life.*

—*Richard Koch*[70]

This advice goes against the grain as self-help authors usually suggest to behave the other way around: think less, and act more. The danger in acting more than thinking is that eventually you'll find yourself working on goals you don't really care that much about or doing things in a less than optimal way.

For example, when I was working on my fitness goals, I acted a lot. I religiously followed my workout schedule and did everything I could to build a strong body, including eating foods recommended for bodybuilders, recording videos of my lifts to improve my technique, and even hiring a fitness coach.

I acted a lot, but thought too little.

It was only when I stopped and reflected on what mattered to me that I realized that I had never wanted to be a bodybuilder. I was following the wrong ideal, chasing something that didn't make me happy or produce any visible results. Upon this realization, I redesigned my entire approach to fitness and started doing something that finally felt natural instead of forced.

Periodically pause and reflect on your own choices. Are you pursuing goals that matter to you? Are you working on your goals in a way that fits your lifestyle, or is there imbalance and disharmony?

# Day 75: On Haters

*Luke! Don't give in to hate. That leads to the Dark Side.*

—***Obi-Wan Kenobi**[71]*

It's a fact of life that when you do something worthwhile, you will have haters. People will criticize you for everything and anything, for a variety of reasons.

People accused me of a lack of respect toward women merely because I wanted to overcome shyness and be able to talk with attractive females. Others criticized me for my efforts to lose weight and build a fit physique. Yet others laughed at my attempts to build a successful business, claiming that I would never accomplish my ambitious financial goals. Today people criticize my books or send me impolite emails because I annoyed them in some unfathomable way.

In the beginning, it bothered me a lot. I wondered if there was something wrong with me, if the people criticizing me knew something that had escaped me. Time passed, and with the growing number of goals I had reached and the trust in myself I had consequently developed, I realized there was no value in the feedback that was coming from haters. Giving in to hate and letting it get to you leads to rancor, a poison that can jeopardize your long-term goals.

I'd love to share with you a secret, foolproof way to deal with haters, but in the end the only solution is the most obvious one —

you ignore whatever insults and malice they throw at you and focus on yourself instead.

We don't know each other, but I know that if you're still reading this book, you're a person who cares about self-improvement and making the world a better place. Don't let the negative individuals instill low self-esteem or doubt in you. I'm sure you have good intentions and the ability to make your dreams come true.

Shield yourself from negativity by surrounding yourself with the Light Side: other people pursuing their goals, empowering books, mentors, and visiting venues or participating in online communities that exhibit positive values.

# Day 76: On Changing Your Mind

*When my information changes, I alter my conclusions. What do you do, sir?*

—*John Maynard Keynes*[72]

I like to say that self-discipline is a powerful force, but only as long as you apply it deliberately in the right circumstances.

Blindly exerting self-control when your efforts are fruitless and unlikely to lead to positive results is dangerous because it's not only a waste of time, but may also lead to bitterness.

"I was so self-disciplined and yet I failed! Self-discipline is overrated, I'm done with it!", a person might exclaim upon realizing that their efforts were for naught, but failing to notice that their self-discipline wasn't to be blamed — it was their wrong use of it that resulted in wasting time.

For example, I once worked in the Search Engine Optimization (SEO) industry. I helped clients build backlinks to their websites so that they could rank higher on Google.

In addition to client work, I built my own sites. At one point, I had 40 sites, each targeting different keywords and covering a different topic. I was extremely self-disciplined about this business, as I was building new sites every week and constantly writing new articles for them.

When my revenue had finally shot up to around $1000 a month, Google introduced an update to their algorithm and my most successful sites dropped in rankings. My income fell by over 50%

overnight. I discovered that it wasn't anything new in the SEO industry. Google periodically introduced new updates and people like me regularly had to rebuild their businesses according to the new rules.

Upon realizing that my business would forever stand on wobbly legs, I stopped working on new sites and retreated from the industry. Choosing to stay self-disciplined would have been the wrong choice, because it would probably never lead me to building the lucrative, *stable* business I was seeking to achieve.

From time to time, revise your goals to factor in any new information you have recently acquired. Does it solidify your reasons to keep going, or is it a sign that perhaps you should alter your conclusions and refocus your efforts on something else?

# Day 77: On Hurting Yourself with Your Own Judgments

*If you are pained by any external thing, it is not this thing that disturbs you, but your own judgment about it. And it is in your power to wipe out this judgment now.*

—*Marcus Aurelius*[73]

When people who are on a diet slip up, it's not that one-off slip-up that causes them to fail; it's their judgment about it, namely persuading themselves that since they made a mistake, all of their prior efforts are now for naught. What follows is self-guilt, which leads to self-doubt, which awakens the need to self-comfort, usually by eating forbidden foods (after all, in their minds they've already lost) and subsequently ruining their entire diet.

A similar phenomenon happens with other goals, too. A person saving money who was forced to spend their entire savings on an emergency expense might consider it a reason to stop saving money. What's the point of saving if one unplanned cost can wipe out the entire fund? Their incorrect judgment of the situation subsequently destroys the positive habit they've built, instead of seeing the situation as a powerful demonstration of how important saving money is.

Whenever you find yourself doubting that you can achieve your goal because you made a mistake or failed to hold out against a temptation, remind yourself that it's in your power to give this event either a negative or a positive meaning; you can consider it as a reason to give up *or* as a valuable lesson that will help you in your future endeavors.

# WEEK 12

# Day 78: On Collaboration

*Life is not a solo act. It's a huge collaboration, and we all need to assemble around us the people who care about us and support us in times of strife.*

*—Tim Gunn*[74]

Even though there's "self" in the word "self-discipline," it doesn't mean that you need to refuse the help of other people or that you need to reinvent the wheel because you can't make your decisions based on the knowledge acquired by other people. It's easier to put up a fight against temptations and stick to your resolutions when others have your back. Learning from the experience of others, regardless if it's in the form of a book or a conversation, makes things easier, too.

I've greatly benefited from the power of social support by participating in online forums. I'm pretty sure that if it weren't for the people I've gotten to know over the years of my entrepreneurial journey, it would have been much harder for me to reach success. Knowing that the people who inspired me also had faced obstacles and were tempted to give up, it was easier for me to keep going when it was me who was facing the immense difficulties.

It doesn't mean that you need to become great at making online friends, though. Most of the people who immensely helped me on my journey don't even know me — it was the breadcrumbs they left in the form of forum posts and articles that changed my life, not my friendship with them.

Another way to collaborate is to find a person who will hold you accountable: a friend who's on the same journey as you or perhaps an online support group.

The key to benefiting from this strategy is choosing the right accountability partner. Go with a person who's strict, rather than lax, so that when you don't feel like doing something, he or she will push you to keep going rather than give you a pass and a pat on the back. Ideally, this person should be great at what you want to accomplish, and if not great, at least slightly better than you.

Last but most definitely not least, if there's a way to accomplish your goal more quickly through working with a reputable coach and you can afford it, do that. I learned the fundamental knowledge about self-publishing in just a couple of weeks, thanks to working with a person who was knowledgeable about the industry. It greatly shortened my learning curve, inspired me, and helped me avoid several obstacles that would have otherwise tested my resolve, if not outright discouraged from entering this business.

# Day 79: On Books

*Books are the quietest and most constant of friends; they are the most accessible and wisest of counsellors, and the most patient of teachers.*

—***Charles William Eliot***[75]

Continuing the topic of support, by far the most important friend on my journey of building self-discipline, developing mental resilience, and working on my long-term goals were non-fiction books that were written by people who have achieved my dreams.

Book were, are, and will always be one of the most valuable things a person wishing to change themselves can learn from to make their dreams come true.

Instead of idle talk about books being incredible — I think I've already made my case clear — today I want to share with you three books I believe you should read for education and inspiration. Here they are:

1. *The Millionaire Fastlane* by MJ DeMarco

*The Millionaire Fastlane* was the book that changed it all for me when it comes not only to business, but also my attitude about work and life in general. In addition to countless lessons about how to start and run a successful business, you'll learn how to become a person tuned in to the needs of others, a skill that will aid you in all kinds of endeavors.

Granted, not everyone equates success with financial success, so if you don't care about achieving financial independence, you can probably skip this book.

2. *The One Thing* by Gary Keller

Richard Koch is the original author of books about the 80/20 principle (stating that 80% of the results come from 20% of the effort). I strongly recommend his books, but when it comes to the most accessible introduction to the topic, Gary Keller's book is the winner.

The premise behind *The One Thing* is answering the following question: "What's the one thing you can do such that by doing it everything else will be easier or unnecessary?" The book delves deep into the details on why and how single focus is so powerful and important for success.

I've made this rule one of the most important guiding principles in my life and I strongly suggest implementing it in your life, too.

3. *A Guide to the Good Life* by William B. Irvine

Roman Stoicism adapted to the modern world by William B. Irvine is one of the most helpful life philosophies you can embrace to live a happier life.

Stoics were also big on self-control, mental resilience and preparedness, so Irvine's book is an all-encompassing guide on how to banish negative emotions, gain more happiness, and become a more valuable member of society.

The most important takeaway for me is practicing your resilience by visualizing bad events. I regularly use this strategy for reducing worry and increasing my peace of mind.

# Day 80: On Cultivating Positivity When Things Go Bad

*Good humor is a tonic for mind and body. It is the best antidote for anxiety and depression. It is a business asset. It attracts and keeps friends. It lightens human burdens. It is the direct route to serenity and contentment.*

—*Grenville Kleiser*

Treating everything seriously is a sure-fire recipe for frustration and depression, particularly when you repeatedly get hit with one obstacle after another with no chance to catch your breath. Negative thoughts can sprout in even the most positive minds, but it's your choice whether you nurture them or pull them out.

When I was struggling to grow one of my businesses, my laptop broke down. I not only had to buy a new computer to be able to continue working, but also pay a steep fee to have my data recovered (I've since learned how important regular data backup is!).

To make matters worse, all of that happened while I was deep in debt. I tried to keep my spirits high, but make no mistake — it was one of the darkest, most hopeless periods of my life. Still, if it weren't for at least trying to be positive about the future, I'm sure I would have had a challenging time sticking to the business that had landed me in so much trouble.

I'm not going to sugarcoat it. You *will* face seemingly hopeless situations and your self-discipline will be tested on numerous occasions. How will you maintain good spirits despite the negative circumstances? What are your most effective techniques to make yourself feel better?

I strongly suggest creating a list of simple ways you can improve your mood that you'll be able to turn to when you find yourself in a distressing situation.

# Day 81: On Identifying Your Resources

> *With every accident, ask yourself what abilities you have for making a proper use of it. If you see an attractive person, you will find that self-restraint is the ability you have against your desire. If you are in pain, you will find fortitude. If you hear unpleasant language, you will find patience.*
>
> —*Epictetus*[76]

For every problem you face, there's an ability or resource you can tap into to overcome it. The key is to discover what it is and immediately put it to use. Unfortunately, many people default to discouragement or frustration rather than adopt a resourceful attitude and look for possible solutions.

Little good comes out of covering your eyes, wishing the problem will go away on its own. The best way to prepare yourself for setbacks is to visualize them and seek solutions before these problems materialize. Not all of your negative predictions will come to pass, but the ones that do won't paralyze you as much if you prepare yourself for them.

For example, if you're on a diet, think of some common scenarios that might jeopardize your adherence to it. What will you do if somebody you always wanted to meet invites you to dinner at a less than healthy restaurant? What will you do if you find yourself starving at the airport while waiting for the connecting flight? What will you do when you fail to resist the temptation to eat chocolate and turn an unplanned treat into a full-blown cheat day?

By creating a list of potential solutions while being at the top of your game and not being influenced by negative emotions, you'll save yourself the time and energy that is wasted on trying to solve problems with a clouded mind.

# Day 82: On Extreme Focus

*Take up one idea. Make that one idea your life — think of it, dream of it, live on that idea. Let the brain, muscles, nerves, every part of your body, be full of that idea, and just leave every other idea alone. This is the way to success.*

—*Swami Vivekananda*[77]

While flawless, 100% focus on a single idea is close to impossible for a modern human being, there's a lot you can gain from focusing as much as you can on just one goal. In fact, I consider it so important that I wrote an entire book about it titled *The Ultimate Focus Strategy*.

There are two primary benefits of making a single idea your life.

The first one is that limiting your focus to a single thing requires a great deal of self-discipline, which subsequently makes it an excellent exercise in cultivating self-control. I've acquired a lot of self-discipline (and finally achieved my goal of building a successful business) thanks to limiting my focus to one business model. Sticking to one thing has taught me the value of patience, dedication, and made me realize how powerful small (and consistent) improvements can be over the long term.

The second benefit of extreme focus is that by centering your life around the one most important endeavor, you'll be more likely to reach it than if you were to spread your attention thin.

You have higher chances of implementing new nutritional habits and losing 20 pounds (or 10 kilos) in the next six months than trying to lose weight while also implementing a new workout routine, building a side business, fighting against your fear of public speaking, saving money for an emergency fund, and learning a foreign language.

If self-discipline is a resource that you can deplete (scientists are still trying to figure it out), it makes sense to spend it judiciously, starting with your most important goal.

# Day 83: On Changing Your Identity

> *Every time you make a decision to stick with your principles instead of indulging your weaknesses, you get stronger spiritually. And eventually this spiritual strength becomes a part of your identity. I don't think of myself as a nonsmoker or "ex-" anything, because smoking and other vices are things I would never do in a million years.*
>
> —*Frank McKinney*[78]

The only way to instill a permanent change is to change your identity. As long as you define yourself by a behavior you want to eliminate, your efforts to change will be in vain because subconsciously, you'll treat your changes as a temporary situation.

I don't define myself as a person who doesn't take drugs — I've never done drugs and never plan on doing them. Why would I define myself as a non-drug user?

In essence, that's what people do when they say they're ex-smokers or ex-convicts. That's behind you. Embrace the present and develop a different, positive definition of yourself that will explain who you are and what you do today, not what you're no longer about or what you're no longer doing.

As a vegetarian, I don't think of myself as a person who used to eat meat. I'm a person who eats a plant-based diet. It doesn't matter how flavorful you tell me this piece of chicken is — I won't eat it.

Your decision to be self-disciplined has to be equally firm. Don't define yourself as a person who used to be lazy or lacking discipline. Define yourself as a person who's doing his or her best to ensure the best future possible. No matter how enticing the temptations are, your self-definition will ensure that you'll stay away from them.

# Day 84: On Work and Chatter

> *The only relationship between work and chatter is that one kills the other.*
>
> *Let the others slap each other on the back while you're back in the lab or the gym or pounding the pavement.*
>
> —*Ryan Holiday*[79]

If you often talk about what you're *going* to do instead of *doing* it, you're not only wasting time you could have spent working on your goal, but also run the risk of not doing anything at all.

Self-congratulatory chatter carries with it the danger that you confuse it with what actually matters: work. Merely *talking* about your goals doesn't turn you into a person who is working on them.

This phenomenon is most visible in entrepreneurship. Entrepreneurs who talk the most are usually the ones doing the least. They attend every seminar, meet-up, workshop, and are heavy social media users, but when it comes to making actual progress with their business, somehow it slips between the cracks. Some of them don't even have an actual business. They're in a never-ending "research phase."

But don't worry, everybody thinks you're taking a lot of action based on how much you talk about business and that's what matters, right? Sadly, while it can gain you points for popularity among the gullible, it isn't a substitute for work and achievement.

To ensure that you actually *do* the work and get the results, be cautious talking about your goals with others. Use a simple rule of thumb: if you're talking merely to show off, save it. If you're talking to gather valuable feedback or get support, do it, but what's more important, actually *act* on the advice you receive.

# WEEK 13

# Day 85: On Experimenting to See What Happens

> *It often feels like everything is so serious — that if you make one mistake, it will all end in disaster. But really everything you do is just a test: an experiment to "see what happens".*
>
> —*Derek Sivers*[80]

I learned how to feel good in spite of failure when I adopted the "let's see what happens" mentality. Now, whenever I want to try something new that has an uncertain chance of success, I tell myself it's an experiment. I assume that whatever I invest in it, I invest it to gather data, and not necessarily to get a return.

For example, I started investing in video courses for my business. In the end, it was a spectacular failure, but I wasn't particularly worried about it because my experiment was still a success: it proved that my business idea wasn't a good one. I also learned a lot working on this goal, and that alone was worth it. I'm not sure if I would have taken action if I had told myself that this endeavor absolutely must deliver a positive return.

You can apply the same mentality to every other goal. For example, if you're afraid that you'll fail to develop a habit of getting up early, consider it a 30-day experiment to see how waking up early will make you feel and whether you'll be more productive. When you think of it this way, you ensure from the get-go that no matter how your experiment goes, it's a success. After all, you aren't trying to make a permanent change: you only want to test a hypothesis.

Usually, if the experiment goes well, it leads to a permanent change anyway, and that's the purpose of adopting this different mindset: you're breaking through the initial resistance by lowering your expectations, and you consequently eliminate the fear of failure.

# Day 86: On the Spillover Effect of Success

> *I've come to believe that success at anything has a spillover effect on other things. You can take advantage of that effect by becoming good at things that require nothing but practice. Once you become good at a few unimportant things, such as hobbies or sports, the habit of success stays with you on more important quests.*
>
> —*Scott Adams*[81]

The first time I discovered that success in one area results in success in other walks of life was when I started exercising. Thanks to my own efforts, I got stronger, lost weight and gained some muscle. This small success made me realize that I had control over my life.

From then on, I embarked on other projects to change my life, including objectives as varied as overcoming shyness and building self-confidence, launching my first business, living in a foreign country, learning foreign languages, and eventually becoming a self-published author.

If you don't believe in your abilities to succeed, heed Scott Adams' advice and pick something that requires nothing but practice to become good at it. Invest several months of your life into it and when you notice progress — based entirely on your own efforts, not "luck" — I'm sure you'll discover in yourself the power to tackle other challenges.

In addition to that, every goal you're consistently working on will help you develop the proper habits and traits needed to achieve success. Whether it's learning how to play chess, dancing, learning Russian, setting up a backyard garden, or mastering table tennis, the real-world experience of going from a complete newbie to a person knowledgeable about the topic will transform you from the inside out.

# Day 87: On Attributing Failure to External Factors

*When interpreting their own failures (...) individuals tend to make external attributions, pointing to factors that are outside of their direct control (such as luck). As a result, their motivation to exert effort on the same task in the future is reduced.*

—*Bradley R. Staats*[82]

Failure can offer valuable feedback that will help you achieve your goal. Unfortunately, many people lose the learning opportunity by attributing the failure to an external factor, such as luck.

Consequently, instead of identifying the root cause in something *they* did, they wrongly assume that they had no control over the situation. This not only makes them less likely to exert equal effort during subsequent attempts (which in itself reduces their chances of success), but also increases the risk they'll repeat the same mistakes over and over again.

As a result, they enter a downward spiral: each failure makes them less motivated to try again, and soon they give up, frustrated at how unfair the world is. It wasn't really the world that was responsible; it was their own failure to take responsibility for their failure and learn from it.

Make sure that whenever you fail, you always look for the cause of the failure in something that *you* did, and not in something that you couldn't control.

Even when it looks as if something was indeed outside of your control, it doesn't mean that you didn't make any mistakes that might have increased the chances of such an outcome. Identifying those mistakes — even if they were only partially responsible for the failure — will help you in future attempts and prevent you from developing the unhelpful mindset that you don't have direct influence over your life.

For example, if you weren't hired by your dream company, perhaps it wasn't your fault. Maybe there was a better candidate, the hiring manager didn't like you, or the company later decided against hiring a new employee.

However, even in such a case, it's valuable to ponder whether there was anything you could have done better. Perhaps you could have improved your resume, asked better questions during the interview, or been better prepared for the questions you had assumed were unlikely to be asked.

Maybe it still wouldn't have resulted in success, but at least that way you will have learned something new that will increase your chances of getting hired the next time, and consequently, you get to lift your spirits and boost your determination.

# Day 88: On the Comfort Zone

> *People will do almost anything to stay in their comfort zones. If you want to accomplish anything, get out of your comfort zone. Strive to increase order and discipline in your life. Discipline usually means doing the opposite of what you feel like doing.*
>
> —*Dave Kekich*[83]

I used to be terrified of heights. When I was a teenager, I remember shaking with fear while I stood on top of a 130-feet (40 meters) tower, afraid to approach the railing. Today, I hike through the high mountains and climb cliffs up to the same height as that of the tower. I jumped out of the airplane, visited the tallest building in the world as of 2017 (Burj Khalifa in Dubai) and flew in a hot-air balloon — things I would have never done in a million years if it weren't for my consistent attempts to face my fear of heights.

Don't get me wrong: I still experience fear, but it has greatly diminished, thanks to years of stepping outside of my comfort zone. Exposing myself to heights was the opposite of what I felt like doing, but I knew it was necessary to help me grow. What started as a mere desire to get rid of a fear of heights turned into a full-blown personal transformation.

Whether it's a fear of heights, an aversion to exercise, or any other kind of animosity toward the uncomfortable, scary, or out of the ordinary, stretching your comfort zone by gradually exposing yourself to such stimuli will lead to immense personal growth.

I strongly recommend regularly stepping outside your comfort zone in both little and big ways.

Little ways can include something as simple as pushing a little bit harder during a workout or working for a little while longer when you feel like you're about to fall asleep.

Big ways include things like skydiving if you're afraid of heights, camping in the wilderness if your biggest love in life is your warm, comfortable bed, or learning public speaking when you're terrified of speaking in front of more than two people.

As uncomfortable and difficult it is to step outside your comfort zone, it pays incredible dividends in the long run. Make it an inherent part of your life to expose yourself to discomfort and face your fears head on. Few things will change your life more than going outside of your comfort zone.

# Day 89: On Not Making Excuses

You have to deliver results when making excuses is an option.

—*Dan Waldschmidt*[84]

Self-discipline comes down to choosing between instant and delayed gratification. Instant gratification feels good today but compromises your long-term goals, while delayed gratification usually doesn't deliver much in the way of instant pleasure, but it can lead to bigger rewards in the future.

Sometimes you'll find yourself in a situation in which you'll be able to make excuses; they may even sound so sensible that (upon hearing your rationalizations) nobody would question your backing out of that situation. However, don't let them fool you — even if there's *some* legitimacy to them, in most cases it's still nothing other than choosing instant gratification.

For example, if you want to establish a habit of jogging three times a week and one day it rains and you're afraid you'll get sick, you have a valid excuse to skip exercise. After all, there *is* a higher risk of getting sick when running in bad weather, right?

However, it sets a dangerous precedent: you're making a decision that your habits depend on the weather. Your self-control (or your lack of it) is now at the mercy of external factors, largely dependent on whether jogging in the given circumstances is easy or not. Is this the right way to build mental toughness and self-discipline?

If you decide to keep going instead of defaulting to the easy choice of using (partly valid) excuses, you'll immensely strengthen your resolve. It takes even more discipline — and consequently offers a greater opportunity to exercise your self-control muscle — to stick to something when you have a good justification to not do it.

# Day 90: On Quitting in a Smart Way

> *Quitting when you're panicked is dangerous and expensive. The best quitters are the ones who decide in advance when they're going to quit. You can always quit later — so wait until you're done panicking to decide.*
>
> —*Seth Godin*[85]

They say that quitters never win, and winners never quit. However, quitting is sometimes more beneficial than stubbornly sticking to something that's not working for you. The key is to quit in a smart way — as the result of a process of logical thinking, not on a whim in the heat of the moment.

For example, after a couple of years of sticking to a bodybuilding routine I'd grown tired of it. I was often so annoyed during the workout that I wanted to stop it and go home. However, doing so would have allowed my temporary state of mind to make the decision — and *that* could have negatively affected my resolve in similar situations in the future where, having once allowed myself to quit on a whim, I would consider it a sensible thing to do again.

I took my time and carefully considered the implications of giving up bodybuilding before I finally parted ways with it. This way, I quit *strategically* instead of *impulsively*.

If you're currently discouraged with a certain goal of yours, make a decision that you won't quit until you can make a logical, educated decision that will take into account all of the repercussions of doing so. After carefully considering your options and their logical consequences, if you still want to quit, you're probably making the right choice.

# Day 91: On Starting Now

*We don't tell ourselves, "I'm never going to write my symphony." Instead we say, "I am going to write my symphony; I'm just going to start tomorrow."*

—*Steven Pressfield*[86]

Here's a principle to introduce today and adhere to it for the rest of your life: whenever you're saying "I'm going to start tomorrow," stop whatever you're doing now and do something — anything — to start *now*.

It doesn't have to be anything big and it doesn't mean you have to be reckless and start working on your goals without any kind of research on how to tackle your new challenge. Just take an action that is in alignment with your new resolution and it will take you at least a little bit closer to accomplishing your objectives.

Let's say you want to start a new diet. Instead of saying that you're going to start tomorrow, take the first action today: inspect your pantry, lay out on the table all of the foods that you're going to give up, and get them out of your house.

If you want to start saving money, don't put it off until your next paycheck. Inspect your house, find things you no longer use and list them online for sale. The money you make from selling your old possessions goes straight to your emergency fund.

Such simple actions are real-world implementations of your new resolution and will greatly diminish the risk that when you wake up the next day, you won't remember your decision to change your life (or tell yourself that you need one more day before you start). They also make it easier to overcome your inertia and begin to develop momentum toward reaching your stated goal.

# WEEK 14
## Day 92: On Pleasure Gained from Abstaining

> *If you are struck by the appearance of any promised pleasure, guard yourself against being hurried away by it; but let the affair wait your leisure, and procure yourself some delay. Then bring to your mind both points of time: that in which you will enjoy the pleasure, and that in which you will repent and reproach yourself after you have enjoyed it; and set before you, in opposition to these, how you will be glad and applaud yourself if you abstain.*
>
> —*Epictetus*[87]

When you delay gratification, it's tempting to think about it in black and white: delaying gratification means no pleasure now in exchange for pleasure in the future. Succumbing to instant gratification means some pleasure now at the expense of your future. In reality, things aren't that simple.

As Epictetus says, there's pleasure to be found in abstaining. When you successfully deny yourself something, even if you feel deprived of it, at the same time you'll feel proud of acting in accordance with your values and long-term goals.

And what might surprise you is that there's some pain found in instant gratification. Yes, you get to enjoy the reward right now, but this also means that you're betraying your future self. You're missing out on the positive feelings you could have gotten by successfully exerting willpower and in the end, the anger you feel at yourself might not be worth the initial pleasure.

# Day 93: On Connecting Dots

*Again, you can't connect the dots looking forward; you can only connect them looking backwards. So you have to trust that the dots will somehow connect in your future. You have to trust in something — your gut, destiny, life, karma, whatever. Because believing that the dots will connect down the road will give you the confidence to follow your heart even when it leads you off the well-worn path and that will make all the difference.*

—*Steve Jobs*[88]

All you need to do to achieve your long-term goals is to stick to them. Easy to say, hard to do, particularly when working on those objectives means months upon months of depriving yourself, making sacrifices and hard choices.

That's why the belief that things will connect in the end is so important for maintaining a high level of self-discipline over the long term. Willpower alone is a precious tool in your arsenal, but if it isn't combined with the confidence that one day it will all be worth it, you may run out of juice well before reaching that point.

When I started my entrepreneurial life, I instilled in myself the belief that no matter what would happen along the way, every sacrifice, hardship, blood, sweat, and tears would be worth it in the end. I had a powerful reason why, and I was confident that I could make it come true.

If it weren't for this belief, I know that I would have given up before reaching my objective. And with a more than fair share of knockout-like failures, this would have probably happened a long time before the dots would have finally connected. It took me seven years before all of my dots — previous experiences and acquired skills — connected and helped me build a successful self-publishing company.

When in doubt, remind yourself that change takes time. What you now see as completely unrelated things can soon connect and form a beautiful picture.

# Day 94: On Overidentifying With Your Emotions

> *People overidentify with their emotions. "I was really mad; I couldn't help it."*
>
> —*Mark Manson*[89]

"I was tired, so I didn't do my workout." But were you really so tired that you couldn't at least try, or did you feel *slightly* tired and consider it a great excuse to skip exercise altogether?

"I was angry, so I shouted at her." But does *feeling* anger mean that you have to *vent* it, or did shouting at your spouse simply feel better than trying to resist the urge to do so?

"I felt so joyous, I had to buy it to celebrate." There's nothing wrong in celebration, but if every joyous occasion leads to unnecessary purchases to treat yourself, isn't your joy really acting as an apparently legitimate excuse for not saving money?

Take notice of whenever you overidentify with your emotions. How often do you use them as excuses for failing to exert self-control? Letting your fleeting feelings control your actions is a sure-fire way to jeopardize your resolve to become a self-disciplined person.

# Day 95: On Early-morning Workouts

*I learned the advantage of training early, before the day starts, when there are no other responsibilities and nobody else is asking anything of you.*

—*Arnold Schwarzenegger*[90]

There's a reason why so many successful people wake up early: early mornings tend to be free of distractions — people asking things of you, emergencies you need to tend to, and dozens of obligations you need to fulfill. By the time other people are awake, the early risers have accomplished more than the rest will accomplish during their entire workday.

One of the best ways to start a day is with exercise. For one, exercising in the morning means that you'll always have time to perform this crucial habit. Leaving exercise for the evening carries the risk of skipping it because of tiredness or other pressing things that require your attention.

Second, exercising in the morning sets a powerful example for the rest of the day: you start the day with a conscious decision to do something that requires self-control and dedication. The way you start your day is usually the way the entire day unfolds.

Last but not least, training early is usually most effective because that's when you have the most energy. It's hard to have the same reserves of willpower and stamina in the evening, after you've depleted a lot of your mental energy on other things.

If possible, try to include exercise in your morning routine. It doesn't have to be an entire workout if for some reason you need to have your workout in the evening. Even just a few reps of some simple exercises, some stretching or a quick walk around the block can provide benefits and start your day on the right note.

# Day 96: On Silence

*Silence is the absolute poise or balance of body, mind, and spirit. The man who preserves his selfhood ever calm and unshaken by the storms of existence — not a leaf, as it were, astir on the tree; not a ripple upon the surface of shining pool — his, in the mind of the unlettered sage, is the ideal attitude and conduct of life. (...) If you ask [him]: "What are the fruits of silence?" he will say: "They are self-control, true courage or endurance, patience, dignity, and reverence. Silence is the cornerstone of character."*

—*Charles Alexander Eastman*[91]

In today's noisy world, silence is uncomfortable. Most of us rarely, if ever, experience true silence. We listen to podcasts when exercising, listen to music when commuting, and interrupt work with a chat or two with colleagues.

Silence is uncomfortable, because it means there are no outside distractions: it's just you and your thoughts. Silence in a conversation is even more uncomfortable because there's an unspoken rule that when people have nothing to talk about, they should come up with any topic just to avoid an awkward silence that might require them to become fully present and aware of how they really feel.

Since silence can bring so much discomfort, it can be a potent tool to improve your self-control.

First, sitting in silence and listening to your inner thoughts without any external distractions can help you slow down and analyze your recent decisions or assess how well you're doing with your new goals. Try to spend at least five minutes a week in silence and you'll be surprised how much valuable feedback you can retrieve from within you.

As a second strategy, embrace silence in a conversation. No, I don't mean that you should make the conversation weird by deliberately not saying anything. I refer to using silence as an exercise in improving your self-control when dealing with other people.

For example, try the following challenge for one day: when talking with somebody who has a different opinion than you do, resist the temptation to immediately attack them and instead listen silently until they have fully presented their arguments. You will have positioned yourself for a more intelligent participation in the conversation, simply because you took the time to listen carefully to what the other person said.

Another exercise is to practice self-control by using fewer words. For one day, focus on *listening* to the other person. Ask as many questions as you can to maintain an interesting conversation and resist the urge to comment or share too many of your opinions.

Both of these exercises will train you to be more focused on the other person and less impulsive during a conversation.

# Day 97: On Treating Yourself Well

*Nearly every human action is in some way an expression of how we think about ourselves.*

—*Gordon Livingston*[92]

If nearly every action of yours is an expression of how you think about yourself, what do your actions say about how you see yourself?

If a person is stuffing themselves with unhealthy food and drinks, do they respect their bodies or is it an expression that they don't value the only vessel they'll ever have in this life?

If a person is constantly playing video games, watching pornography, or trolling on social media, what does choosing to engage full-time in such low-value entertainment options say about their self-esteem? If for one day they were to play host to an important guest — say a successful person they admire — would they entertain their guest in the same way?

If a person is spending money they don't have and never saving even a penny, how much respect do they have for their own well-being, knowing that financial emergencies *do* happen and that, without savings, they can be some of the most stressful events in life?

Consider your actions and ask yourself what they express. Do you treat yourself well or are most of your actions things you would never do to a dear friend of yours?

# Day 98: On Society (Not) Holding You Back

*It's not society that holds us back, it's ourselves. We just blame society because not only is it easier but it's a nearly impossible weight to move. This way, we don't actually have to change.*

—*Neil Strauss*[93]

It's easy to use society as a crutch.

"I can't lose weight because there are billboards of fast food restaurants everywhere, and besides, I just got a free coupon for a burger."

"I can't become more productive because my colleagues laugh at me for making an effort, and besides, my boss won't appreciate it anyway."

"I can't stay faithful to my significant other because dating apps make it so easy to meet sexy people."

Is it the billboard, your colleagues, or dating apps that control your life? If so, is that really how you'd like to live — at the whim of advertisers, other people, or new technologies?

Every time you claim that it's the surroundings that hold you back, ask yourself if it's really your environment or perhaps it's just an easy excuse for you to not act. And if you still think it's your surroundings — because that *might* be the case — then change them.

Nobody forces you to hang out with the same people, install a dating app, or drive by your favorite fast food joints. If your long-term goals are important to you, you can always consider moving to a place that will be more conducive to your personal growth.

# WEEK 15

# Day 99: On Applying Knowledge

*Reading 32 books means you're reading a lot, but does it mean you're applying it?*

—*Darren Hardy*[94]

It's day 99, so you've already read 98 entries, with most of them offering tips you can immediately implement in your life. How many have you applied so far? If the answer is zero and you have no intention of doing so, what's the point of continuing to read this book?

Whenever you're reading a non-fiction book for educational purposes, try to find at least one important lesson that you'll apply in your life. It doesn't have to be anything big — the point is to develop a habit of applying at least *some* knowledge from each book you read.

I'll give you some examples from my own reading list.

When I read *The One Thing* by Gary Keller, I decided to always seek only one key action to improve any given area of my life. In the case of my self-publishing business, it was the decision to stick to a consistent publishing schedule (an activity I discovered to be the one thing that makes everything else easier or unnecessary) and foregoing any other endeavors that take a lot of time, but bring few results (such as participating in social media).

When I educated myself about dividend stock investing by reading some books, countless articles and blog posts, I used their suggestions for building my own portfolio. Within a couple of weeks of educating myself about dividend stocks, I'd already bought some shares.

When I read two practical books about rock climbing, I identified a technique I considered to be a key tool for self-improvement (establishing a specific intention prior to scaling a wall, such as an intention to focus on proper hip-positioning), and started using it during my workouts.

If you finish a non-fiction book and don't act upon any of its suggestions, you've wasted time. When reading, always think about how you can apply the teachings in your own life — not about how you can finish the book faster so you can begin reading another one.

# Day 100: On Being a Leader

*If you wish to control others you must first control yourself.*

—*Miyamoto Musashi*[95]

One good way to boost your willpower when you're struggling to maintain it is to remind yourself of the benefits of self-control. In other words, give yourself an answer as to why you should resist yet another temptation and stay self-disciplined. Failing to find a good answer will make you succumb to the urge, so it's useful to know as many practical benefits of self-discipline as possible.

One overlooked benefit of self-control — or a big weakness in a person who lacks it — is that leadership is impossible without it. If you demand self-discipline from others, you should first have it yourself. Otherwise, you'll lack the credibility that makes other people want to follow you.

This applies not only to the most common use of the word "leader" (such as a business leader), but also to any other role in which you're responsible for the well-being of another person of a group of people — being a parent, being in a relationship, being a part of a local community, etc.

Whenever you're struggling to stay disciplined, think of people whom you consider your loyal "followers," whether they're your colleagues, your children, your friends, or your neighbors.

What would they think of you — and would they still be willing to follow you — if they knew that you'd failed to embrace the quality that they admire in you so much that they consider you an important person in their lives?

# Day 101: On the Ultimate Excellence in Self-Discipline

> *Ultimate excellence lies not in winning every battle, but in defeating the enemy without ever fighting.*
>
> —*Sun Tzu*[96]

Some people wrongly believe that self-discipline is a never-ending series of battles with temptations. Today you're battling against the temptation to drink wine, tomorrow you'll battle against the temptation of laziness, and the day after tomorrow you'll struggle with a temptation to eat pizza instead of steamed vegetables. In the meantime, you'll have dozens of smaller skirmishes, each attacking you from a different front.

In reality, if your life looks like that, there's little chance that you'll stay self-disciplined in the long haul. The ultimate goal is to design your life in such a way that you'll rarely fight against temptations. There are three primary tools you can use for that:

1. Identity change. When your identity changes, you no longer need to desperately fight against temptations because you don't see them as such. If eating potato chips daily is no longer a part of your identity, there's no temptation to defeat; previously overpowering urges are now a non-issue because they are incongruent with your new identity.

2. Habits. Unlike identity change, you might still need *some* self-discipline to act or to overcome a temptation, but it will be only a

modicum of what had been necessary before you established your routine. Instead of a full-blown battle, either you won't need to fight at all, or it will be a short brawl at most.

3. Avoiding temptations. If you don't want to eat fast food, avoid fast food restaurants. There's little benefit in needlessly exposing yourself to temptations, particularly when you know that the enemy is hard to beat.

# Day 102: On the Deeper Meaning Behind Temptations

*Monastic rules that advise renouncing liquor, renouncing sex, and so on are not pointing out that those things are inherently bad or immoral, but that we use them as babysitters. We use them as a way to escape; we use them to try to get comfort and to distract ourselves.*

—*Pema Chödrön*[97]

Deconstructing a temptation piece by piece can uncover interesting facts about why you engage in them at all. Of course, you can say that you eat chocolate simply because you enjoy its taste. However, what if there's a deeper meaning behind it, a need it fulfills beyond the need for something sweet to eat? If you address this need in a different, more positive way, you'll no longer need to eat chocolate.

I'll share with you a personal example of mine. I was once going through a period in which I couldn't control my eating. I would eat a big meal that would normally satisfy me for the entire day, and then would continue eating afterward — sometimes a few snacks, sometimes another large meal an hour or two later.

I discovered that the primary reason behind this behavior wasn't hunger in itself; I ate a lot because I didn't have anything productive to do, and I didn't have anything productive to do because I felt slightly depressed. I was in a downward spiral: I was low-spirited and demotivated, so I didn't take any actions that led to boredom.

Then, because I wanted to fill my days with *something*, I filled them with food. When I came up with a new business goal and started working more, the problem soon disappeared.

Think about your problematic behaviors and temptations and seek a deeper meaning behind them. Why do you use these particular methods to comfort or distract yourself? Why do you need to comfort or distract yourself in the first place? What is the trigger or emotional need that leads to the negative behavior and what kind of emotional payoff do you expect to get out of engaging in it?

# Day 103: On Controlled Burn

*Small forest fires periodically cleanse the system of the most flammable material, so this does not have the opportunity to accumulate.*

—*Nassim Taleb*[98]

Fire is a natural part of the forest ecology. Regular small fires serve a cleansing purpose, reducing the amount of fuel build-up and consequently lowering the likelihood of a potentially large, disastrous fire.

Fires promote the growth and biodiversity of surviving healthy vegetation when the old, sickly trees burn and the ashes add nutrients to the soil. Moreover, burned trees provide habitat for the wildlife which often grows in numbers after a fire.

A controlled burn is a strategy that foresters around the world use to regulate plant and animal life, usually as a way to reduce the risk of a larger, uncontrolled fire.

You can use a similar strategy: give yourself some slack every now and then to prevent yourself from a massive, uncontrollable loss of self-discipline.

The most obvious application of this technique is in dieting: allowing yourself a cheat meal every now and that will help you avoid an unplanned cheat day or cheat week that could result in disastrous consequences for your long-term progress.

You can use a controlled burn in any other endeavor that requires you to maintain high levels of self-discipline for a long period of time. For example, if you're working hard on your business, every other week give yourself an entire day to slack off instead of working your fingers to the bone and burning out.

Controlled burns, as long as they remain *controlled* and limited to a defined period of time, can increase your long-term discipline, so don't feel guilty about scheduling one every now and then. You might temporarily lose some momentum, but in the long haul it will be worth it.

# Day 104: On the Past Predicting the Future

*The best predictor of future behavior is past behavior.*

—*Phil McGraw*[99]

If yet again you're telling yourself that you'll do something once X or Y happens, stop fooling yourself; the pop psychology maxim of past behavior being the best predictor of future behavior is absolutely correct for that situation.

This cynical rule isn't always right. If it were, nobody would ever be able to change. However, it holds true whenever you've been thinking of doing something for years and always ended up by putting it off, thinking that when the conditions would change, you'd certainly do it.

There's only one way to get out of this trap: when you catch yourself making a list of the right conditions before you act on your goal, tear the list up and take action now.

If you're telling yourself that once the conditions are right, you'll surely do it, count how many times you told yourself the same thing before (and didn't ever do it at all) and add one more instance — because that's what most certainly will happen this time, too.

# Day 105: On Predicting When You'll Give In

> *People who think they have the most willpower are actually the most likely to lose control when tempted. Why? They fail to predict when, where, and why they will give in.*
>
> —*Kelly McGonigal*[100]

If you don't know yourself well, you'll struggle with building self-discipline because temptations will often catch you unprepared.

A key practice you should embrace in your everyday life is to make a note of when, where, and why you give in to temptations. This knowledge will help you structure your life in such a way that you'll reduce the chances of a similar situation happening again or help you become prepared to overcome the urge when it arises again.

For example, I know that when I take a nap during the day, I'll most likely wake up hungry. I have no idea why; all I know is that if I fall asleep during the day, it's almost guaranteed that I'll wake up so hungry that I'll have to eat something — and while it's usually a piece of fruit and some nuts, often (in my still groggy state) I'll overeat.

Consequently, whenever I feel tired and know that I'll need to take a nap, I mentally prepare myself for the hunger when I wake up. If I can, I simply eat less prior to taking the nap so that when I wake up, I won't eat more than my intended daily calorie ration. Alternatively, I try to set up a meeting with a friend so that when I wake up, I'll immediately have to leave, with no time to spare for a visit to the pantry.

Think of some of your most common slip-ups and figure out when, where, and why they happen. What can you do when you're most likely to give in to the temptation? What can you do to avoid visiting the venue where they're most likely to happen? Why do you think you're succumbing to this temptation and is there any other way in which you can address the need this temptation fulfills, without actually giving in to it?

# WEEK 16

# Day 106: On Valuing Your Own Opinion

*I have often wondered how it is that every man loves himself more than all the rest of men, but yet sets less value on his own opinion of himself than on the opinion of others.*

—*Marcus Aurelius*[101]

Publicly refusing instant gratification — such as ordering a salad when everybody around you orders a pizza — can result in criticism from other people. If you lack trust in yourself, this negative feedback can cause self-doubt and compromise your long-term goals.

As Marcus Aurelius points out, it's a curious fact that even though we consider ourselves the most important people in our lives, we still often value the opinion of others more than our own.

Usually people who are the opposite of what you want to accomplish criticize you out of fear of being inferior to you. If you manage to reach success, what does it say about them? Consequently, even if they aren't malicious by nature, you may sense resistance coming from their direction, often masquerading as good-hearted advice, but intended to make you conform to the status quo.

While I doubt that there is a foolproof way to stop valuing the opinion of others more than our own (and I doubt that it would be smart to assume that we know everything best) forever, there is a way to protect yourself from self-doubt upon hearing criticism.

It's really quite simple. Whenever somebody criticizes your choices, ask yourself if they can serve as a model for you. If your overweight friend ridicules your resolution to stop eating fast food, is his or her opinion valuable for you? Does he or she set a positive example and have the credibility to change your mind? If not, why listen to him or her?

# Day 107: On the Innocent Distractions

*Distraction and displacement seem innocent on the surface. How can we be harming ourselves by having fun, or seeking romance, or enjoying the fruits of this big, beautiful world? But lives go down the tubes one repetition at a time, one deflection at a time, one hundred and forty characters at a time.*

—*Steven Pressfield*[102]

While it may seem that I place self-discipline as the most important thing in life, I want to clarify that that's not the case. We weren't made for work alone and it's important to celebrate what life has to offer, particularly as a reward after a job well done.

However, we weren't made for constantly entertaining ourselves and engaging in low-quality pleasures, either. These innocent distractions can make life more pleasurable, but at the same time a monster hides behind the innocence: developing an erroneous belief that there's nothing wrong with exceptions.

An exception *every now and then* won't hurt you, but when you do it regularly, it isn't an exception anymore; it's a habit. And that's how people continue to drink fizzy drinks, while they said a long time ago they'd stop; how people continue spending money they don't have, even though they vowed to make smart purchases; and how people watch TV instead of learning for their next exam.

"Doing it just one more time" quickly converts into another, another, and yet another exception, and soon the exception becomes the new norm. Every time you catch yourself saying that you're going to do it for the last time, remember that (as Steven Pressfield nicely put it), lives go down the tubes one exception at a time.

# Day 108: On Following a Routine

*I only write when inspiration strikes. Fortunately it strikes at nine every morning.*

—*William Faulkner*[103]

If you depend on inspiration to act on your goals, don't expect to achieve them quickly (if ever).

The only way to ensure that you consistently advance toward your objectives is to establish a routine and force inspiration upon yourself. It works in the same way as with people who always feel hunger at the same time: they've accustomed their bodies to eating at the same hour every day.

My preferred time to write is early morning. That's when inspiration strikes me — but it's only so because I established a routine and followed it religiously for years. Likewise, an inspiration to improve my foreign language skills strikes me at nine in the morning because that's when I usually have language classes. Again — I don't rely on fickle and elusive motivation; I rely on a routine.

You can benefit from routines when working on virtually any other goal.

Always exercise at the same hour, and soon you'll train yourself to be ready for exercise at the same hour.

Always meditate right after waking up, and soon you'll find yourself automatically inspired to meditate upon getting out of your bed.

Always set aside a fixed portion of your income each week or each month, and soon you won't even think twice before sending it away to your emergency fund.

Making your life predictable by sticking to a set of routines might seem boring, but imagine how exciting it will be to finally accomplish your goals, thanks to following those routines! It also uses less energy when you follow the routines as a habit, so you can accomplish more with less energy, leaving you more time and energy for other things that increase your pleasure in the journey itself.

# Day 109: On the Size of Containers

*Moviegoers who were given fresh popcorn ate 45.3% more popcorn when it was given to them in large containers. This container-size influence is so powerful that even when the popcorn was disliked, people still ate 33.6% more popcorn when eating from a large container than from a medium-size container.*

—*Brian Wansink*[104]

Sometimes weird tips can go a long way toward helping you accomplish some common goals, such as losing weight.

In the cited study, the size of the popcorn containers affected how much people ate from them. What's interesting is that, even if they didn't like popcorn, when they were eating it from a larger container, they still ate more than people who were eating from a medium-size container.

Conclusion? If you want to eat less, and consequently, increase your chances of success when dieting without the need for more willpower, consume in smaller containers: smaller plates, bowls, and glasses. When the plate is bigger than the food on it, it looks like there's less food than when it's a small plate filled to the brim with a smaller amount of food.

As a bonus random dieting tip for today, if you're struggling not to eat something, go and brush your teeth. For some strange reason, brushing your teeth — at least in my experience — makes you less likely to indulge, probably because you don't want to lose the freshness you now feel in your mouth (plus things don't taste well immediately after brushing your teeth, so it gives you time to pause and think before you cheat).

# Day 110: On Moving Yourself Closer to the Finish Line

> *People find it more motivating to be partly finished with a longer journey than to be at the starting gate of a shorter one.*
>
> —*Chip and Dan Heath*[105]

Think of the difference between having run the first 5 miles (or kilometers) out of 25 and having just taken the first steps of a 5-mile or 5-km run. Even though they're so similar, according to bestselling authors Chip and Dan Heath, people are more motivated when they're facing the first option.

Based on my own observations, I think the main reason for their findings is that people usually find it difficult to start something challenging, so if they can get past the first barrier and are partway there (with some achievements under their belt), they're fired up to continue.

You can benefit from this observation by moving yourself closer to the finish line — yes, even if you've just set a new goal for yourself. The idea is to fool yourself that you're actually somewhere along into the journey, and not just about to start it — a proposition many people find so discouraging that they don't even begin.

How do you do it? If you want to build a financial emergency fund, you can convince yourself that you're already on the right track because you have some source of income (while others have to find it first), or if not, that you have some things you can sell that are actually just money waiting to be converted into physical cash (you surely have something you could sell, so this always works). Just like that, you're no longer just getting started with the goal — you're already partly finished.

Let's go with another example. Imagine you want to have a flat stomach or become more muscular. You're already partly finished with this goal when you can perform basic bodyweight exercises (people who can't need to learn them first), if you've read some articles or books about exercise (people who haven't have to educate themselves first), or if you have fit friends and support (others need to find it first), etc.

Whatever your starting point is, think of what you already have or what you've already accomplished and use it as a way of seeing that you're closer to the finish line than you thought.

# Day 111: On Patience With Mindset Changes

*Nothing important comes into being overnight; even grapes or figs need time to ripen. If you say that you want a fig now, I will tell you to be patient. First, you must allow the tree to flower, then put forth fruit; then you have to wait until the fruit is ripe. So if the fruit of a fig tree is not brought to maturity instantly or in an hour, how do you expect the human mind to come to fruition, so quickly and easily?*

—*Epictetus*[106]

Here's a rule everybody would be wise to remember: don't expect to change the negative habits you've been engaging in for years over the course of a few days or even a few weeks. Mindset changes — in both positive and negative directions — take time to develop.

At the very least, it will take you months or even years to eradicate negative habits and traits from your life. Getting angry at the timeline is futile because you can't change the past. All you can do now is do your best to stay faithful to your new resolutions and be patient.

If you're starting from zero, without a vice you first need to get rid of, it will obviously take you less time to acquire the virtue you're seeking, as you don't have to reverse the negative effects of the vice. Even so, it doesn't mean that you'll be able to implement a permanent change overnight.

Just as it takes time for fruit to ripen, so it takes time for a mindset to mature. A new trait or habit only becomes firmly ingrained in your identity with the passage of time and a growing number of experiences that reinforce it.

Think of it as learning how to play basketball. No matter how much talent you have, you still need to take thousands upon thousands of shots to build muscle memory and develop a sixth sense for shooting the ball. Since you can't shoot hoops 24/7, it usually takes years to become a great player, and there's no way to shortcut the process.

Mindset changes are the same. One successful shot doesn't make you a great basketball player. A consistent series of successful shots does — and for something to be considered consistent, it needs to be repeated over a long period of time.

# Day 112: On Self-Licensing

*Past good deeds can liberate individuals to engage in behaviors that are immoral, unethical, or otherwise problematic, behaviors that they would otherwise avoid for fear of feeling or appearing immoral.*

—*Anna C. Merritt*[107]

Self-licensing, also known as moral licensing, is a phenomenon in which doing something good makes you more likely to do something bad. This irrational behavior is visible in many walks of life, including political correctness, prosocial behavior, and consumer choice.

Being aware of this danger and remaining vigilant when it's most likely to manifest can help you avoid it. Basically, it comes down to monitoring your actions when a good behavior inflates your ego (say, you resisted a temptation to eat a piece of cake at work), or when you're telling yourself that you've earned the right to indulge yourself, just because you did something you consider good for your goals.

Here are several situations in which self-licensing can rear its ugly head:

- seeing a great deal when shopping and thinking that, since you're going to save so much money, it's intelligent to buy it (but you don't realize that you don't actually need it),

- going through an aisle with healthy food and buying something with a "healthy" label, and then proceeding to buy some sweets because, after all, you're eating healthy, so why not indulge yourself every now and then?

- eating a huge post-workout meal to "recover" after exercise and fooling yourself that you've burned so many calories that one meal isn't going to replenish them (while in fact you're eating twice as much as you burned during exercise).

# WEEK 17

# Day 113: On a Lack of Time

*Instead of saying "I don't have time" try saying "it's not a priority," and see how that feels.*

—*Laura Vanderkam*[108]

"I don't have time" has to be the biggest and most common lie people tell themselves daily. It's never about a lack of time, because it's you who controls how you spend it, and you can always forego one thing in favor of another.

Telling yourself that you don't have time to exercise means that *nothing* that you have in your schedule is less important than your health. With all due respect, I doubt that you (or anyone else, for that matter) do super-important things 24/7 and that there's not even a single low-value activity in your routine that you could easily eliminate to make time for exercise.

I strongly suggest eliminating the phrase "I don't have time" from your vocabulary. People repeat it so often and so freely that it only serves as a convenient excuse — and self-disciplined individuals shouldn't make any excuses.

The next time you want to claim that you don't have time, tell yourself instead that it's not your priority. Now consider what that means for you: if exercise (and subsequently, your own health) isn't your priority, then what is? If you don't have time to attend your child's first play but still work overtime even though you don't have to, then what is more important? If you're too busy to read books, then what do you prioritize over education if you still spend time watching TV?

# Day 114: On Fulfilling Your Own Standards

*It's far better when doing good work is sufficient. In other words, the less attached we are to outcomes, the better. When fulfilling our own standards is what fills us with pride and self-respect. When the effort — not the results, good or bad — is enough.*

—*Ryan Holiday*[109]

When your motivation depends on the results of your labor, it poses a big challenge: if the results are slow to come, you'll most likely give up well before you see your efforts bear fruit.

When you set new goals, think not only of the results you want to achieve, but also your own standards that you want to fulfill. While you're waiting for the results, draw inspiration from your efforts to do your best. Even if the results don't materialize for this particular goal, in itself this appreciation of your own efforts will help you to build a disciplined work ethic that will benefit your entire life.

For example, for me as a writer, I know when my writing is up to my standards and I always strive to make every book better than the one before. Even if a book I consider to be my best work turns out to be a commercial flop — as has already happened a couple of times — it doesn't discourage me from writing new books. I know that I fulfilled my own standards and did my best. If I were motivated only by the results for each new release, I would have given up a long time ago.

Do you know what your standards are and do you strive to fulfill them, even when there's no hope for gratification in the foreseeable future?

# Day 115: On the Cost of Indulgence

> *The cost of a thing is the amount of what I call life which is required to be exchanged for it, immediately or in the long run.*
>
> —*Henry David Thoreau*[110]

When succumbing to a temptation — or after having done so, when you're analyzing what you did to avoid making similar mistakes in the future — think of the entire cost of your indulgence, both now and in the long run.

This delicious cake? Right now, it can deliver a sugar rush and make you feel happy as it hits your taste buds. However, it's also additional calories that you probably don't need and will need to burn off. In the long term, this one cake alone can lead to another, another, and yet another delicious cake, resulting in gaining more weight, and then requiring even more time to lose it again.

And what do you exchange for this indulgence today? Your life — the time that you have here on Earth to do something more exciting and fulfilling than eating a cake. Is it really worth it? Are you fine with the fact that an indulgence today can rob you of weeks or months of your life?

# Day 116: On Taking the Low Road

*The problem with making an extrinsic reward the only destination that matters is that some people will choose the quickest route there, even if it means taking the low road.*

—*Daniel Pink*[111]

Being obsessed about the outcome can help you achieve it more quickly, but it carries the risk of achieving unsustainable results, or worse, ruining your life in the process by taking the low road.

For example, consider a person who wants to build a successful business. Their end goal — making a million dollars — is more important than anything else. They don't care about the why or how; it's only money that counts. Whenever there's an opportunity to make money, even if it's unethical, they'll take it. After all, the end justifies the means, right?

Taking the low road is yet another temptation you must battle on your journey toward success. There's no glory in building a business the unethical way, ruining your body with an unsustainable, unhealthy diet just to be slim, or ruining your body forever by taking steroids and other unsafe medications just to become more muscular.

One way to prevent this from happening is to always think of something bigger than an extrinsic reward as a source of motivation. Think how working on your goal — not merely reaching it — can improve you as a person. How much fun it can be or how much meaning it can give to your life. Focus on those internal rewards in the first place, and you'll greatly reduce the risk of giving in to the temptation of taking the low road.

# Day 117: On Dressing New Things in Old Habits

> *Whether selling a new song, a new food, or a new crib, the lesson is the same: If you dress a new something in old habits, it's easier for the public to accept it.*
>
> —*Charles Duhigg*[112]

You'll find it easier to change your current negative habits if you make your new, positive habits seem similar to your original, disempowering patterns.

For example, if you're a huge fan of potatoes (more specifically, French fries), and now your diet forces you to give them up, it might prove to be too big of a challenge for you to eliminate them just like that.

What if you allowed yourself to eat potatoes, but in a healthier form? Instead of eating French fries, you could eat baked potatoes that were sliced in a similar way as your beloved fries.

It's an improvement to your diet, it gives you some positive momentum, and yet it shouldn't cost you that much in terms of willpower.

If you want to start jogging and you're a fan of listening to podcasts, why not tell yourself that you're going to listen to some podcasts and in the meantime, move a little? It doesn't sound like such a big, difficult change, does it?

Whenever you can, find a way to link a new change or make it as similar as possible (in appearance, not consequences) to your previous negative habit. That way, it will more easily become a permanent routine in your life.

# Day 118: On Free Things

*Most transactions have an upside and a downside, but when something is "FREE!" we forget the downside. "FREE!" gives us such an emotional charge that we perceive what is being offered as immensely more valuable than it really is. Why? Because humans are intrinsically afraid of loss. The real allure of "FREE!" is tied to this fear.*

—*Dan Ariely*[113]

"Free" is the ultimate marketing method, and it's also the one that can do the greatest damage to your resolutions, primarily those of the financial and fitness kind.

From now on, whenever you see that something is free and you want to act on it, ask yourself whether you really need it. If you were to pay for it, would you still want it or do you want it simply because you don't want to miss out on a freebie?

The first practical application is for people who are on a diet and gorge on food whenever they find themselves at a party with free snacks. What are you gaining by eating all this food and what are you losing? Unless food is scarce in your world (and it probably isn't if you're on a diet), the only thing that you're gaining is avoiding the fear of missing out. And what are you losing? Your dream, your hard work until now, and possibly your future. Are the free snacks worth it?

The second application is for people who want to exert more self-control when it comes to their finances. When shopping, if there's a deal where you can get one thing for free, ask yourself whether you'd pay for this thing if it weren't offered for free and if you're really going to have a use for it. If not, what's so special about this deal? It might be a deal to someone who would buy the thing on sale anyway, but it isn't for you.

There's nothing you're losing out on if you don't purchase something that has no use for you. And if you do buy it, you're losing a lot: your money, space in your house, time needed to maintain it, etc.

# Day 119: On Hatching the Egg

*We shall sooner have the fowl by hatching the egg than by smashing it.*

—*Abraham Lincoln*[114]

In today's world of abundance, there's always the next hot thing, a new miracle solution, a cure for it all. It's no wonder that so many people lack the self-discipline to stick to one thing and constantly jump from one thing to another, deluding themselves that the new thing will surely be better than the one they have now.

If we think of pursuing your goals as being in the business of breeding chickens, how big will your fowl empire get if you constantly smash all of the eggs you have, thinking that those other eggs you've seen online will hatch more quickly?

In essence, that's what a person is doing when they are constantly changing their mind. An important aspect of self-discipline is the discipline to stick to the specific strategies you've chosen to follow, in order to get the results.

If the strategy you're following has been proven to work for other people (as in the case of following popular healthy diets, tested workout plans, personal finance strategies, etc.), switching out of it to another one only because you think the other one could be better is nothing but an act of self-sabotage.

If you're currently thinking about giving up your current strategy because you're tempted to try something else, remind yourself of the metaphor with the egg. Nobody has ever accomplished anything by constantly destroying the fruits of their labor. If your strategy has been proven to work for many people, dedicate yourself to it for at least a year before you even consider the thought of trying something else.

# WEEK 18

# Day 120: On Handling Interruptions to Your Routine

*Planning a variance, make it concrete, black and white, and specify exactly when the variance will end. For example, instead of doing your regular gym routine while traveling through Europe, you commit to do twenty pushups every morning, and then as soon as you return home, resume your normal routine.*

—*Tynan*[115]

Things change and routines get disrupted, with travel being one of the most common culprits. Whenever I can, I try to maintain the exact same routine as I follow when I am back home. If I can't, as Tynan suggests, I come up with an alternative that is specifically to be used during the time of the disruption.

For example, in a few days I'm going to travel to Cyprus, an island country in the eastern Mediterranean. I have no idea whether I'll have access to any fitness equipment there, including something as simple as a pull-up bar.

Consequently, I plan to take advantage of the surroundings as much as I can to maintain my shape: swim in the sea, take long walks or run at the beach, hike in the mountains, and if I find the time, perform some simple bodyweight exercises that don't require any kind of equipment whatsoever.

This way, when I come back home, I won't feel as if I've lost my normal routine. And I won't — it will only be *altered* for the special occasion, but I'll still perform it, and consequently, won't run the risk of falling off the bandwagon.

When you know about an approaching situation that's likely to disrupt your routine, prepare yourself beforehand. Think if there's any way that you can maintain your routine despite that situation, and if you can't, come up with an alternative routine modified for the special circumstances. Even if your best idea is not a great one, at least you'll still be sticking to your routine in some way, and that will prevent you from losing it.

# Day 121: On the Mark of a Champion

*The mark of a champion is the ability to win when things are not quite right — when you're not playing well and your emotions are not the right ones.*

—*Carol Dweck*[116]

At the time I'm writing these words, I'm struggling. Instead of following my usual routine of writing in the early morning when I'm the most productive, I spent the entire day catching up with other tasks that all popped up at the same time. Now it's 8 p.m., I find it hard to focus, and I'm only beginning to write my daily word count.

And yet, I'm sitting here in front of my laptop and pushing myself to stick to my resolutions and yes, I'll sit here until I get it done. Wouldn't it be better to take it easy and just start again tomorrow? If I were sick and barely able to work, then yes.

However, in my case, even though I don't feel even half as creative and mentally prepared for work as in the morning, I'm going to persist because it's when you struggle and things aren't quite right that you can strengthen your self-discipline the most.

I know that once I finish my work today — even if it takes me several hours of strenuous work in the late evening (when I'm usually asleep) — I'll feel good, knowing that I've kept a promise I made to myself.

If you're struggling while reading these words, please remember that the mark of a champion is to keep going, under all circumstances. Sometimes it will be hard, sometimes it will be easy, and since you can't control it, the best thing you can do is to keep going, regardless of what's happening.

I promise you that after a long, hard day of struggling, you'll still be happier than you would be if you decided to take it easy and then had to deal with the guilt of not having done your best.

# Day 122: On Making Agreements With Yourself

*Agreements you make with yourself: When you make an agreement and you don't keep it, you undermine your own self-trust.*

—*Roy Baumeister*[117]

I strive to value the agreements I make with myself as much as the ones I make with other people. The reason is simple: just like when you lose the trust of another person when you fail to keep your promise, so you lose your trust of yourself when you don't keep an agreement that you made with yourself.

Without self-trust, it's impossible to have the self-discipline and self-confidence to achieve big goals and change your life. Your doubts will nag at you and you'll sabotage yourself because, deep down, you'll believe that you can't trust yourself anyway.

Whenever you make commitments with yourself, honor them just like you honor the word you give to other people, if not more. If you frequently betray yourself, you'll make it harder and harder to rebuild trust with yourself, and soon, it will take many months of consistent wins before you get to regain self-trust.

Your brain rewires itself according to your repeated actions, and if you teach it to expect that you go back on your word, it will get better at exactly that skill: backing out of your agreements.

# Day 123: On Doing This or Nothing

*The important thing is that there should be a space of time, say four hours a day at the least, when a professional writer doesn't do anything but write. He doesn't have to write, and if he doesn't feel like it, he shouldn't try. He can look out the window or stand on his head or writhe on the floor. But he is not to do any other positive thing, not read, write letters, glance at magazines, or write checks. Either write or nothing... I find it works. Two very simple rules, a: you don't have to write. b: you can't do anything else. The rest comes of itself.*

—*Raymond Chandler*[118]

If you're struggling to get to work, give yourself two options: for the next several hours you can work or do nothing.

Entertaining yourself with your smartphone, social media, Internet, talking, listening to music or anything else that serves as a distraction isn't allowed. You can walk around the room, sit, look out of the window, or stare at the monitor, but you can't do anything more exciting than that.

This technique gives you a license to goof off, but since you can't do anything remotely interesting, sooner or later you'll probably get to work. And that's the purpose of this trick: you aren't forcing yourself to work, and hence, there's no resistance that you need to overcome. If you spend an hour bored out of your mind, even the most despised task you need to do will be a relief.

# Day 124: On Daily Gratitude

*The more you regularly experience gratitude, the more self-control you have in various areas of your life.*

—*David DeSteno*[119]

Research suggests that daily gratitude boosts self-control. Researcher David DeSteno says that expressing gratitude for little everyday things, such as the kindness of a stranger, functions like a vaccine against impulsiveness. It enhances self-control and makes you more oriented toward the future.

In addition to boosting your self-control, expressing thankfulness daily makes you a more positive person, and that in itself is a huge benefit that can affect your ability to stick to your goals when the going gets tough.

Each morning or evening express gratitude for five small things. For example, I'm now sitting outdoors (one thing to be grateful for is our beautiful planet), enjoying sunny weather, and doing work I like. I'm grateful because I was able to spend a few hours climbing today and because (after I finish my work for the day) I'll cook myself a tasty, healthy meal.

Such simple things are what makes life great. Why not regularly express your gratitude for them and become happier, develop more mental resistance, reduce impulsiveness and gain more self-control?

# Day 125: On Going Away From Work

> *Every now and then go away, have a little relaxation, for when you come back to your work your judgment will be surer. Go some distance away because then the work appears smaller and more of it can be taken in at a glance and a lack of harmony and proportion is more readily seen.*
>
> —*Leonardo DaVinci*

A productive, self-disciplined person isn't afraid of taking a break and relaxing a little. They know that if they *don't* do it, they won't recharge and soon their greatly decreased creativity and problem-solving skills will ruin their resolve.

I strongly suggest traveling — even if it's just a weekend trip — to get away from your work, forget about it for a while, gain a fresh perspective and return ready to solve the challenges.

Often when you're struggling with the same problem for weeks or months on end, it's because you're too close to it and unable to see the forest for the trees. An act of what you might consider a lack of self-discipline — taking it easy and going on a trip — is ultimately a smart technique to ensure maximum productivity and persistence for the long haul.

# Day 126: On Shedding Light on the Dark Things

*Much as we must keep returning to the gym and pushing weight against resistance in order to sustain or increase our physical strength, so we must persistently shed light on those aspects of ourselves that we prefer not to see in order to build our mental, emotional and spiritual capacity.*

*—Jim Loehr*[120]

Who likes to think about their flaws, let alone put them on full display? We hide our dark side — our mistakes, our failures, temptations we couldn't overcome, and so on. Instead, we focus on our strengths and proudly talk about our successes.

While bombarding yourself with self-guilt or embarrassment isn't a particularly bright strategy for success, sometimes it's necessary to shed light on the dark side and pick a weakness to address or a temptation you finally need to face and overcome.

Self-denial is ultimately a self-sabotaging strategy. By telling yourself that you don't have anything to worry about, you might feel better temporarily, but the flaws and weaknesses don't go away. You're missing out on the opportunity to overcome them.

Right now, spend a few minutes thinking about your unpleasant traits — the ones that you always ignore, or worse, don't even admit that you have them. If you're good at accepting criticism from other people, ask your friends what they think your biggest flaws are — and work on fixing them.

# WEEK 19

# Day 127: On Cold Exposure

> *Take cold showers first thing in the morning. As soon as you get up. Jump in the shower. Close your eyes and turn the temperature to cold. Not just cold. Not ice cold. Try we-just-piped-this-water-in-from-Antarctica-because-the-penguins-won't-swim-in-it-cold. Do this for thirty days in a row. I call it Cold Shower Therapy because it, quite literally, is therapy.*
>
> —*Joel Runyon*[121]

Doing a two-month challenge of only taking cold showers was one of my first deliberate endeavors to improve my self-control. Unlike other goals that I pursued for the specific benefits that they would give me, my cold shower challenge was primarily about testing myself.

During those two months, I learned a great deal about how to overcome temptations and how my own mechanisms of self-control work (and when they cease to function).

I strongly recommend taking up a similar challenge to push your limits and toughen up. Is an entire month or two necessary to benefit from this exercise? Not really. Even just a few cold showers can be valuable lessons that will strengthen your self-control. Willingly exposing yourself to such a torture is something very few people are capable of doing, so this in itself is a great accomplishment.

If your health doesn't allow you to take cold showers (and as a side note, please note that you should always speak with your doctor before making any decisions of such a nature), try other ways of cold exposure.

Underdress in cold weather, submerge the lower part of your body in a cold bath, or turn your thermostat down. Voluntarily exposing yourself to the discomfort you feel when you're cold, no matter if it's a cold shower or something less extreme, will still be an excellent way to improve your impulse control and become tougher.

# Day 128: On Principles

*Principles are fundamental truths that serve as the foundations for behavior that gets you what you want out of life. They can be applied again and again in similar situations to help you achieve your goals.*

—*Ray Dalio*[122]

Do you follow a set of principles in your life? If not, it's time to design them and adapt them as an inherent part of your decision-making process, to ensure that you make better choices.

For example, I have ten fundamental rules that guide my overall life and many more that I apply to different aspects of my life. Here are three examples of my general principles that are applicable to every endeavor:

1. I never give up on anything that's important to me.

2. Time is my most important asset. I always focus on achieving more in less time.

3. Growth happens outside one's comfort zone. Security leads to mediocrity.

These rules ensure that I live my life according to my most important values and help me avoid making decisions that favor instant gratification.

For example, following the first rule means that if I establish that something is important to me, I won't give up on it, no matter what. Embracing the second rule means that I resist the temptation to do things mindlessly and always seek a more effective way of doing something. Living by the third rule means that I face my fears and resist the urge to stay complacent. This way, I'm always growing and reduce the risk of becoming too comfortable.

These are not just mere words — I consider them as important as promises made to somebody else, so I need to fulfill them. What rules do you want to embrace in your own life? Make a list of your own fundamental truths that will help you get what you want out of life and treat them as agreements that you can't break.

# Day 129: On Everyday Practice

*I mistakenly only associated the word "practice" with art forms such as music, dance or painting. I did not see dealing with a cranky child, an over-burdened work schedule, or a tight monthly budget as actions that required applying the same principles as did learning music.*

—*Thomas Sterner*[123]

You can view everyday annoyances in two ways: as frustrating experiences or as opportunities to practice your willpower.

A stranger bumped into you and didn't apologize? Practice your self-control by wishing him or her a good day.

Your child is misbehaving and you feel like being a parent is sometimes too much to handle? Consider it an exercise in manifesting mental toughness.

You have so much work to do and then your car breaks down, an unexpected bill comes, and a friend needs your help? Don't wish there were more than 24 hours in a day — accept it as a challenge in improving your productivity so that you can get everything done on time despite new difficulties thrown at you from every direction.

If you take advantage of every problem and look at it as a means of self-improvement, you'll improve your self-discipline and mental resistance just by going about your day.

# Day 130: On Working on Laziness

*If you are smart, but not lazy, work on laziness. To do everything, simply because you can, lowers effectiveness. Concentrate on the really important things that get amazing results. Do only the few things with greatest benefit.*

—*Richard Koch*[124]

As contradictory as it sounds, some self-disciplined people need to work on laziness to get to the next level of personal growth. Just like it takes discipline to work on the hard things, it also takes discipline to resist the temptation to work on unnecessary things.

For example, as a self-published author there are countless ways for me to promote my books. I dabbled into different marketing methods, but in the end had to limit my focus to only the few things that offered the greatest benefit. Doing everything would have perhaps portrayed me as a more hard-working author, but it wouldn't increase my effectiveness, and most likely would only reduce it.

Restlessness can be a good thing to inspire a person to take action, but if it leads to mindless work for the sake of work, you're wasting your potential and resources you could have spent on another area of life where increased effort would have led to noticeable improvements.

Periodically assess tasks you perform most frequently and ask yourself if you're not only exerting willpower to keep working, but also showing restraint when it comes to performing tasks that add little or nothing to your life. Crossing off unnecessary tasks from your to-do list might feel good, but it's just another form of instant gratification that ultimately compromises your long-term objectives.

# Day 131: On Building an Ark

*It took Noah 20 years to build an ark. And people said he was being silly because the skies were beautiful. And of course, the whole time, he looked stupid — until it started raining. You can spend a long time building an ark while everybody else is out there enjoying the sun.*

—*Peter Bevelin*[125]

Your efforts to improve will draw criticism or ridicule from people who don't care about self-improvement. It's possible you'll spend a long time doing things without a reward and start wondering whether your goal makes sense.

Is it worth it to spend several years working so hard to get a degree, build a business, or move up the ladder in your company while others are partying and enjoying their lives on credit?

During the process you might face doubts and even feel tempted to give up. However, five or ten years from now, the ones who were wasting time will get the short end of the stick when they realize that they wasted their time on ultimately meaningless pleasures. Now they're in debt, worried about how to pay their bills, and doubting that they'll ever have a successful career, while you're enjoying the fruits of your labor.

Whenever you're in doubt, remind yourself that you're building an ark and that rain *will* come. Maybe now you aren't enjoying yourself as much as others are, but in the grand scheme of things, it's better to be prepared and suffer a little now to prosper in the future than live in sweet denial and one day realize it's too late.

# Day 132: On Being Willing to Be Bad

> *To get good, it's helpful to be willing, or even enthusiastic, about being bad.*
>
> —*Daniel Coyle*[126]

An expert is a person who has made all of the most common mistakes in their field and learned from them. They embraced being bad so that they could get good.

For example, in rock climbing I noticed that if I stick to routes that are within my abilities or only slightly above them, I improve less quickly than if I climb routes that are well beyond my current limits.

Sometimes I make a fool out of myself because I can't even start the route, and sometimes I surprise myself when I climb 50%, or sometimes even 75% of the route before it defeats me.

The great benefit in climbing such difficult routes is that I make many more mistakes than when I climb easier routes. This is good, because it reveals my weaknesses and gives me more opportunities to learn.

If you only stick to routes with easy holds, you'll never learn how to properly climb when the holds are no bigger than your finger tip. If you only climb on routes with easy footholds, you'll never learn the proper footwork that a route with sparse, slippery footholds requires.

It's tempting to climb routes within your abilities because they make you feel good and capable, but ultimately it's nothing but instant gratification. It's the hard routes that will defeat you that teach you the most in the long run, even if you hate climbing them at the very moment you are doing so.

If you only set easy challenges for yourself (the ones that will never make you look bad or show you your deficiencies), you'll hamper your progress or even bring it to a halt.

Overcome the temptation to lower your bar. Come up with difficult challenges — the ones that make you doubt you'll succeed — and get to work. Get as bad as you can now, so that you can become as good as possible in the future.

# Day 133: On Self-Caring

*Self-discipline is self-caring. If we feel ourselves valuable, then we will feel our time to be valuable, to organize it and protect it and make maximum use of it.*

—*M. Scott Peck*[127]

The way you look at what self-discipline is can affect how self-disciplined you are. If you think of self-discipline as *punishing* yourself in return for some possible benefits in the future, how likely are you going to be eager to maintain it in your life?

Instead, what if you embraced self-discipline as self-caring, a way of manifesting that your time is valuable to you and that you want to make the most of it?

Now, instead of seeing every temptation as something pleasant that you must avoid for the possible future benefit, you'd look at it as a threat to your well-being. For example, upon adopting this outlook on life, you'd understand on a deeper level that watching TV for hours on end is not entertainment; it's killing your valuable time, and in the case of low-quality TV, killing your brain cells.

And the other way around: things that you currently consider torturous (such as waking up early, eating vegetables, saving money, expanding your comfort zone, and so on) would all become manifestations of self-care. You'd understand on a deeper level that waking up early makes you more productive, and consequently, creates more time and energy for you — even if it isn't always fun.

# WEEK 20

# Day 134: On Staying Congruent

*Immediately prescribe some character and form of conduct to yourself, which you may keep both alone and in company.*

—*Epictetus*[128]

If there exists a "hack" for quickly embracing self-discipline as a part of your identity, it's clearly communicating to everyone around you how important this value is for you — and then taking actions that are congruent with that decision.

The key is to maintain that behavior both when you are around other people and also when you're alone — we're not talking about faking it in public. The beautiful part is that when others associate you with a certain positive trait, you'll want to maintain it.

Think of a child who's considered to be tough by other kids. The next time he or she scrapes his or her knee, will he or she cry or try to remain congruent with his or her public image and walk it off? Obviously, we're adults now, but the basic premise doesn't change: humans need to stay congruent, particularly around other people.

All of my friends know that I'm a bit of a freak when it comes to self-discipline (okay, not a *bit of a freak*, I *am* a freak about that!) and consequently, this form of conduct is pretty much forced on me. I don't want to be incongruent with myself and I don't want other people to think that I'm saying one thing and doing another.

For example, if there's a challenge in front of me and I know that my friend is thinking that I'm going to face it instead of quitting, I'll face it (obviously only after I ensure that it's relatively safe).

Then, when I'm alone dealing with a self-imposed challenge, I'll be less likely to give up, too — after all, I don't want to lose the respect I have for myself, and most certainly don't want my friends to be disappointed in me upon learning that I'm a different person around them and a different person when I'm by myself.

# Day 135: On Staying in Love With Your Goals

> *Skipping around from one kind of pursuit to another: grit is about working on something you care about so much that you're willing to stay loyal to it. Not just falling in love — staying in love.*
>
> —*Angela Duckworth*[129]

It's easy to fall in love, but hard to stay in love, particularly when the waters get rough. It takes constant recommitment, sacrifice, and a willingness to deeply care for what you already have. In a sense, falling in love is like immediate gratification, giving you butterflies and all that jazz without any unpleasantries, while staying in love (although it's rewarding in the long run) is sometimes an act of sacrifice that requires a great deal of self-control.

When you set your goals, do you tend to stick to them for the long haul, or do you let the temptation to change things decide for you?

If you constantly jump from one thing to another, perhaps you don't care about your goals enough to stay loyal to them. Ask yourself if that's the case, and if so, how you can find new, stronger motivators or if perhaps you should give up altogether.

If it happens with every objective of yours, even when you deeply care about it (like it was for me when I was constantly launching one business after another), it's probably not a question of not caring enough, but about a failure to exert self-control when faced with the shiny object syndrome.

The shiny object syndrome is the inability to maintain focus on one thing, mistakenly believing that the grass is greener on the other side. Instead of investing all of your resources in just one thing (for example, a specific relationship, business, diet, etc.), you constantly replace the thing you have now with something else, just because it's new and shiny. What you fail to realize, though, is that by constantly "upgrading," you never get to build something that lasts, so you fail to achieve your long-term goals.

The next time you find yourself researching a new diet, workout plan, business model, way to save money, technique to stay productive, and so on, remind yourself that unless your approach is clearly not working at all (and for that, you need to stick to it in the long term), all you're doing is falling under the spell of instant gratification that will endanger your long-term goal .

# Day 136: On the Desire for Happiness Replacing the Need for Self-Discipline

*Pitching is what makes me happy. I've devoted my life to it. (...) It determines what I eat, when I go to bed, what I do when I'm awake. It determines how I spend my life when I'm not pitching. (...) If it means in the winter I eat cottage cheese instead of chocolate chip cookies in order to keep my weight down, then I eat cottage cheese. I might want those cookies but I won't ever eat them. That might bother some people but it doesn't bother me. I enjoy the cottage cheese. I enjoy it more than I would those cookies because I know it will help me do what makes me happy. (...) Life isn't very heavy for me. I've made up my mind what I want to do. I'm happy when I pitch well so I only do those things that help me be happy."*

—*Tom Seaver*[130]

If something makes you extremely happy, the desire to do it as much as you can will replace or at least greatly diminish the need for self-discipline. Obviously, the thing that you love must be good for you — eating French fries may make you extremely happy, but devoting your life to them won't be a good idea.

For example, in my case, one of the things that currently determines many of my choices and replaces the need for self-discipline is rock climbing. It's the number one reason why I perform hard bodyweight workouts (to be stronger to climb better), why I maintain low weight (because it's easier to climb if you weigh less), why I constantly expand my comfort zone (because it improves my mental game when I'm climbing), and so on.

The thing that makes you happy doesn't have to be a sport, but it does need to have a positive influence on you.

If you already have such a big passion in your life, link it to your new resolutions. There's always a way to combine a positive change with an improved ability to engage in your passion (for example, eating better will make you more energetic, which will make you better at everything you're doing, including your passion), so tap into this resource and let your desire to engage in your passion render self-discipline unnecessary.

# Day 137: On Waiting for Ten Minutes

> *For a cooler, wiser brain, institute a mandatory ten-minute wait for any temptation.*
>
> —*Kelly McGonigal*[131]

Telling yourself that you're going to get something in ten minutes satisfies your craving for the next ten minutes. After all, you *are* getting your reward; you just need to wait ten minutes.

A curious fact is that after ten minutes, it's likely that you'll no longer remember the craving or it will have diminished to such a level that you'll be able to handle it. And if not, you can tell yourself yet again that you'll have it in ten minutes and repeat the process until the urge is gone.

If you find the urge overpowering, use a stopwatch and stare at it the entire ten minutes before succumbing to the temptation. After ten minutes, even if you still reward yourself, at least you'll have exercised your self-control muscle a little.

Note that you can wait for ten minutes for any temptation in both directions: either by waiting for 10 minutes before you give in to something, or by giving yourself 10 minutes to do something and then allowing yourself to stop.

For example, if you're facing the challenge of unpleasant, but necessary and urgent work to do, tell yourself that you'll only do it for ten minutes and then you can quit. More often than not, you'll continue. And if not, as with waiting for 10 minutes before giving in to a temptation, you'll still have exercised your willpower.

# Day 138: On Nature Boosting Your Focus

> *Nature, which is filled with intriguing stimuli, modestly grabs attention in a bottom-up fashion, allowing top-down directed-attention abilities a chance to replenish. Unlike natural environments, urban environments are filled with stimulation that captures attention dramatically and additionally requires directed attention (e.g., to avoid being hit by a car), making them less restorative.*
>
> —*Marc G. Berman*[132]

Research suggests that spending time in nature regenerates your ability to concentrate. What's interesting is the finding that even viewing *pictures* of nature can be restorative.

If you're struggling to concentrate on an important task and no amount of self-control helps, head out for a walk in a forest or any other non-urban environment.

I take regular forest walks at least three times a week and consider it pretty much a necessary part of my weekly routine. When you spend your entire days in environments filled with stimulation, your ability to focus will be greatly diminished. Give your mind some time to rest and seek places where you can be by yourself, without blinking signs, crowds, cars, noise, and pollution.

If you can't afford or don't have easy access to the wilderness, at least try to spend some time in quasi-natural environments like a city park or even just your own backyard. If even that is not possible, put on your headphones and turn on a video of natural scenery.

# Day 139: On Tolerating an Absence of Novelty

> *(...) the use of a distracting service does not, by itself, reduce your brain's ability to focus. It's instead the constant switching from low-stimuli/high-value activities to high-stimuli/low-value activities, at the slightest hint of boredom or cognitive challenge, that teaches your mind to never tolerate an absence of novelty.*
>
> —*Cal Newport*[133]

The ability to thrive in low-stimuli environments, such as when working without distractions, is one of the most powerful demonstrations of self-control. Sadly, most people don't possess it, because they have developed a habit of constantly interrupting their focus with low-value, highly-stimulating activities, such as browsing social media or shopping online.

If you're unable to tolerate an absence of novelty, you'll be unable to focus on anything for long enough to see it through to the end. Therefore, it's key to develop the willpower to resist the temptation to entertain yourself when things get boring or too challenging for your mind.

I suggest a simple practice: follow the Pomodoro technique of time management in which you work for 25 minutes and then give yourself 5 minutes to distract yourself with whatever you want. Once the 5 minutes are up, you have to get back to work, and after 25 minutes more of work, you can yet again let yourself enjoy high-stimuli, low-value activities for 5 minutes.

The Pomodoro technique works so well because it doesn't force people to exert incredible amounts of willpower. It's only 25 minutes of work, so even if you're usually interrupting work every 10 minutes, you'll only need to wait for 15 minutes more before you can indulge.

After following this technique for several weeks or months, you should notice an improvement in the quality of your work. Soon, 25 minutes of highly-focused work will no longer be a challenge for you, and you'll greatly strengthen your self-control.

# Day 140: On Longing for Paradise

*The problem with longing for paradises is that it distracts us from our efforts to extract pleasure and meaning from the present.*

—*Gordon Livingston*[134]

In the pursuit of success, it's easy to forget that we live in the present moment. The struggle is certainly less attractive than the ultimate reward you're after, but it doesn't mean that you should let the vision distract you from the present.

There's a danger in romanticizing the outcome: when you compare this beautiful mental picture to the struggle you're going through now, you may become discouraged because of the painful contrast between what *could* be and what currently *is*.

By all means, if it inspires you to work, from time to time indulge in the fantasy, but don't forget that the future lies ahead, and it's the present moment you should focus on to ensure that that future actually materializes.

Obsessing about the final outcome means robbing yourself of the pleasure and meaning of the powerful, difficult process that you're going through right now.

The next time you catch yourself dreaming about the future, refocus on the present moment. Notice the small but positive changes that have occurred (thanks to your struggle), look at your progress so far, and draw inspiration from your sacrifices and your resolve to keep going, despite all of the hardships.

# WEEK 21

# Day 141: On Punctuality

*A person who cannot keep appointments on time, cannot keep scheduled commitments, or cannot stick to a schedule cannot be trusted in other ways either.*

—***Dan Kennedy***[135]

Punctuality is another facet of a self-disciplined person, while tardiness is often a sign of a preference toward immediate gratification.

A person who's late doesn't give themselves a margin to arrive on time, so they get the instant gratification of gaining a few minutes of time at the expense of straining their relationship or their chances of making a good first impression. Meanwhile, a person who arrives earlier might lose a couple of minutes, but in the long haul enjoys the reputation of being a punctual, trustworthy person.

If you're often late, realize that being late to an appointment doesn't differ from breaking a promise; it's still an act that can cost you the trust of another person. In addition to that, it demonstrates that you lack organizational skills and self-discipline. Is this the message you want to display to the world? Is being late something that will help you realize your full potential or stand in your way?

Set a new self-discipline challenge for yourself: resolve to always be at least five minutes early for every appointment in the next 30 days. After a full month, it should become a new norm for you, and you should benefit from improved relationships, as well as newly-gained self-respect for having developed the reputation of being a punctual person.

# Day 142: On Keystone Habits

*Typically, people who exercise, start eating better and becoming more productive at work. They smoke less and show more patience with colleagues and family. They use their credit cards less frequently and say they feel less stressed. Exercise is a keystone habit that triggers widespread change.*

—*Charles Duhigg*[136]

A keystone habit is a habit that results in other positive changes in your life without directly focusing on them. For example, the decision to start exercising will affect your diet, productivity, patience, and overall well-being.

Instead of focusing on several different habits, you can concentrate on making one change and, as if by magic, it will lead to other improvements that are introduced virtually without effort.

If you want to get the best return on your efforts, focus on establishing keystone habits first and only work on other routines when you already have established the keystone habits as habits. Some keystone habits include:

- regular exercise;
- making your bed every morning;
- tracking what you eat;
- saving money;
- meditation;
- waking up earlier;
- expressing gratitude;
- regularly getting enough quality sleep;

- trying a new thing every day.

# Day 143: On Falling in Love With the Idea of Starting

*What was the use of doing great things if I could have a better time telling her what I was going to do?*

—*F. Scott Fitzgerald*[137]

There's an inherent danger in sharing with everybody what you're going to do: you might fall in love with the idea of starting something at the expense of actually doing it.

Telling others about your plan can be addictive because it delivers a reward without you having done any meaningful work: you boast about what you're going to do, people are impressed, and you get a sense of accomplishment.

For example, I used to talk about starting to travel more, but whenever I was faced with an opportunity to go on a trip, I was scared.

It was easier and more pleasant to talk with my friends about all the exciting places I would go to. Today, while I still feel some resistance prior to going on a trip (particularly a more demanding adventure, such as visiting an exotic country), I almost never talk about my plans until I actually book the flights and the trip converts from being a wish into becoming a real-world action.

Are there any goals of yours that you "started" working on a long time ago, but which in fact still remain in the realm of unmaterialized plans? An easy way to figure this out is to think of your recent conversations and find a topic that you frequently talk about, but never actually act upon.

# Day 144: On the Work of a Human Being

*In the morning when thou risest unwillingly, let this thought be present — I am rising to the work of a human being. Why then am I dissatisfied if I am going to do the things for which I exist and for which I was brought into the world? Or have I been made for this, to lie in the bed-clothes and keep myself warm? — But this is more pleasant. — Dost thou exist then to take thy pleasure, and not at all for action or exertion?*

—*Marcus Aurelius*[138]

Marcus Aurelius argues that we haven't been made for embracing the comfort of a warm bed. Is sleeping in more pleasant than doing work? Obviously it is; otherwise nobody would ever do it.

Yet sleeping in is only more pleasant *in the beginning* or when you've *earned it*. Making your life revolve around comfort and laziness doesn't lead to happiness in the long term; it leads to depression. Taking action and exerting yourself rarely feels good *at first*, but upon completing valuable work, the pleasure of sleeping in can hardly match the pleasure of being productive.

The most powerful proof of the fact that human beings cannot thrive if they don't act and exert themselves is the research on retirement.

For example, according to a report published by the Institute of Economic Affairs in association with the Age Endeavour Fellowship, retirement increases your risk of clinical depression by

41% and the probability of having at least one diagnosed physical condition by 63%.[139] What's more, the adverse effects increase as the number of years spent in retirement increases.

Obviously, the effect of retirement depends on how the retired person approaches retirement. Sadly, when facing a new reality in which they no longer have to work, a lot of people stop being active and disengage from life — and that's what leads to the disturbing findings of the study. The ones who feel that their golden years are indeed golden are the ones who continue to be active, whether it's helping their families, volunteering, working part time, or embracing new hobbies.

Whenever you find yourself discouraged, remind yourself that while succumbing to laziness feels good at first, ultimately it will only worsen your situation and make you even less ready to face challenges. Embrace discipline, stay active, constantly grow, and you'll find both fulfillment and meaning in life.

# Day 145: On Complicating the World for Profit

> *To earn a fortune in the diet and exercise industries, there is a dictum: complicate to profit.*
>
> —*Tim Ferriss*[140]

Fitness companies make a fortune on persuading people that exercise or diet is complicated. The same situation applies to the investment world. The more complicated something appears to be, the more people will decide that it's better to hire an expert to help them than do it themselves.

Consequently, many don't start at all because they're convinced that they'll fail without help — and help, whether it's for fitness or in the investment world, is expensive. This provides a legitimate excuse not to start. It also makes you more likely to fall victim to the claims that some product —designed by the world's top experts, of course — is a miracle solution.

In reality, most things are simpler than you think. You don't need to attend expensive aerobics classes to become fit. There's no need to buy pricey home-delivered meals designed by some renowned doctor to lose weight. An investment advisor can often deliver worse results than if you were to educate yourself with free articles and invest on your own.

Whenever you want to make a change in your life and find that everywhere you look, companies involved in the industry make it complicated, step aside and review the fundamentals.

Somehow people were still fit before the advent of commercial gyms. They still managed to build successful businesses without Internet gurus. It was still possible to eat healthily in a world where bookstores weren't filled to the brim with diet books.

Don't use the fact that the industry makes things complicated as an excuse not to make a change. Educate yourself about the basics and draw your own conclusions. For you to make a change in your life, no expensive coach is necessary.

# Day 146: On Decision Avoidance

*I saw myself sitting in the crotch of this fig tree, starving to death, just because I couldn't make up my mind which of the figs I would choose. I wanted each and every one of them, but choosing one meant losing all the rest, and, as I sat there, unable to decide, the figs began to wrinkle and go black, and, one by one, they plopped to the ground at my feet.*

—*Sylvia Plath*[141]

Not making a decision is also a decision, and usually the worst one. While you're torn between one choice and another, you're losing time you could have spent taking action — any action — and then figuring out whether it was the right choice or not.

People often decide to not decide, or they put off their decisions because of a fear of missing out. Choosing one thing means *not* choosing another. However, not choosing either of them means losing both.

It's also tempting to avoid making a decision because it creates an illusion that you still have the freedom to choose. And while it's true that you *do* retain this freedom, there's *more* freedom in commitment, as it frees you from inertia and gets you closer to determining where you want to go.

If you're hesitant about whether you want to pursue a certain goal or not, figure out a low-investment way to get started. You can't get much additional insight by waiting for an excessive period of time, while you can gain an immense amount of knowledge by going ahead and testing the waters.

# Day 147: On Walking by Your Mistakes

> *Far too often we let little things slide. But just turn on the news and listen as the anchors lament an auto-part defect leading to deaths and multibillion-dollar recalls or a small leak in a gas pipeline causing an explosion that endangers wildlife. Recognizing when something is wrong, big or small, and holding people accountable can save industries billions and citizens their lives. Sergeant Bowen instilled in me instantly that if you do walk by a mistake, then you just set a new, lower standard.*
>
> —***Ann Dunwoody**[142]*

When you make an unimportant mistake, there's a temptation to let it go and ignore it. After all, it isn't a big deal, so why bother? If your dishes aren't pristinely clean, it won't change much in the grand scheme of things, and most certainly won't hurt anybody.

The problem is that walking by your mistakes sets a precedent of tolerating small errors. You're also missing out on a valuable exercise in self-control: making sure that all that you do is done with the utmost care.

I'm the last person to say that from now on you need to make sure that everything that you do is flawless. I'm fully aware that it isn't feasible, and I'd be a hypocrite to say that; my favorite tea mug is never entirely free of tea stains!

However, whenever you can, try to exercise a little bit of self-control and correct a little thing that you consider unimportant. It can be a small tweak in your posture, making sure that you sit properly in front of the computer. It can be making an effort to speak more clearly and improve your articulation. It can be ensuring that your bed is made properly or slicing a loaf of bread with more precision.

I often spend several minutes trying to fix a paragraph that I don't consider up to my standards. In the grand scheme of things, one single paragraph doesn't mean much. However, when the little things are repeated over and over again, it does have an effect on the final outcome and carries the risk of establishing a precedent — in this case, of my being lazy with my writing.

# WEEK 22

# Day 148: On Fear

*Action cures fear.*

—*David Schwartz*[143]

Many put off acting on their goals because they're afraid. Instead of facing the challenge head on, they choose a more comfortable option: withdrawing until they gain the courage to take action.

The sad truth is that courage never appears out of the blue, magically manifesting itself if you only wait long enough. Brave people aren't immune to fear; they also feel it, but decide to act in spite of it. And in this very act of refusal, fear goes away and they get to do incredible things.

As a rock climber, fear is my regular companion. Fear makes you question whether you can climb a particular route, or when climbing, makes you back out from a challenge.

While fear *does* serve an important purpose in situations like climbing, when there sometimes *is* a risk of injuring or killing yourself, it's often a wrong counselor. The key is to ask yourself one fundamental question:

Is there a statistically-significant chance of harming myself?

In climbing, a potential fall is often safe, so any fear that makes you question your abilities is unfounded. If a fall is safe, you might as well try and fall; nothing bad will happen. However, sometimes the decision to continue climbing needs to be carefully calculated, especially when a potential fall can be dangerous. Then fear can actually save your life.

However, in most everyday applications, fear is unfounded. There's almost no risk involved in chatting up that attractive stranger, launching a side business on a shoestring, applying for a new job, starting a diet, or implementing any other change of a similar nature.

This means that unless you're engaging in any higher-risk activity, you need to go past your fear. I know — it's not pleasant, it's paralyzing, it causes so much pressure that all you want to do is get away from it. However, if you want to strengthen your self-discipline and build mental toughness, there's no better exercise than to repeatedly face your fears.

By regularly facing my fear of heights, I was able to largely cure myself of it. If I were continuously avoiding it, hoping that one day the fear would disappear by itself, I'd never have become a rock climber.

# Day 149: On the Weak Point in Your Armor

> *The individual can attain self-control in great things only through self-control in little things. He must study himself to discover what is the weak point in his armor, what is the element within him that ever keeps him from his fullest success. This is the characteristic upon which he should begin his exercise in self-control. Is it selfishness, vanity, cowardice, morbidness, temper, laziness, worry, mind-wandering, lack of purpose? — whatever form human weakness assumes in the masquerade of life he must discover.*
>
> —*William George Jordan*[144]

Inspect your armor and find its weakest point, the common thread that leads you into most temptations or poses the biggest barrier to achieving your goals.

For example, in my case, one of my weakest points is patience. If I do something, I want to go all out and get results as quickly as possible. While it often serves as a strength, it's also a common reason why I fail to achieve some of my goals.

I follow rigid routines and am sometimes so strict with myself that eventually I can no longer continue because I burn myself out. What follows is a full-blown cheat day (after following too strict of a diet), an inability to write (after writing too much for too long), or an injury (after exercising too hard).

My inability to be patient with the process was also one of the reasons why I failed to build a profitable business for several years.

Instead of accepting the fact that all businesses need the owner's undivided focus for a long period of time, I constantly launched one business after another, thinking each time that the new business model would surely provide a breakthrough.

Having discovered my weak point, when setting new goals I now focus on sustainability. I try to accept the fact that it's better to take the longer path with fewer pitfalls than choose the quick route with a high chance of failure or delude myself by thinking that switching my strategy (for no reason) will lead to success.

What are your own weak points? How do they affect your goals and what can you do to fix those weaknesses, to prevent them from continuing to affect your life in a negative way?

# Day 150: On Indulgences Charging You Interest

*It's this great paradox that only a few people understand, but ultra-performers have realized that procrastination and indulgence are like these creditors that charge us interest. They make us feel good now, it's easy in the short term, but it's what creates the more difficult life.*

—*Rory Vaden*[145]

Metaphors can serve as useful tools to better understand and embrace concepts that otherwise don't produce an emotional effect.

If I tell you that putting things off and indulging yourself affect you negatively in the long term, perhaps you'll agree with me and stay away from them. Or perhaps you'll ignore me, because the statement in itself isn't emotionally-charged and memorable.

Instead, what if you embraced the metaphor that procrastination and indulgence are like your creditors? They extend you some credit today, but don't fool yourself — they *will* be back, asking you to give the money back along with interest.

The more you overeat today, the more time you'll have to spend in the future in a caloric deficit. A cake today is so tasty and nice to have, but don't let it fool you — under the friendly face hides a ruthless banker.

The more time you spend playing video games, the harder it will be in the future to give up the habit and become more productive.

Indulging yourself feels good today, but there *will* be a price to pay for it!

What are the interest rates your indulgences charge you? The next time you're about to succumb to a temptation, ask yourself if you want to place yourself in debt, in exchange for a fleeting moment of pleasure.

# Day 151: On Changing Your Character

*If you make disciplined, caring choices, you are slowly engraving certain tendencies into your mind. You are making it more likely that you will desire the right things and execute the right actions. If you make selfish, cruel, or disorganized choices, then you are slowly turning this core thing inside yourself into something that is degraded, inconstant, or fragmented.*

—*David Brooks*[146]

If you currently don't see yourself as a self-disciplined person and your desires and actions prioritize instant gratification over sacrifices that lead to bigger rewards in the future, you may feel as if there's no way you'll ever change. After all, it's been your way of doing things for a long time, and it's probably already part of your nature now.

Fortunately, while your character takes time to change, it *is* possible to change it — with thousands of little decisions and by embracing certain thoughts over others.

For example, today you may not have a tendency to desire healthy food, but rest assured that if you eat it for long enough, you *will* develop a desire for it.

I'm speaking from my own experience; initially I couldn't stand the taste of many vegetables, such as broccoli, Brussels sprouts, or cauliflower. As for the other vegetables, I was neutral about most of them, which meant that — given a choice between eating vegetables and something else, I'd go for something else. Today, I often crave vegetables. I no longer need to force myself to eat them. A tendency to consume them regularly is now a part of my character.

This little example is only one change that was engraved in my mind after making disciplined choices over and over again. No matter which area of your life you are talking about, what now feels like a difficult act of deprivation or a sacrifice will eventually turn into something you consider essential in your life.

# Day 152: On the Future Value of Money

> *If an item was listed at fifty dollars, consider the potential value of that same fifty dollars after it has been invested for twenty years. Ask, "Is this item worth $250?" If it's worth $250 to you today, then it's worth buying.*
>
> —*Darren Hardy*[147]

Money has present and future value. At the very moment, 50 bucks is 50 bucks. However, when invested over a long period of time (with a rate or return that exceeds inflation) , it can grow several times or more.

If you're struggling to maintain self-discipline with your finances, use Darren Hardy's mind trick to reduce the number of unnecessary purchases and assume that each purchase costs you five times more over the long term.

Alternatively, think of any purchase as hours of your work. 50 bucks is just a number that has little, if any, emotional charge. How about two or three hours of your life? Would you buy this new trinket with two or three hours of your time, instead of paying with a $50 bill? What if it's actually the same thing as losing fifteen hours of your life over the long run? Is it still worth it?

# Day 153: On Spontaneity

*As he walked across the farmyard toward the hen house, he noticed the pump was leaking. So he stopped to fix it. It needed a new washer, so he set off to the barn to get one. But on the way he saw that the hayloft needed straightening, so he went to fetch the pitchfork. Hanging next to the pitchfork was a broom with a broken handle. "I must make a note to myself to buy a broom handle the next time I get to town," he thought...*

*By now it is clear that the farmer is not going to get his eggs gathered, nor is he likely to accomplish anything else he sets out to do. He is utterly, gloriously spontaneous, but he is hardly free. He is, if anything, a prisoner to his unbridled spontaneity. The fact of the matter is that discipline is the only way to freedom; it is the necessary context for spontaneity.*

—*John Guest*[148]

When you think of spontaneity, you might think of it as something positive and fun. Going on an unplanned road trip. Dancing in the rain. Saying yes to random invitations.

Spontaneity can be positive, as long as you don't mistake it with impulsiveness. Whenever you justify your uninhibited behaviors with spontaneity, ask yourself if that's what it really is or whether your unplanned actions are in reality caused by a lack of self-control.

Another danger you need to be aware of is when people use spontaneity to lure you in to betray your resolutions. For example, imagine you're on a diet. When you're out having fun with your friends, at midnight suddenly one of them announces that you're all going to go get some pizza. If you back out, you may be called uptight or a killjoy.

At that moment, it's important to realize that your friend's accusations are unfounded because they mistake disinhibition with spontaneity. You can still be spontaneous without ruining your goals. For example, instead of eating a pizza, you can eat something less caloric (like a salad), eat just one or two small slices, or if you decide to eat the entire pizza, schedule a strenuous workout the next day (or reduce your caloric intake for a day) to burn off the excess calories.

If you're wondering if self-discipline is going to make you a boring person, realize that you *can* make an exception from time to time — just don't do it when you're being pressured into doing it.

# Day 154: On the Value of Doing Things Yourself

*Know the pleasure of workmanship, the joy that comes from things made well by your own hands, the happiness which comes from closer touch with the fundamental things of life and the consciousness of being of value to the world.*

—*Ernest Thompson Seton*[149]

In today's world, nobody is self-sufficient. Everybody is doing what they do best and they rely on others to satisfy their other needs and desires. Division of labor has led to prosperity, but it has also made us lazy: whatever you want, you can buy it and get it almost instantly delivered to your door.

Have a backyard? Hire a gardener to tend to it. Don't want to clean? Hire a maid. Don't have the patience to learn how to fix your sink? Call a handyman.

There's nothing inherently wrong about it and in fact, more often than not it's a smart approach. Why waste time doing something you're not good at if there are people who would be happy to take care of the problem for you?

However, if you develop a habit that whenever you're facing a problem, you need to call somebody else to fix it, what will happen to your problem-solving skills? How likely will you be to keep going when problems emerge in your line of work and it will be you who will need to deal with them?

Lastly, by avoiding doing things yourself, how many opportunities are you missing out on to learn something new or face a difficult situation head on and solve it yourself?

At the moment I'm writing this, I'm in the process of remodeling my apartment. I debated on hiring an interior designer to handle the entire process: design the apartment, buy materials, hire contractors, and manage it all.

However, even though I could afford it, in the end I decided against it, realizing that in addition to financial savings, it was a good opportunity to learn something new. Remodeling can be a frustrating and difficult undertaking, so it can also serve as a valuable exercise in self-control. In the end, doing it myself will not only save me money, but also lead to personal growth — and that's the primary reward of doing things yourself.

# WEEK 23
## Day 155: On Broadening Your Horizons

*What do you know of history, biology, evolution, ethics, and the thousand and one branches of knowledge? "But," you object, "I fail to see how such things can aid me in the writing of a romance or a poem." Ah, but they will — not so much directly as by subtle reaction. They broaden your thought, lengthen out your vistas, drive back the bounds of the field in which you work. They give you your philosophy, which is like unto no other man's philosophy, force you to original thought.*

—*Jack London*[150]

Jack London's advice is for writers who want to improve their craft, but it can also apply to any other domain. Expanding your knowledge and exposing yourself to different disciplines is not only a fantastic way to become a more educated person, but also a powerful way to become more successful.

Random bits of information from one domain can help you achieve success in another. Likewise, experience gained in one field can provide the foundation for another endeavor.

I'm an inquisitive person by nature and I'm always interested in learning about new things from various domains. I often randomly stumble upon powerful life lessons while learning about fields that are completely unrelated to personal development.

For example, rock climbing has taught me the value of taking things one step at a time. When climbing a difficult route, you focus only on the next handhold or foothold. You slowly advance, with your vision limited to the immediate surroundings. The same approach is effective when working on your goals — instead of worrying whether you get to the top, you focus on what's right in front of you.

The experience and skills I gained when climbing are now useful to me in every other sport, and thanks to that, I can learn them more quickly.

On a completely unrelated note, the experience of off-road driving has taught me the power of momentum. It's difficult to gain traction with nothing but sand under your wheels, but once you start, you can traverse difficult terrain. If you stop, it will be hard to start yet again. I don't think I need to tell you how much that applies to the world of personal development.

Draw parallels between different fields and strive to always expand your knowledge. Becoming erudite can dramatically improve your ability to learn quickly and achieve success with many different endeavors.

# Day 156: On Wanting What We Already Have

*One wonderful way to tame our tendency to always want more is to persuade ourselves to want the things we already have.*

*—William B. Irvine[151]*

I'm a follower of intermittent fasting, a type of eating in which you regularly alternate between eating and abstaining from food.

In addition to daily fasts of 16 to 20 hours, I sometimes fast for 40 hours or more. When you fast for such a long time, your senses are heightened. Smells are more intense and flavors more explosive.

In this state, you learn to want things you already have. A simple apple tastes like heaven and is more than sufficient as a food source. I don't need an apple pie, a caramelized apple sprinkled with cinnamon, or apple pancakes covered with apple-horseradish sauce.

You can persuade yourself to want the things you have by abstaining from them for a period of time or imagining they're no longer available for you. It doesn't apply just to food. Things can disappear in a blink of an eye — including your house, car, clothes, family members, spouse, a comfortable bed, a warm shower, or your health.

When you feel the threat of losing something you hold dearly, you'll start wanting it with more intensity than ever before. As a result, you'll work harder to keep it in your life and stop craving other things.

The applications of this practice for self-discipline are endless and go beyond the example with fasting.

Stop driving for a few days and imagine you'll always have to commute by bus or bike. Suddenly you might realize that you actually love your current car and there's no need to strain your finances and buy a new one.

Imagine — and I'm sorry for the horrid mental picture — that your loved one died in a car accident right after you had an argument with them. How terrible would you feel if it was your anger — and not your expression of love — that would accompany them in their last moments? Wouldn't such a morbid reminder make you less prone to anger attacks and more likely to exert willpower to not shout at your partner, child, parent, or other loved one?

In many aspects, your life is already incredible. You just need to remind yourself that you can lose it, so that you can relearn its value for you.

# Day 157: On Remembering Death

> *Remembering that I'll be dead soon is the most important tool I've ever encountered to help me make the big choices in life. Because almost everything — all external expectations, all pride, all fear of embarrassment or failure — these things just fall away in the face of death, leaving only what is truly important. Remembering that you are going to die is the best way I know to avoid the trap of thinking you have something to lose. You are already naked. There is no reason not to follow your heart.*
>
> —*Steve Jobs*[152]

In the face of death, what does pride or fear of embarrassment mean? What will you regret more in your last days: not going after your goals out of a fear of failure or voluntarily putting yourself in uncomfortable situations that might result in embarrassment in exchange for eventually making your dreams come true?

It's not a particularly pleasant practice to remember that you're going to die, but it can serve as a powerful reminder that — in the grand scheme of things — there's little you can lose and a lot you can gain by chasing after your dreams (and on the other hand, a lot to lose and little to gain by not shaping your life the way you want it to be just because you're afraid of failure or embarrassment).

# Day 158: On Learning From the Greats

*You do not win in a big fight by any patent device. There is not any way by which you can turn your hand and conquer in a time of great trial. You have got to conquer as your fathers and grandfathers conquered before you. You have got to conquer as strong men have conquered in every struggle of history, and draw on whatever fund of courage, of resolution, of hardihood, of iron will that you have at your command, and you can conquer only if you draw on just those qualities.*

—*Theodore Roosevelt*[153]

Whatever problems you're facing today, somebody has already faced them in the past. Perhaps not in the exact same way as you, but close enough that the story of this person will resonate with you.

That's why I find biographies (particularly autobiographies) so inspirational — you're getting to know the stories of great individuals and discover that no matter what period of history they took place in, people always employed the same or similar ways to achieve success. What's so powerful about it is that you can apply their lessons in your own life and have a reasonable chance that if it worked for them, it will work for you.

It might sound like I'm opposed to the use of self-help literature (obviously I'm not; otherwise I wouldn't write my books!), but I strongly believe that you're often better served by reading biographies of people you want to emulate, rather than yet another generic book about personal development. (And yes, you have my blessing to close this book now, if you have a good biography waiting for you on the bookshelf!)

Here are some biographies I strongly recommend, listed in no particular order:

1. *Losing My Virginity* and *Finding My Virginity* by Richard Branson.
2. *Shoe Dog* by Phil Knight.
3. *Elon Musk* by Ashlee Vance.
4. *How to Fail at Almost Everything and Still Win Big* by Scott Adams.
5. *On Writing* by Stephen King.
6. *How to Get Rich* by Felix Dennis.
7. *Let My People Go Surfing* by Yvon Chouinard.

# Day 159: On Having Options

*Always have options. Options are a primary source of power.*

—*Dave Kekich*[154]

Here's an easy way to sabotage yourself: limit your thinking to black or white. It's either A or B. You either do it or you don't. Having only two options takes away your power to choose and makes you susceptible to decision avoidance. This, in turn, makes you less likely to introduce important changes in your life.

Rarely, if ever, are there only two options.

For example, let's imagine you're now working 9 to 5, but you'd like to become an entrepreneur. Black or white thinking makes you believe that you only have two options: keep your job or give notice and start your business. With only two (opposite) directions to choose from, you can't make it any harder for you to decide.

What about continuing your career while building a side business? How about asking your boss if you can work from your home office? What about changing your form of employment to become a contractor instead of an employee? What about finding a job in a startup that is looking for a cofounder with your experience?

Suddenly you have other options, and those options can empower you to introduce a change instead of having to choose between the status quo and making an irresponsible decision.

Whenever you catch yourself thinking that you only have two options, think again. Black-or-white thinking is mental laziness.

Always find at least one more alternative and give yourself a better chance of making the right decision.

# Day 160: On Deliberate Practice

*Doing things we know how to do well is enjoyable, and that's exactly the opposite of what deliberate practice demands. Instead of doing what we're good at, we insistently seek out what we're not good at. Then we identify the painful, difficult activities that will make us better and do those things over and over. After each repetition, we force ourselves to see — or get others to tell us — exactly what still isn't right so we can repeat the most painful and difficult parts of what we've just done.*

—**Geoff Colvin**[155]

Concentrating on what you aren't good at instead of exclusively doing what you do well can dramatically speed up your progress rate, particularly in a complex endeavor that has many moving pieces.

It's tempting to stick to doing what you're good at and ignore the rest. It feels enjoyable, and if it's a skill you can show off to others, that's another reason to stick to what you do well. However, ultimately you can find little growth in repeating (over and over again) what you've already mastered, while other aspects of your performance leave something to be desired.

For example, in rock climbing one of my weaknesses is climbing routes that rely heavily on finger strength. I could choose to ignore any routes of this nature, but doing so would mean dramatically slowing down my progress, if not bringing it to a halt. Even though it gives me great pleasure to climb routes with easier handholds and climbing the ones requiring finger strength is often a nightmare, I know that ultimately, it's the *uncomfortable* routes that will make me a better climber.

Focusing on your strengths and ignoring or bypassing what you aren't good at is a form of instant gratification. Meanwhile, identifying the painful, difficult activities that will address your weaknesses requires sacrifice, but ultimately leads to bigger rewards in the future. Go with the latter.

# Day 161: On Addressing the Real Mistakes

*When expert putters miss, they don't say, "I am a terrible putter." They say, "I picked the wrong target."*

—*John Eliot*[156]

Proclaiming that you suck simply because you made a mistake is not only being unfair to yourself. You also rob yourself of the opportunity to improve, and increase the risk of developing learned helplessness.

Learning can't happen if you believe that improvement is beyond your control. Yet, that's precisely what you're doing when you're pointing the finger at yourself instead of at a specific action that you took.

Imagine an instructor who tells their student that they're a terrible tennis player. What does such kind of feedback accomplish besides demotivating the student? The only effective way to teach is to deliver specific feedback pertaining to a concrete aspect of their game, not by criticizing the person playing it.

Do what expert putters do. Instead of wrongly criticizing *yourself*, address the real mistakes in the form of specific *actions* you took that didn't result in the desired outcome.

# WEEK 24

# Day 162: On Inverse Paranoia

> *Inverse paranoid: someone who believes the world is conspiring to do him good. Sees every situation as being heaven-sent to teach some valuable lesson or make him successful. This is the most outwardly identifiable quality of a high-performing person.*
>
> —**Brian Tracy**[157]

Cognitive reframing is a process in which you change the meaning of a difficulty, hardship, or failure and give it a positive slant.

For example, if you were injured during a workout, you can think of it as the worst thing that could have happened to you or you can reframe it by looking at it as an opportunity to recharge and focus on performing the exercise more safely in the future, perhaps preventing an even worse injury by doing so.

If you cheated while on a diet, you can think of it as a stupid move on your part. However, it would be better to look at it as a lesson by asking yourself why, where, and when it happened, and what you can do to avoid doing it again in the future.

If you're ready to take cognitive reframing to the extreme (and I strongly recommend you do so), develop what Brian Tracy calls "inverse paranoia": the belief that the world is conspiring to do you good and that everything that happens to you contributes to your success.

Living with such a mindset not only makes you happier. It also makes you more mentally resilient (because you know that everything happens for a good reason) and consequently, less likely to become discouraged and give up.

# Day 163: On Angry Comebacks

*Never respond to an angry person with a fiery comeback, even if he deserves it... Don't allow his anger to become your anger.*

—**Bohdi Sanders**[158]

Anger is one of the most infectious emotions. When somebody attacks them verbally, for many people the urge to offer a nasty, angry comeback is so overpowering that they do it automatically. Before you know it, you're engaged in a verbal fight. Working on controlling your anger can provide great benefits when it comes to strengthening your impulse control.

Every time somebody attacks you, resist the temptation to engage in a fight by either finding something funny about the situation, deflecting the attack (for example by thanking the attacker for expressing their opinion, which might then strike you as humorous), or if those are not possible, walking away from the situation.

Remember that in the grand scheme of things you gain nothing — and risk a lot — by responding with a fiery comeback. As good as venting feels at that moment, losing your temper is not worth it when you consider the potential longer-term cost, such as losing your job, your reputation, a key relationship, or even just ruining your mood for the entire day.

Refusing to respond with anger is a *simple* exercise, but not *easy*. And that's why, combined with the fact that most of us deal with aggressive people at least once a week, it can be a valuable opportunity for you to increase your self-control when interacting with others.

As a bonus quote for today, ponder the words of Hazrat Inayat Khan:

"Very often in everyday life one sees that by losing one's temper with someone who has already lost his, one does not gain anything but only sets out upon the path of stupidity. He who has enough self-control to stand firm at the moment when the other person is in a temper, wins in the end. It is not he who has spoken a hundred words aloud who has won; it is he who has perhaps spoken only one word."[159]

# Day 164: On Easing Yourself Into the Pain

*One painful duty fulfilled makes the next plainer and easier.*

—*Helen Keller*[160]

If you have a few unpleasant tasks to perform and you have no idea where to start, begin with the least unpleasant task to ease yourself into the pain, so to speak. Once you cross off the first task, working on the next task — even if it's more painful than the first one — should be easier because you'll be warmed up, carried forward by the positive momentum.

It's like taking a brief, 10-second cold shower prior to jumping into a cold swimming pool (something I used to do when I was a regular at my local swimming pool). You've already exhibited some self-control, warmed yourself up for discomfort (I know, "warming yourself up" isn't really a good choice of words here) and now the more unpleasant act of submerging your body in cold water should be easier. After all, you've already taken the first step and gained some momentum.

If even the least unpleasant task on your list is still so overwhelming that you don't want to get to it, warm yourself up to discomfort by doing virtually anything else that's slightly uncomfortable, such as doing the dishes, performing a quick set of squats, or cleaning your desk.

This way, you'll slowly transition from being comfortable into being a bit less comfortable, and eventually, into the unpleasant task you need to perform.

# Day 165: On Not Living Up To Your Ideals

> *Our behavior sometimes falls short of our ideals not because we're bad people and not because our self-interest outweighs our benevolence, but because we don't realize we're not living up to our ideals.*
>
> —*Russ Roberts*[161]

Self-awareness is an important part of the process of making any change. If you don't pay enough attention to your actions, you won't be able to ensure that you live up to your ideals.

Each week, perform a quick review. Ask yourself if your actions during the past week were congruent with your ideals, values, and goals.

For example, if my goal is to become a calmer, more understanding person, each week (or each day), I'll ask myself if I exuded those emotions or let myself go — and in *both* cases, specifically when I did so, and how and why.

Knowing when you make mistakes will help you avoid them in the future and encourage further improvement. Don't focus on mistakes alone, though. For motivational purposes, it's also important to think about when you *did* live up to your ideals and feel proud of your progress.

Implement self-monitoring and periodic reviews in your routine, and you'll increase your chances of making a new change stick. If you don't evaluate your behavior, you'll make everything harder.

# Day 166: On Handling Emotions

*People with a strong physical constitution can tolerate extremes of hot and cold; people of strong mental health can handle anger, grief, joy and the other emotions.*

—*Epictetus*[162]

While people usually associate self-discipline with the ability to resist temptations (such as laziness or overeating), another equally (if not more) important benefit of self-control is the increased ability to control your emotions.

Both negative and positive feelings make our lives more exciting, but they can also jeopardize our long-term goals if we let them influence our behavior too much.

For example, if you're impatient and tend to rush things, one wrong, emotionally-motivated decision can destroy the progress of many months or years.

A more disciplined approach to impatience — recognizing the difference between when the emotion can actually inspire positive change and when it's a sign of dissatisfaction with something you can't control — would serve you more than letting impatience dictate all of your behaviors.

Positive emotions, as pleasant as they feel, can also affect you negatively. For example, being overjoyed with your results carries the danger of self-congratulation and subsequent complacency, which places you at risk of losing the habits that you had to develop to reach that success.

A more disciplined approach to joy — expressing your happiness and gratitude for your success, and then reminding yourself that you still have a lot to learn and promptly looking for another challenge — would serve you more than jumping from joy and assuming that now that you've accomplished your goal, you're a world-class expert and now nothing will ever stand in your way.

Be vigilant of both your positive and negative emotions and understand the risk they can carry with them when left unchecked.

# Day 167: On Routines Overcoming a Bad Mood

*A solid routine fosters a well-worn groove for one's mental energies and helps stave off the tyranny of moods.*

—*Mason Currey*[163]

I'm a big proponent of daily routines, not only because they ensure that you steadily advance toward your goal, but also because they reduce the likelihood of negative moods ruining your progress.

Let's not fool ourselves — we're humans, and sometimes we feel bad. If you don't have a daily routine and wake up in a bad mood, it's almost certain that you won't care much about your current resolutions and forego them for the rest of the day. Handling your negative mood will be more important than any other objectives you might have had.

However, if you've established a daily routine and it's now instilled in your mind, the risk that you won't perform it is much lower. Why is that so? Because the beautiful thing about a daily routine is that once it's automatic, you feel bad when you don't do it. This means that if you're in a bad mood, not performing your routine will make you feel even worse, so the best choice is to stick to your routine in spite of your bad mood.

When setting important long-term goals, also create daily routines that will steadily move you toward achieving them. Once established, they will be some of your biggest allies.

# Day 168: On Wasting Your Energy When You Don't Have Important Rituals

*There is no more miserable human being than one in whom nothing is habitual but indecision, and for whom the lighting of every cigar, the drinking of every cup, the time of rising and going to bed every day, and the beginning of every bit of work, are subjects of express volitional deliberation. Full half the time of such a man goes to the deciding, or regretting, of matters which ought to be so ingrained in him as practically not to exist for his consciousness at all.*

—*William James*[164]

Continuing on the topic of routines that we discussed yesterday, the more routines you have (particularly routines for the most important parts of the day), the more time and energy you have for making decisions.

Many top performers follow specific routines, but they all differ wildly. For example, Pablo Picasso worked between 3 p.m. and 2 a.m., with a one-hour break at 10 p.m., while Victor Hugo spent most of his day on leisure, except for a 2-hour writing session between 6 and 8 p.m. Benjamin Franklin woke up at 5 in the morning, while Pablo Picasso didn't wake up until 11 a.m.

This demonstrates that what's most important is not following somebody else's specific routine, but following *some kind* of a routine that fits your personality.

At a minimum, develop at least three routines in your life that will eliminate indecision and improve your control of the day:

**1. When you wake up and when you go to bed.** Life is unpredictable and things will happen, but you can choose your working hours and ensure a highly predictable weekly schedule.

**2. What you do in the morning to ensure a good day's start.** Discover what types of mornings usually lead to happy, productive days and repeat the same actions daily.

**3. When you work.** Most applicable to entrepreneurs and other people with flexible work schedule. If you don't have a flexible schedule, at least dedicate a set period of the day for the most important part of your work.

# WEEK 25

# Day 169: On Stopping at the Right Moment to Help You Tomorrow

*The best way is always to stop when you are going good and when you know what will happen next. If you do that every day when you are writing a novel you will never be stuck. That is the most valuable thing I can tell you so try to remember it.*

—*Ernest Hemingway*[165]

One simple trick a writer can use to help him or her resume writing the next day is to stop in the middle of a sentence that leads to a clear conclusion. This way, when they sit down to write the next time, there won't be any writer's block: they can gain momentum right away by finishing the sentence.

This advice can be helpful for non-writers, too.

Each day when you're finishing your work, leave an easy, unimportant task half-finished so that you can immediately begin to work on it the next day with little to no resistance.

If you're reading a book about an important skill you want to learn, stop in the middle of an easy chapter, not a difficult one.

If you want to improve your nutritional habits but your busyness often leads you to eat less than healthy breakfasts, prepare a small, healthy breakfast the evening before.

Make it easy for you to resume your activity the next day, and you'll rarely, if ever, struggle to get started.

# Day 170: On Supply and Demand

*Supply and demand: the more people do something, the less valuable it is.*

—*Derek Sivers*[166]

An often-overlooked benefit of self-discipline is that it's a rare trait. Consequently, it makes you a more valuable employee when compared to your lazy colleagues, a more respected boss when compared to a boss who demands a lot from others but not from themselves, or a more trustworthy business partner when compared to a person who doesn't mind cutting corners.

Since self-discipline is so hard to attain, there will always be more demand than supply. This can indirectly lead to more opportunities and a better financial situation.

If you still find it hard to resist temptations, emotions often get the best of you, and you can't overcome the allure of instant gratification, try to give self-discipline a monetary value.

The fact that you're becoming more productive (thanks to more self-discipline) increases your chances of being promoted at work. More self-discipline means that you'll improve more quickly at a skill that you plan to monetize soon. And if you're an entrepreneur, it directly affects how much income you generate.

It probably sounds ridiculous to suggest that you can become a more self-disciplined person by linking self-discipline with higher income, but can you deny that money is a powerful motivator for many people?

If I were to give you $100,000 if you eliminated three bad habits from your life, I'm pretty sure that no matter how many times you had failed to get rid of them before, this time you'd succeed.

Think of self-discipline in the same category as any other skill or credential you could list on your resume or in a sales brochure. It doesn't cost anything (other than your time and energy) to develop this ability, and the return on this investment can be higher than any other lucrative endeavor you might pursue.

# Day 171: On Stress

> *Stress — including negative emotions like anger, sadness, self-doubt, and anxiety — shifts the brain into a reward-seeking state. You end up craving whatever substance or activity your brain associates with the promise of reward, and you become convinced that the "reward" is the only way to feel better.*
>
> —*Kelly McGonigal*[167]

There are two types of stress: *distress*, which is negative stress in the common usage of this word, and *eustress*, the good type of stress in which you respond to stress with healthy, positive feelings (for example, during an athletic competition or riding a roller coaster).

Distress, and particularly chronic distress, is one of the biggest enemies of willpower. When you're under stress, your ability to withstand pressure diminishes. This means that you can no longer exhibit the same kind of mental toughness and self-discipline as when you're your normal self. It's like expecting your car (you) to have the same acceleration when there's a semi-truck (stress) attached to it.

As Kelly McGonigal notes, stress puts you into a reward-seeking state where your priority ceases to be about personal growth (such as overcoming a temptation), and becomes all about gaining comfort, often at the expense of your long-term goals. And it makes a lot of sense: why would a person who's stressed out seek more stressors?

Chronically elevated levels of stress will not only have a negative effect on your health and well-being, but also on your entire life. If you often get stressed, make it your priority to relax daily, even if it's just five minutes of cuddling with your partner, reading a book, or taking a short walk.

In addition to that, avoid setting any new challenges for your willpower and conserve your energy when you're going through a tough period. It's better to deal with the stress first and then (having recovered) focus on personal growth yet again, than it is to put too much burden on your shoulders and collapse under the weight.

# Day 172: On Having More Than One Identity

> *Those who gain their sense of identity from many areas are more resilient when failing in any one area. For example, a professional tennis player is more likely to be upset by losing a match than is an amateur player for whom tennis is only one of many activities in the week.*
>
> —*Neil Fiore*[168]

If you define yourself by only one role — an entrepreneur, a surfer, a writer, or a pianist — your self-image might be heavily dependent on your performance in this role. This can make you incapable of effectively processing big failures in that area.

For this reason, it's good to define yourself by at least several roles. Then, even when you fail in one domain, there will still be other areas in which your performance might still inspire hope and help you recover from the failure in that other thing.

For example, if I have a bad day when rock climbing, it won't affect my well-being very much if I'm still doing well as a writer or have recently improved my language skills or strengthened a key relationship. If I considered myself exclusively a rock climber, each failure would crush me.

How many roles do you have? How many of them affect your self-image? If you have only one or two defining roles, consider adding an additional identity or two. That way, you'll disperse any negative emotions over several domains and improve your ability to quickly bounce back from any failure in one of them.

# Day 173: On Eating Alone

*Meals eaten with one other person present were 33% larger than meals eaten alone, whereas 47%, 58%, 69%, 70%, 72%, and 96% increases were associated with two, three, four, five, six, and seven or more people present, respectively.*

—John M. de Castro[169]

Here's a super simple way to improve your self-control when eating: eat alone. When people eat with others, they eat more — and the greater the number of people who share the meal with you, the more you eat.

However, studies suggest that this phenomenon isn't related to the amount of time spent eating.[170] It's the companionship in itself that makes humans more likely to eat more when they are around other people than when alone. The same happens with animals. With chickens, for example, a full chicken will continue eating if a hungry chicken starts eating with it.

If you're currently on a diet and you frequently have a bite with other people, ask yourself how important it is for you to spend time eating with them. Perhaps you could forego or reduce the number of shared meals while you're on a diet and find a different activity that you could do together.

Sometimes such simple tweaks can quickly produce big results, so give it a go for at least a few weeks and see whether it can help you achieve your goals more quickly.

# Day 174: On Experiencing Life

*Accept what life offers you and try to drink from every cup. All wines should be tasted; some should only be sipped, but with others, drink the whole bottle.*

—*Paulo Coelho*[171]

While this book and most of my other books glorify self-discipline and make it sound like the most important thing in the world, I don't want you to think that a life of deprivation is the right one. In fact, I believe that unless you espouse self-discipline in a healthy way, it might be close to impossible to maintain it in the long haul.

However, what *is* a healthy approach to self-discipline? It's the attitude that self-discipline exists to support you in your goals, but it shouldn't prevent you from fully experiencing life.

For example, I'm now on an overseas trip. While I'm still largely following my routine by waking up early and working in the morning, I also make exceptions: I work less, my diet is not as strict, and I allow myself to be lazier. I'm still working toward some goals, but I put some on a temporary hold. I can always work on them later, while pushing myself now would mean that I wouldn't be able to experience the trip to the fullest and recharge my batteries.

I want you to be as self-disciplined as possible, but I don't want you to skip eating spaghetti, pizza, or ice cream while in Italy, avoid eating a piece of birthday cake at your best friend's party, or to not enjoy sunny weather and goof off at the beach every now and then.

However, as the quote from Paulo Coelho's says, please note that you should experience some things only a little, while others are there to be enjoyed to the fullest. There are also experiences that you can skip without any regrets. For example, you don't have to take hard drugs to know that it's a bad idea, while indulging in unhealthy food *every now and then* (ideally when celebrating something with your loved ones) isn't that bad.

Lastly, don't treat it as a permission to cheat. You shouldn't go on a trip while in the middle of your diet just so you can indulge in unhealthy food or get lazy because it's sunny outside while you have an urgent job to do.

Accept with welcoming hands what life has to offer, but make sure that you drink from the right cups, and in the right amount — not too little, and not too much.

# Day 175: On Improving Self-Control by Using Your Other Hand

*Using the mouse, stirring your coffee, opening doors. This requires people to practice self-control because their habitual tendency is to use their dominant hands.*

—*Thomas Denson*[172]

One interesting exercise to improve your self-control is to start using your other hand for the things you usually do with your dominant one. For example, use your non-dominant hand for brushing your teeth, pouring drinks into a cup, washing yourself, doing the dishes, opening jars, stirring coffee, or opening doors.

Psychologist Thomas Denson had people use their non-dominant hand for two weeks for any task that was safe to do that way. After two weeks, people in the group using the non-dominant hand controlled their aggression better.

What does it have to do with self-control? It's because aggression, or virtually any other thing you control by exerting self-discipline, is an impulse. Just like you automatically open doors with your dominant hand, so do you impulsively reply with anger, grab a cookie, or choose the elevator instead of the stairs.

Conscious change in your automatic behaviors, such as intentionally using your non-dominant hand, can then help you improve your ability to control impulses, and by extension, make you more self-disciplined. I know, it's a wild theory, but why not try it? Even if it only produces small improvements, it's still a fun experiment.

# WEEK 26

# Day 176: On Jotting Things Down

*The palest ink is more reliable than the most powerful memory.*

—*Chinese proverb*

It's all fine and dandy to tell yourself that you're going to achieve this and that goal. However, in the end, our memories are fickle. You can forget about some goals, or stop working on them simply because they were never *real* in the first place — you've never written them down, so they only existed in your head and if something is only in your head, you can conveniently make it disappear without a trace or simply forget it without intending to.

Develop a habit of writing down your goals, even if it's only one sentence or two. Thanks to the habit of tracking your goals on paper, you'll look at your objectives as real-world resolutions and not just mere ideas floating through your head that you can disregard whenever you feel like doing so. It's more difficult to do the same if your goals are written, because erasing them — regardless if it's by deleting a text file or tearing up a piece of paper — will make it painfully clear that you're giving up on them.

In addition to writing down your goals, write down specific routines that you plan to follow in order to achieve them. For example, for this book, I have a spreadsheet in which I note down how many daily entries I write each day. That way, I can hold myself accountable and compare my performance today to that of the past. Moreover, it makes it clear to me how close I am to achieving my goal, and all of that boosts my motivation to keep going. It also lets me see if things are going as planned and if the plan itself needs revision in order to improve the results.

# Day 177: On Sleep

*Good sleep habits could refuel a person's ability to make more difficult choices instead of opting for the easier choice or the easier task.*

—***June J. Pilcher***[173]

Sleep is one of the needs that you can't control no matter how self-disciplined you are. You can choose to go without food for a few days and you'll be fine. If you've been going without sleep for, say, 48 hours, even in a situation like driving (when falling asleep means certain death), you still won't be able to control it.

For this reason, sleep is king and you should do all in your power to ensure that you have a good night's sleep. Studies show that a lack of or poor sleep can negatively affect self-control. I don't think I need to cite research to convince you that it's true. You probably have plenty of empiric evidence from your own life, and so do I.

If you're half-asleep the entire day, your only priority will be to go to sleep as quickly as possible. Who cares about dieting, exercise, money, etc. if they can barely think straight, their mental capacity reduced to zero.

There are several key things you can do to improve your sleep:

1. Make sure you have a comfortable mattress. Most mattresses should be replaced at least every ten years.

2. Make sure you sleep in silence. Any noise will dramatically reduce the sleep quality. Use earplugs if there's no way to soundproof your bedroom.

3. Make sure you sleep in the right temperature. The most beneficial temperature for sleep is 60-67 degrees Fahrenheit (15-19 Celsius).[174]

4. Make sure you reduce the amount of blue light you receive in the evening, especially during the last hour before you want to be asleep. This means not using electronics before sleep, and if not possible (as is the case for most of us), put on blue-blocking goggles and make sure to expose yourself to bright light during the day.

5. Make sure your racing mind is asleep. If you have any lingering thoughts, write them down and resume thinking about them the next day. You won't have to revisit them during the time you should be sleeping because you will have written them down.

6. Make sure you don't consume caffeine when it's less than six hours prior to sleep (it takes three to seven hours for caffeine to metabolize[175]). Caffeine-induced sleep disorder is a real thing, and even if you can fall asleep after drinking tea of coffee, it doesn't mean your sleep is of high quality.

7. Make sure you don't consume a big meal prior to going to sleep. Give your body at least two hours after eating before you go to sleep.

# Day 178: On Losing Momentum

*No matter what your goal/project, never allow yourself to miss two days in a row.*

—*Leo Babauta*[176]

Momentum will carry you forward almost automatically for as long as you stick to your resolutions every day. Missing one day every now and then isn't that dangerous, but if it's two or more days without any action taken to get you closer to your goal, the risk of giving up on your goal dramatically increases.

What I've found from my personal experience is that you don't necessarily have to always stick to your resolutions exactly as they are stated. If, for example, you have a goal to write 1,000 words a day and for a weekend you can only write 100 words each day, you should still be able to resume your regular routine on Monday easily. If, however, you skip writing altogether, resuming your routine will be much more challenging.

The same happens with exercise, where even a super brief 5-minute workout will still be better than not exercising at all, or when changing your nutritional habits, where adding even one tiny vegetable to your plate is better than only eating junk food.

Whenever you find yourself in a situation where it's hard to stick to your goals, take one full day off if you need it, but on the next day perform at least one tiny action associated with your goal. That way you'll still maintain some momentum and ensure that it will be easier to resume your regular routine when you're ready.

# Day 179: On Effort Generating Satisfaction

> *We like sitting in a garden but don't want to get sweaty and dirty digging up a garden space or mowing the lawn, so we pay a gardener to cut the grass and plant some flowers.*
>
> *We want to enjoy a nice meal, but shopping and cooking are too much trouble, so we eat out or just pop something into the microwave.*
>
> *Sadly, in surrendering our effort in these activities, we gain relaxation, but we may actually give up a lot of deep enjoyment.*
>
> *It's often effort that ultimately creates long-term satisfaction.*
>
> —**Dan Ariely**[177]

On day 154 we discussed the value of doing things yourself. We focused on the fact that resisting the temptation to delegate everything can help you learn new things and ultimately grow as a person.

Today I'd like to approach this subject from another perspective — that effort leads to long-term satisfaction. By choosing what now feels like a choice that maximizes your happiness (delegating the work), not only do you miss potential opportunities to learn, but you also lose the positive feelings you can get from expending the effort yourself.

As I've already stated, it's not possible for most people to do everything themselves. However, whenever you can afford to do so, overcome your laziness and inertia, exert some willpower and, instead of having somebody else do something for you, do it yourself.

Yes, in the beginning it probably won't feel as nice as the relaxation you could get from somebody else handling it for you, but in the end the expended effort will probably make you happier; this will also improve your ability to discipline yourself instead of defaulting to delegating the work to others.

# Day 180: On Paying the Price as Fast as Possible

*No matter how long a situation continues, there's always a way to get out. But the sooner you handle it, the easier it is.*

*Whenever I can I choose to pay in advance. But if I become aware of a mistake, I want to pay the price as fast as possible and clear the record. I've become fanatically intolerant of permanent irritants.*

—*Harry Browne*[178]

Small irritating things tend to grow into bigger problems the longer you let them continue. Moreover, the longer the situation continues, the more difficult it is to resolve it.

For this reason, it's important to develop a habit of paying the price as fast as possible: engage in something a little unpleasant today to resolve the situation before it gets worse and more difficult to handle.

To share an example with you, there was a time when I used to carry a large textile bag and a duffel bag for each outdoors climbing session. I was too lazy to take my climbing gear out of my gym bag and put it into a travel backpack that was more suitable for transportation between one crag and another.

I used to complain about it, but I didn't do anything about the situation because it was only a small irritant. Usually it didn't take more than a couple of minutes to access the crag, so it wasn't a big deal to carry the gear this way.

Then one sector required a twenty-minute walk on a hiking path with steep declines and inclines. I quickly discovered how stupid and uncomfortable it was to carry climbing gear in something other than a backpack.

On the next occasion, I overcame my laziness and put my climbing gear into a backpack. It took me just a few minutes to repack my things, and now I could comfortably walk from one crag to another. Paying the price as fast as possible — the first time I realized there was a problem — would have helped me avoid unnecessary discomfort.

This and other similar lessons have taught me that it's best to act as soon as you realize that there's a problem or an unpleasant thing to do. Use your self-control to handle any irritants, no matter how small they might be, right away. You'll not only get rid of the problem, you'll also exercise your willpower muscle each time you decide to act immediately instead of postponing it.

# Day 181: On the Disciplined Pursuit of Less

> *If success is a catalyst for failure because it leads to the "undisciplined pursuit of more," then one simple antidote is the disciplined pursuit of less. Not just haphazardly saying no, but purposefully, deliberately, and strategically eliminating the nonessentials.*
>
> —*Greg McKeown*[179]

It takes work to simplify one's life, and perhaps that's why most people are engaged in the undisciplined pursuit of more rather than less.

Saying no is uncomfortable, so by default they say yes to new obligations. They don't pause and ponder on how they use up their energy because it takes too much work. There's always something urgent to do, and hence they never take the time to deliberately eliminate what's unessential in their lives so they can focus on what matters.

It's particularly important to remedy a situation in which your non-priorities dominate your priorities. For example, when you spend several hours a week cleaning your house and then don't have time and energy for exercise, it's a clear case of nonessentials robbing your priorities. Harness the power of self-discipline to make some uncomfortable changes, such as hiring a cleaning person so that you can free up your time and energy to focus on what matters more — your well-being.

If you want to retain control over your life, embrace the strategy of deliberately pursuing less. Instead of thinking how you can add more to your life, figure out what you can eliminate from it, in order to make more time for what matters most for you. Think twice before you accept any new obligations or add new events to your calendar.

# Day 182: On Saying No

*Don't do anything you don't want to do. When you agree to do something you don't want to do, you will resent the person who asked you to do it.*

—*James Altucher[180]*

Saying yes to something you don't want to do can save you the discomfort of saying no, but ultimately it's like cheating on a diet. You get fleeting pleasure (or in the case of saying yes, temporarily escape discomfort) now at the expense of your long-term well-being. In addition to that, in the case of saying yes, you risk feeling resentful toward the person who asked you to do something you didn't want to do.

Practice your self-control by saying no when you're tempted to say yes just to avoid awkwardness. It doesn't mean that from now on you'll never help somebody just because you don't feel like doing it; give a helping hand whenever people need you, but establish boundaries and respect them.

If you have trouble saying no, start small at first. For example, offer your help, but in a limited way, or put some conditions on it. After all, you're the one being *asked* for help, so even if you don't use your right to refuse, you can still exert your right to say when you're available or what you can and cannot do for another person.

# WEEK 27

# Day 183: On Shocking Your Body

*"Your body needs to be shocked to become resilient," Eric explained. Follow the same daily routine, and your musculoskeletal system quickly figures out how to adapt and go on autopilot. But surprise it with new challenges — leap over a creek, commando-crawl under a log, sprint till your lungs are bursting — and scores of nerves and ancillary muscles are suddenly electrified into action.*

—*Christopher McDougall*[181]

One of the most common reasons why people don't succeed at introducing a permanent exercise habit in their lives is because their workouts are boring. They do the same things over and over again, and even if they work in the beginning, the body quickly adapts to them and stops responding to them in the same way as in the beginning.

When the effectiveness drops down and a person gets tired of doing the same things, the outcome is predictable: you no longer want to work out anymore.

That's why I'm so strongly against any kind of structured fitness classes at the gym that you attend because you think it's the only way to exercise.

Seek something enjoyable and exciting that won't feel like dreadful exercise. If you can't find it, keep looking until you do. Ultimately, it's the only way to successfully maintain an exercise habit in your life.

However, please note that even if you're doing something exciting, no matter how fantastic it is in the beginning, if you don't change your routine every now and then, it also might get boring.

Mixing it up every now and then by focusing on a different aspect of the activity, doing it in a different place, with different intensity or with different people will boost your excitement, shock your body, and ensure that you'll stick to physical activity for the long haul.

# Day 184: On Creating Value

*Vow: "I will create value for society, rather than extract it."*

—*John C. Bogle[182]*

In today's world of consumerism, it's easy to extract value without creating much yourself. Millions of office workers all over the world pretend they're hard at work, while on their screens you can see solitaire, social media sites, memes, or any other distraction that helps them to pass time until they can go home.

Instead of supporting somebody else's efforts or creating something themselves, millions of people pass time by hating the things that were created by others. For example, watch pretty much any video on YouTube and you're guaranteed to see critical (if not blatantly hate-filled) comments, no matter how high the quality of the content and presentation is. Look at other comments that were posted by the same people, and you'll often find that their primary occupation in life is (unconstructively) criticizing the work of others without ever creating anything themselves.

Instead of bettering themselves and encouraging others to do the same, millions seek to live their lives in the easiest way possible, even at the expense of their moral principles.

Harness the power of self-discipline to create more value than you extract. In addition to making the world a better place, it will serve as a powerful exercise in self-control and transform your mindset to that of a producer, a person who will always be valued in society, regardless of the economy or location.

For example, whenever you ask somebody for advice, share the knowledge with two or more other people. At work, try to do your best — and if your job doesn't excite you enough to do so, do everybody a favor and find a different job that will let you contribute to the world in a better way. Support other creators instead of criticizing them. Don't always wait for somebody else to take the initiative: step forward and organize something yourself.

Resist the temptation to consume without ever contributing much yourself. The more value you create, the better off everyone is — and the more that eventually comes back to you.

# Day 185: On Staying With Problems Longer

*Students who were forced to struggle on complex problems before receiving help from teachers outperformed students who received immediate assistance.*

—*Brad Stulberg and Steve Magness*[183]

Here's a simple mindset change that can help you improve your problem-solving skills and make you more persistent: whenever you face a problem, stay with it for a good while before you ask anyone for help.

If you're immediately seeking outside help the instant you find you can't deal with something, you're robbing yourself out of the opportunity to struggle and figure it out yourself.

Obviously, this doesn't apply to life-or-death situations. I don't want you to spend a little while longer trying to figure out how to help a victim of a car accident — call the ambulance right away. Practice staying with problems longer only when it's safe and sensible to do so.

For example, if something is not working properly on your computer, before you call for IT help, seek answers yourself and only get help if you've tried several possible solutions and nothing has worked.

If you're learning a new skill and can't figure out how to do something, try to deconstruct it, piece by piece. If you still can't figure it out, seek assistance from your teacher.

By rejecting the impulse to ask for help right away, you'll also practice your self-control. The downside is wasting a few minutes on a problem you can't solve. The upside is developing more trust in your own abilities, becoming more patient, and learning something new.

# Day 186: On Simple Rules

> *Simple rules are shortcut strategies that save time and effort by focusing our attention and simplifying the way we process information. The rules aren't universal — they're tailored to the particular situation and the person using them.*
>
> —***Donald Sull***[184]

I'm a big fan of using rules to simplify my life. In today's world, we have too many choices to make. Many of those choices are trivial, but because we don't want to miss out, we waste precious time deciding where we want to go for dinner, whether we want to drink blueberry, raspberry, strawberry, or blackberry juice, and then waste even more time choosing a meal we want to eat.

And that's just one common situation in a sea of choices. Which brand of bread to eat? Which fitness regimen to follow? Where to go for a vacation? Which book to read? The choices are endless, and they're all sucking energy that you could spend on something more constructive and useful.

Embrace some simple rules in your life to pare down your choices to the bare minimum.

For example, I have a simple rule when it comes to traveling: I never travel to cold places. If it's less than 60-70 degrees Fahrenheit (15–20 degrees Celsius) there, I'm not going. This greatly limits my choices, I know that the weather will be relatively good, and I get to spend more time planning the actual trip rather than choosing the destination.

Another example, more from the realm of personal development, is my rule of never giving up on anything that's important to me. Having established that something is important to me, I don't give up. I can't break my rule, so I'll stick to a goal for as long as necessary or until it stops being important to me.

My other rules include things like not taking group classes (I find it to be an extremely ineffective way of learning when the attention of the teacher is spread out over several students or more), rejecting interviews and social media (I'd rather spend my time by writing a new book), and always choosing solutions that minimize my *time* investment, even if they're financially more expensive (such as choosing more expensive airport parking to be closer to the terminal or buying more expensive products to reduce the risk of them breaking down).

What are your rules? Think of some common decisions you often have to make — including the important choices related to your goals — and think of simple rules you could establish to simplify your life and your decision-making process.

# Day 187: On Not Judging Too Quickly

*Realize that other people think their behavior is more responsive to situational factors than you're inclined to think — and they're more likely to be right than you are. They almost certainly know their current situation — and their relevant personal history — better than you do.*

—*Richard Nisbett*[185]

You can develop your self-control while working on your most important goals, but you can also practice it in everyday situations —when judging people, for example.

Virtually all of us have done it at least once: you assume you know what's best for another person, while in fact you know nothing about their background or approach to the current situation, yet you judge. It's hard to resist this temptation; after all, we look at the world through our own filters and consider them suitable for everything and everyone.

Whenever you catch yourself judging someone harshly, pause and ask yourself if you understand this person's personal history, motives, and current situation.

A driver who honked at you might have been a jerk, but he might also have just been diagnosed with cancer, late to an important meeting or driving to the hospital to visit a relative.

An overweight person might be lazy, but he or she might also struggle with difficult family issues, health disorders, or be battling against depression.

You never know the entire picture, so the best approach is to refrain from judging. You'll improve your "people skills" and at the same time you'll be practicing your self-control.

# Day 188: On Pride

*All men make mistakes, but a good man yields when he knows his course is wrong, and repairs the evil. The only crime is pride.*

—*Sophocles*[186]

Pride has a positive connotation. You're proud of your achievements, proud of your children, or proud of your country.

However, pride often serves as an excuse to stick to the wrong path or deny responsibility for your wrongdoings. It's also dangerous when it converts to egotism, a state leading to complacency and overestimating your abilities.

Embrace a healthy approach toward accomplishment: appreciate your successes, but don't put pride on the pedestal and discontinue further efforts just because somebody acknowledged your triumphs.

I sometimes receive emails from my readers telling me that my books have changed their lives. I'm happy to hear that they've found my work valuable, but — as strange as it may sound — I refuse to feel proud of my books. My books might have been the spark, but it's the reader's efforts that have helped them change their lives. If I were to convince myself that my books are so incredible, I would have probably become complacent or let the success go to my head.

Another aspect of pride is stubbornly following the wrong path. A common demonstration of this behavior is particularly common among men: when they get lost, they'll put off asking somebody for directions for as long as they can, while they continue their journey in the wrong direction.

Instead of acknowledging the mistake, swallowing their pride, and asking for help, they waste time and energy just because they're too prideful.

If you recognize such a behavior in yourself, vow to never again let pride make you overinvest in the wrong endeavors. The moment you realize you're following the wrong path, stop. Go back to the drawing board, prepare new plans and start again. In the grand scheme of things, your pride is of small importance when compared to achieving your large long-term goals.

# Day 189: On Adventures

*So many people live within unhappy circumstances and yet will not take the initiative to change their situation because they are conditioned to a life of security, conformity, and conservatism, all of which may appear to give one peace of mind, but in reality nothing is more dangerous to the adventurous spirit within a man than a secure future. The very basic core of a man's living spirit is his passion for adventure. The joy of life comes from our encounters with new experiences, and hence there is no greater joy than to have an endlessly changing horizon, for each day to have a new and different sun.*

—*Jon Krakauer*[187]

Boredom is dangerous not only because it's unpleasant, but also because it usually means having the worst kind of security in life — complacency. It's good to feel satisfied with what you have, but the moment you get stuck in a rut, afraid that any change will ruin the security you now enjoy, you lose the opportunity for immense joy and personal growth.

Adventures spice up life. Without new experiences, life is boring and there's little growth to be attained. When you're bored, you're less likely to feel inspired to make changes in life, so it leads to a downward spiral.

Embark on new adventures as often as you can. Traveling always means encounters with new experiences, but you don't necessarily have to leave your hometown every week to live an adventurous life. Learning new interesting skills can be an adventure in itself. Hiking to a nearby wilderness area or spending the night in a tent outdoors can get you out of a rut, too.

Lastly, to actually be considered adventures, they are usually at least slightly uncomfortable or dangerous, and that also means an opportunity to practice self-discipline and toughen up. Plan your next adventure now!

# WEEK 28
## Day 190: On Being Specific About Your Resolutions

*Instead of saying "I'm never going to cheat again," say, "Today, I'm not going to do that thing that makes me feel weak and shameful about myself again."*

—*Neil Strauss*[188]

When setting a new resolution, be specific about it, and particularly about the way a certain behavior you want to give up makes you feel.

For example, saying "I'm not going to eat pizza anymore" isn't going to be as visceral as saying "I'm not going to eat that thing that makes me bloated, obese, and tired anymore." The former is a weak, non-emotional statement; the latter is a strong resolution that reminds you about the reason why you want to stop engaging in a given activity.

This strategy works the other way, too. Instead of saying "I'm going to write 1000 words a day," say "I'm going to write 1000 words a day, the activity that makes me feel so energized, creative, and hopeful about the future in which I'm a bestselling author."

A more specific, emotionally-charged resolution will stick in your mind better, and that will help you keep going or pause and think before breaking a resolution.

# Day 191: On Futile Determination

*If any man is able to convince me and show me that I do not think or act right, I will gladly change; for I seek the truth by which no man was ever injured. But he is injured who abides in his error and ignorance.*

—*Marcus Aurelius*[189]

Determination can change your life, but it can also lead to a lot of wasted time if you stubbornly keep going when everyone around you who's knowledgeable about the goal you want to reach tells you that you're following the wrong path.

Obviously, if the only people who are trying to convince you that you're wrong have no idea about what you're doing, you can safely ignore their advice. If, however, people who have reached the goals you're striving to achieve are trying to correct your ways, heed their advice.

I sometimes offer advice to new entrepreneurs who have big dreams, but the word "realistic" doesn't seem to be a part of their dictionary. I tell them to listen to the experts, get their feet wet with a simple business model and slowly build real-world experience. Unfortunately, many of them ignore this advice only to return months or years later, this time with more humility and a desire to apply their immense desire and determination in a way that it can actually lead to results.

Don't get me wrong — I'm all for bold undertakings, but often what those entrepreneurs do is waste time and energy, investing their vast reserves of determination into a project that was doomed to fail from the get-go because they had no real-world business experience to make it succeed.

I know how it works, because I was such a person, too.

The first time I read *The Millionaire Fastlane* by MJ DeMarco (a book that eventually changed my life), I didn't heed the author's advice about not pursuing money-making schemes. I thought I knew better, and foolishly stuck to SEO (Search Engine Optimization) and affiliate marketing. I had to suffer from several more failures before I was ready to listen to people who were more experienced than I was.

If you want to save yourself from unnecessary failures, be open to feedback from people who have achieved the goals you'd like to reach. Don't abide in error and ignorance, digging for gold like a mad man where hundreds of people had dug before you and didn't find anything.

# Day 192: On Being in It for the Long Term

*Tests compared new musicians who saw themselves as in it for the long term, versus just trying it. With the same amount of practice, the long-term-commitment group outperformed the short-term-commitment group by 400 percent. The long-term-commitment group, with a mere twenty minutes of weekly practice, progressed faster than the short-termers who practiced for an hour and a half. When long-term commitment combined with high levels of practice, skills skyrocketed.*

—*Daniel Coyle*[190]

There's something about long-term commitment that makes it immensely more powerful than doing something once-off, even when the amount of time spent practicing is the same in both cases.

What matters is not putting in the same number of hours every now and then, but putting in time consistently, even if it's a small amount of time. In other words, the winning strategy is that of a marathoner, running long distances slowly, and not that of a sprinter, running short distances quickly.

For example, as a writer, I currently follow a routine of writing at least 1000 words a day. I wouldn't be able to do my best work by not having a schedule and writing in a random fashion instead. It's the everyday habit that keeps my writing sharp, and whenever I take a longer break from writing, I need at least several days to get back into the groove. Consequently, I make sure that even if I can't write 1000 words for some reason, I at least write *something*.

Are your goals designed in such a way that you're working on them regularly or are you doing them from time to time, in an erratic fashion? How can you develop a system that will ensure that each day or each week you practice for a set period of time?

# Day 193: On Becoming a New Person

> *If you want to be a new man you have to stay in new places, and do new things, with people who never knew you before. If you go back to the same old ways, what else can you be but the same old person?*
>
> —*Joe Abercrombie*[191]

Changing yourself doesn't necessarily mean throwing away your old life, cutting ties with your family and friends and moving to another corner of the world. If, however, certain aspects of your old life clearly hold you back, it *is* necessary to replace them with something new to enable your identity to change.

If, for example, your primary way of spending time is going to nightclubs and partying, don't expect to become highly productive until you get rid of that habit and embrace a new, less exciting, lifestyle. Some of your friends will probably resent you for it, but if they're against you doing what you need to do for your personal growth, are they truly your friends?

Likewise, pursuing important long-term goals often means becoming a part of a new community, visiting places you've never been to before, and embracing habits that you've never thought about. It's understandable to feel some resistance toward destroying your old ways and replacing them with something new, but ultimately it's how you become a new person.

For example, I was apprehensive about terminating my bodybuilding workout regimen and switching to an entirely different, bodyweight-based approach to exercise. I had to follow new experts, perform new exercises, and train in a different environment.

There's no way around it; if you want something new in your life, something old has to go, no matter how sentimental you are about it or how scared you are that the new thing might not work well for you.

# Day 194: On Pain and Quitting

*Pain is temporary. Quitting lasts forever.*

—*Lance Armstrong*[192]

Pain, particularly during strenuous exercise, is often so overpowering that you can barely think straight. However, it's through this pain that we grow, and it's a necessary part of the process, just like embracing discomfort in general is essential for rejecting instant gratification in order to accomplish your long-term goals.

Whenever you feel tempted to give up because of momentary pain, do your best to remind yourself that pain passes, but the disappointment you'll feel upon quitting will accompany you for a long time. Giving up will give you some relief right now, but the price you'll have to pay will be ultimately more painful than bearing the pain a little while longer.

If you think that there's no way you can handle the pain — something that will probably happen to you during the first several weeks of exercising, for example — tell yourself to only bear it for three seconds longer and then give up. Often, pain is a fleeting high-intensity burst at the moment you first feel it, and then it quickly recedes as your body adapts to it — something I experienced in numerous workouts, as well as when I took cold showers. Waiting for three seconds before you give up can be enough time to enable you to withstand the pain and keep going.

As a quick disclaimer, please don't mistake the kind of pain that's safe, signaling you're pushing yourself, with the kind of pain that's the signal of an injury. Whenever you are pushing your limits, always prioritize safety over everything else.

# Day 195: On Procrastination as Your Ally

*If I defer writing a section, it must be eliminated. This is simple ethics: Why should I try to fool people by writing about a subject for which I feel no natural drive?*

—*Nassim Taleb*[193]

People consider procrastination an enemy and seek ways to eliminate it from their life. What if I told you that procrastination can be actually one of your greatest allies?

In essence, when you're putting something off, it's because you don't care about it enough to take action now. If there's no natural drive to get it done, then it means you're forcing yourself into doing something that isn't right for you.

Perhaps it's the wrong action or you're thinking about it in the wrong way. Regardless, in both of those circumstances, procrastination tells you that you're lacking the right motivation.

If you woke up in the early morning in a burning house, would you put off getting up for later?

Likewise, if you cared deep down about building a business, would you procrastinate about doing the necessary work? Playing video games instead of working would be a clear signal that you've yet to uncover a strong enough reason to give up gaming in favor of doing something more productive.

The next time you catch yourself delaying action, reassess your motivators. If you're constantly putting it off, your chances of success are slim. Discover better reasons why, or give up and do something else that won't result in constant procrastination.

# Day 196: On Impermanent Motivation

*Of course motivation is not permanent. But then, neither is bathing; but it is something you should do on a regular basis.*

—*Zig Ziglar*[194]

Don't assume that if you're motivated now, you'll be motivated forever, and if the motivation is gone, it's time to give up on your goals.

You should draw your motivation from your personal reasons why (such as your desire to build a successful business to offer your family the best of what life has to offer), but you'll have to periodically do some spring-cleaning and revise your motivators.

Resist the temptation to give up just because you temporarily lack motivation. Instead of treating it as an excuse to discontinue your efforts, come up with practical solutions that will recharge your motivation.

Just like you need to wash your body regularly to keep it clean, you need to regularly take care of your motivation. Replenish it whenever it drops and always look for new ways to strengthen it.

I strongly suggest creating a document in which you're going to put anything that fires you up. For example, I save articles I find inspirational, jot down songs I find motivating, and download images that inspire me. Whenever I feel under the weather, I can access my "inspiration bank" and lift my spirits.

# WEEK 29

# Day 197: On Eliminating a Negative Attitude

*I will eliminate hatred, envy, jealousy, selfishness, and cynicism, by developing love for all humanity, because I know that a negative attitude toward others can never bring me success.*

—*Napoleon Hill*[195]

All but a few enlightened individuals engage at least periodically in behaviors and emotions like hatred, sarcasm, envy, jealousy, selfishness, miserliness, cynicism, or indifference.

Fighting against those emotions is a battle that never ends, because no matter how self-disciplined you are, those behaviors are often impulses appearing out of the blue. What you *can* do is to be vigilant for them and whenever they appear, instead of letting them linger in your head, replace them with the opposite thought or regard them as mere useless distractions.

It's important to note that you need to see the pleasure you get out of engaging in negative emotions and behaviors as the worst type of instant gratification.

Yes, in some twisted way it's pleasant to hate somebody, use sarcasm to hurt them, or be indifferent. However, if you engage in those behaviors without any restraint, you're training yourself to not control your impulses. Is this something that will help you exhibit self-discipline in other areas of your life or will it hurt your efforts to do so?

# Day 198: On Your Maxims

*The maxims of men reveal their characters.*

—*Luc de Clapiers*[196]

We've already talked about living in accordance with your principles and using simple rules to improve your decision-making process.

Today I'd like to talk about a related topic: the importance of life maxims.

I've already told you that metaphors can help instill a change better than any amount of specific step-by-step instructions — and so can the maxims you live by.

Ponder the common statement that life is hard. If you truly believe that life is hard, then how does it affect your character? Are you going to be a cheery, optimistic person or adapt a defeatist outlook on life?

How about thinking that a stranger is a friend you haven't met? Will this make you more likely to be a friendly person and develop a supportive circle of friends or close you off to new opportunities to connect with like-minded individuals?

What about adopting the maxim that everything in life is possible as long as you refuse to listen to reason? Okay, you won't become the President of the United States if you weren't born in that country (and a few other things), but other than that, would you say that living by such a maxim will hinder your growth or perhaps empower you?

Your maxims expose your character. If you want to be successful, make sure that your maxims are empowering and positive. Make a list of the most important truths you live by — consciously or unconsciously — and ask yourself if they all serve you to become a better person. If they don't, discard them and replace them with different, more advantageous ones.

# Day 199: On Your Inaction Hurting Others

> *If you were meant to cure cancer or write a symphony or crack cold fusion and you don't do it, you not only hurt yourself, even destroy yourself. You hurt your children. You hurt me. You hurt the planet.*
>
> —*Steven Pressfield*[197]

If you can't shake yourself out of inaction for your own benefit, perhaps you can do it by having others in mind. This type of motivation is called *prosocial motivation*; it means taking action for the benefit of somebody or something beyond yourself: your family, your favorite charity, your community, the environment, etc.

Spend some time thinking how your inaction hurts the people around you. For some people, the negative motivation they can get from such an exercise is more powerful than any words of encouragement. The guilt they feel upon realizing they're betraying their family or harming the planet can be a more enticing motivator than getting the rewards for themselves, whether they're internal or external ones.

It's a technique I sometimes use to motivate myself to write. I've developed the skill of writing and people seem to enjoy and benefit from my books. If I don't write more books, I'm hurting them by depriving them of the education and possibly valuable insights that they could get by reading my works.

If you're the type of a person who often cares more about others than yourself, this sort of motivation can turn you into a high achiever, However, be cautious not to overdo it: the point isn't to spend your life working yourself into the ground, forever feeling guilty that you could do even more. Strive to produce value for everyone, including yourself.

# Day 200: On Fretting About Yesterday's Problems

*"If a ship has been sunk," Admiral King went on, "I can't bring it up. If it is going to be sunk, I can't stop it. I can use my time much better working on tomorrow's problem than by fretting about yesterday's. Besides, if I let those things get me, I wouldn't last long."*

—*Dale Carnegie*[198]

So many people waste time living in the past. They feel guilty because of the mistakes they made last year, regret not making a different decision last week, or wishing they could have somehow foreseen a failure five months ago.

What's the point?

Like Admiral King says, if a ship has been sunk, it's not like you can bring it up and set sail again. If you made a mistake, it's not like you can undo it. You can fix some of its consequences, but you can't turn back the clock. Likewise, you can't change the decision you made a week ago; all you can do is make a different decision today. Nor can you foresee the future; all you can do is try to do your best and prepare for the worst.

Tap into your resources of willpower whenever you catch yourself fretting about yesterday's problems. Instead of ruminating about them, think about what you can do today — right here and right now — to improve your life. Ultimately, the only control you have is over what you're doing now, so make sure you're making the right choices today.

# Day 201: On Teaching Others

*Teach others what you are learning. You become what you teach. You teach what you are. When you attempt to articulate and explain a new concept to someone else, you understand it and internalize it better yourself.*

*You only really know something to the degree to which you can teach it to someone else, and have them understand and apply it in their own lives.*

*—Brian Tracy[199]*

Here's an ingenious way to become more self-disciplined: while learning how to strengthen your self-control, regularly share your lessons with other people. Teaching is a powerful way to make the knowledge you already have in your head become more organized and better internalized.

Guess why I write books about self-discipline! Just kidding, though writing has definitely helped me clarify my ideas and better understand them myself.

The next time you find yourself in a conversation with somebody who is wondering how to instill more self-discipline in their lives, don't hesitate to share your experiences or even serve as their unofficial coach and mentor.

Another wonderful way to teach others is to participate in online forums or on social media sites. Teach others how you succeeded with your goals or how you successfully overcame a recent temptation, and you'll not only help them achieve *their* dreams, but also solidify your own success.

Last but not least, if you aren't willing to teach others, teach yourself by journaling. Jotting down your insights, lessons, and conclusions will also serve as a valuable tool for self-improvement.

# Day 202: On Accepting the Worst

*True peace of mind comes from accepting the worst. Psychologically, I think it means a release of energy.*

—*Lin Yutang*[200]

If you can't stop worrying, accept that the worst will happen and let it go. Having released this negative energy, you can now think of constructive ways to deal with the aftermath instead of wasting your time fearing the worst.

This technique sounds simplistic, but it's actually a powerful way to escape from fear-driven paralysis.

For example, if you're constantly worried that your business will not succeed and you're procrastinating about getting started, assume that it *will* go bankrupt.

What can you do to ensure that the failure of your business won't have a big impact on your life? Make a list of potential solutions, such as starting your business on a shoestring or working on it only during the weekends, without it negatively affecting your day job.

Now, if your business actually fails, you'll know how to cope. And if it doesn't, being prepared won't hurt you. In the end, thanks to accepting the worst, you can escape indecision and be better prepared both for success and failure.

# Day 203: On Maintaining Composure

> *Those who have accomplished the greatest results are those who never lose self-control, but are always calm, self-possessed, patient, and polite.*
>
> —*Ryan Holiday*[201]

Being calm, self-possessed, patient, and polite are all traits that everyone interested in building self-discipline should aspire to have. Let's go through them one by one and offer some pointers on how to develop them.

Staying calm means being free of nervousness, anger, and other negative emotions that can take away your self-control and make you do things you'll later regret. In essence, staying calm comes down to mindfulness and the clear logical thinking that comes from that.

One of the best ways to become calmer is to engage in some type of a meditative practice. Whether it's traditional meditation, engaging in a high-focus sport, or doing something that captures your full attention, it will serve as an exercise in mindfulness and thinking clearly. Being calm is a skill; the more often you put yourself in a calm state, the easier it will be to access and maintain it in your everyday life.

Being self-possessed means that you can navigate difficult situations with grace and remain in control of your feelings in circumstances in which a person lacking such an ability would lose their head. By far the best way to develop this ability is by deliberately putting yourself in uncomfortable situations. The more you stretch your comfort zone, the less future situations will overwhelm you. A person who's already been in a disagreeable situation several times, out of their own volition, will be less likely to lose their head when they involuntarily find themselves in such circumstances in the future.

A person who's unable to remain patient — whether it's with other people or when waiting for results to materialize — is more likely to make impulsive decisions that will sabotage their long-term goals. You need to train patience like a muscle. One way in which you can exercise your patience muscle is by engaging in activities that require patience or by learning a skill that takes a long time to develop. Slow progress will help you develop more humility and understand that some things can't be rushed, no matter how hard you try to push them.

Being polite seems unrelated to the topic of self-discipline, but there's one aspect of this trait that does affect your self-control: treating everyone as your equal. People who are impolite are in essence putting themselves above others, thinking that they're superior. This arrogance can lead them to unnecessarily putting themselves in situations that test their willpower, which carries a higher risk of failure.

How do you become more polite? Easy. Assume that you aren't better than others and try to learn from everybody. It's impossible to be impolite toward a person you consider your mentor, because that's what every person can become for you when you embrace humility.

# WEEK 30

# Day 204: On Psychological Limits

*The limit I thought existed was purely psychological. Now that I'd seen someone doing a thousand pounds, I started making leaps in my training. It showed the power of mind over body.*

—*Arnold Schwarzenegger*[202]

Our limits come primarily from our surroundings. If your role model of financial self-discipline is your uncle Jimmy (who somehow managed to save $500 this year), his example will set your own threshold — after all, he's the only person you know who has managed to save money, so $500 saved in a year has to be a huge accomplishment.

Let's imagine that your uncle has been networking with the movers and shakers and invited you out to a dinner with Bob, an owner of a local chain of bakeries. Bob instantly takes a liking to you, and answers all of your questions with enthusiasm.

When you ask him how much a person should save during a year, he says that everyone can easily save at least $5000 a year, and that's actually what he did for several years, in order to save enough money to bootstrap his business. Suddenly your psychological limits stretch and now in your mind, it's $5000 that's a lot and $500 feels like nothing.

The same effect happens in virtually all areas of life, whether it's finance, fitness, health, learning new skills, eradicating deeply-rooted negative habits or introducing new challenging ones.

Exposing yourself to high performers can be a wonderful way to push your psychological limits and show you what's possible. Reading stories of average people like you or me who have managed to achieve their goals despite having no natural talent, resources, or any other hidden advantages works almost like brainwashing. What belonged to the realm of impossible is now something you know can be achieved.

# Day 205: On Treating Hate as an Exercise

*I have no time to quarrel, no time for regrets and no man can force me to stoop low enough to hate him.*

—*Laurence Jones*[203]

Critics can get the best of even the world class top-performers with millions of fans.

Sadly, most of us have a tendency to focus more on a single instance of hatred than on a multitude of people expressing their love for ourselves or our work.

Fortunately, encountering hate can serve as a valuable exercise in building self-control. As Laurence Jones points out, it's your choice as to whether you stoop low enough to radiate hate back, or ignore it and focus on something else that is more important.

When you meet with criticism, skepticism or sarcasm, receive it as an opportunity to practice self-control. Instead of responding to it, think of it as a minor annoyance that tests your patience. You have just "down-sized" it to a level where it's just not worth your time or energy.

Just like you can practice restraint when you're stuck in traffic, you can improve your self-control by disregarding hate. That way, you'll get two benefits: you'll improve your willpower and avoid ruining your mood by engaging in negative emotions.

# Day 206: On Vice Fasts

*Go on a "vice fast." Pick one vice and abstain for thirty days. Proving to yourself that you're still in charge.*

—***Darren Hardy***[204]

30-day vice fasts can be a great way to kickstart your self-control after a period of decreased self-discipline. Since it's just a 30-day challenge and not a lifetime change, you'll feel less resistance to starting it.

Even though it's such a short period, it can still serve as a great way to exercise your willpower. Some ideas for 30-day vice fasts include:

- 30 days without alcohol;

- 30 days without sugar in any form (or without processed sugar alone);

- 30 days without the snooze button;

- 30 days without watching TV;

- 30 days without watching pornography;

- 30 days without using social media;

- 30 days without spending money on anything besides necessary expenses, such as food, transportation costs, and bills.

# Day 207: On Enthusiasm and Endurance

*Enthusiasm is common. Endurance is rare.*

—*Angela Duckworth*[205]

In a perfect world, everyone who is pursuing their goals would be an endless source of enthusiasm for themselves and always be ready to pump themselves up when things get difficult. Unfortunately (or perhaps fortunately), life isn't so simple.

No matter how passionate you are about your goals today, there will come a day when everything will suck and all you'll want to do will be to give up. On that day, it won't be feel-good enthusiasm that makes you continue. It will be dogged determination and the tenacity to finish what you begin that will carry you forward.

In a sense, enthusiasm is a fair-weather friend. By all means, you can have a great time with it when things are going well, but if you're having problems, the only people you'll be able to turn to would be your true friends, or in this case, perseverance.

I once spent a weekend in miserable conditions, on the brink of hypothermia, learning outdoor first aid — something I was initially enthusiastic about.

I can't even begin to describe how tempted I was to end that torture and go back home. Nobody forced me to stay there. At any moment, I could have said that I was unwell and announced that I had to leave the camp early.

However, doing so would have been to act against my most important values and to miss out on an opportunity to instill endurance in myself. In the end, I saw it through to the end. Even though the experience was hellish, I reinforced my habit of keeping going and staying the course, even when everything inside me is screaming to let it go and quit.

To train your endurance, vow to always see things through to the end. This will help you develop an empowering habit of sticking to your resolutions, come hell or high water.

# Day 208: On Profiting From Your Losses

> *The most important thing in life is not to capitalize on your gains. Any fool can do that. The really important thing is to profit from your losses. That requires intelligence; and it makes the difference between a man of sense and a fool.*
>
> —*William Bolitho*[206]

In an ideal world, everybody would succeed more often than fail. In reality, failures are more common than triumphs, and so it means that the key skill is to learn how to profit primarily from your losses, not your successes.

And how do you do that? Simple. Whenever you fail, don't just shrug it off and try again; carefully analyze what happened, what worked well and what didn't, and what ultimately led to a failure. If you fail to do so, you'll miss out on a valuable learning experience and probably repeat your mistakes in the future.

As an author, I track my books' sales performance. If a book doesn't perform well, despite my following the exact same marketing approach as I had used with my previous successful releases, I know that I probably made a mistake when I chose its topic and won't write about it again.

When it comes my nutritional habits, I try to track how each food affects me. That way, I discovered that potatoes always make me feel unwell, and that no matter how many strawberries or blueberries I eat, I'll still be hungry. Such simple discoveries can have a huge impact on your diet, because you'll know the potential dangers and, instead of unconsciously exposing yourself to them over and over again, you'll correct your approach.

Don't discount the value of a failure. There's a hidden treasure underneath each setback and struggle. Dig it out and use it to help you get closer to your goals.

# Day 209: On Finishing Quick Tasks Right Away

*My rule is never to lay down a letter until I have answered it. I dictate the reply to my secretary at once.*

—*William L. Sadler*[207]

There exists a big temptation to put off quick tasks. After all, they're easy and fast to do, so why do them now? Better to batch them and take care of them later.

However, ultimately this strategy can generate more work. The reason is simple: whenever you procrastinate about a quick task, you're actually creating two tasks: the task in itself, and the task of remembering to do it. True, you can note it down, but it's still another task to do. In the end, keeping track of it can cost more time than simply doing the task right away.

Moreover, quick tasks have a tendency to accumulate, and what originally would only take 5 minutes can ultimately take 3 hours, and then it suddenly becomes a problem to find so much time to get it all done.

Finally, whether it's a quick task or not, putting it off just because you don't feel like doing it now creates a habit of procrastination. Remember that all of your behaviors contribute to who you are as a person. Procrastinating about small tasks leads to procrastinating about big goals.

The next time you find yourself thinking about postponing a quick task, do it right away. Anything important that takes less than 5–10 minutes should be attended to immediately.

# Day 210: On Deferring Happiness

*I have found that one of the commonest causes of unhappiness among my patients is that they are attempting to live their lives on the deferred payment plan. They do not live, nor enjoy life now, but wait for some future event or occurrence.*

—*Maxwell Maltz*[208]

It's important to be future-oriented and prioritize future rewards over instant gratification. However, this statement is only valid to a certain point. If you live exclusively in the future, thinking that achieving some goal in the future is the only way to bring you happiness, chances are you won't be happy either now or when you reach your goals — by then, you'll come up with yet another event that must happen in order for you to be happy.

For this reason, it's important to ensure that while your focus is on the future, it isn't a condition for you to be happy.

For one, if you're unhappy today, it will affect your well-being and make you less likely to reach your goals. Positivity breeds more positivity, while negativity spawns more negativity. A lack of happiness today can ruin your chances of making your future vision turn into reality.

Second, happiness is a habit — and just like any other habit, it requires some self-control to practice it. Activities like expressing gratitude for what you have, reframing negative events into valuable experiences, and drawing pleasure from the little things are all essential practices you need to engage in regularly to stay in top mental shape.

Last but not least, if you're always waiting for some future occurrence, thinking that it will change your life, you're essentially delegating the responsibility for your own happiness to some event happening (or not) in the future. Does that sound like a behavior of a successful person?

# WEEK 31

# Day 211: On a Simple Adherence Hack

*Photograph all meals or snacks prior to eating. Subjects who use food diaries lose three times as much weight as those who don't.*

—*Tim Ferriss*[209]

Photographing all that you eat will make you more aware of what you put in your mouth. It will make you pause and think before you cheat because there will be a clear consequence of it: a picture that proves beyond a reasonable doubt that you didn't stick to your resolutions.

Such a simple hack can provide tremendous benefits or even be the single thing that will finally make you stick to your diet in the long term.

I can attest to the benefits of this approach: when I was on a diet, I used to track my food intake to make sure that I hit my nutritional targets for the day. If I ate something, it had to be noted in the spreadsheet. This made it more difficult to cheat because I could immediately see when and how much I was exceeding my planned caloric intake for the day.

This trick doesn't just apply to dieting. You can also use it successfully for other goals. For example:

- If you want to become an early riser, take a picture of your clock the moment you get out of bed.

- If you want to become more fit, record a video of your every workout or jot down the exercises you did, the amount of weight that you lifted, the number of reps, sets, and the duration of your session.

- If you want to save more money, photograph any purchase that isn't a necessity.

# Day 212: On Learning From Your Illness

*When you become ill, regard your illness as your teacher, not as something to be hated.*

—*George Ivanovich Gurdjieff[210]*

Nothing in life is more important than health, but we fail to understand this fact until we become ill and lose what we've been taking for granted for so long. At first, you deny it. Then you start wondering, "Why me?" Then you start hating it, and the more that negative emotions breed inside you, the more difficult it is to battle against the illness.

Many illnesses are preventable, or at least you can greatly reduce your risk for them by adopting healthy habits. Other illnesses can fall upon anyone, making your life miserable without it being your fault.

In both cases, setting aside the obvious fact that it would be better not to have it at all, an illness can serve as a teacher. In fact, regarding your illness as a mentor is the only way in which you can effectively cope with it. Denial, hate, regret, or frustration ultimately only work against you.

If you're currently dealing with an illness, look at it as an opportunity to review your life, your lifestyle choices, and your priorities. Take advantage of the fact that now you understand on a visceral level how important health is and make those healthy changes you've been postponing for so long.

Finally, think of the illness as a challenge to overcome, and if it's chronic and incurable, seek examples from people who live their lives to the fullest despite not being in the best health or physical condition: Nick Vujicic (a motivational speaker who was born without all four limbs), Sean Swarner (the first two-time cancer survivor to climb the seven highest peaks of the seven continents), Randy Pausch (a professor given three months to life who gave an inspiring lecture entitled "The Last Lecture" which went on to become a global phenomenon), or Jessica Cox (the first pilot without arms).

# Day 213: On Sudden Trials

> *The art of life is more like the wrestler's art than the dancer's, in respect of this, that it should stand ready and firm to meet onsets which are sudden and unexpected.*
>
> —*Marcus Aurelius*[211]

Preparing yourself for possible temptations and avoiding situations in which you're likely to encounter them is a solid strategy, but it won't eliminate one of the most formidable enemies: sudden and unexpected trials.

During my krav maga workouts (an Israeli self-defense system), my coach often reminds me that during an attack in the street, I'll be unlikely to be prepared for it. I may be carrying shopping bags, coming home after a tiring workout, feeling sick, or have my mind so occupied that I won't notice the threat until it's too late. Consequently, during our workouts, we sometimes imitate such situations so that I can be better prepared during an unexpected attack.

Self-discipline is similar to self-defense in this regard. It's one thing to remain self-disciplined when you're mentally prepared or perform a self-defense technique during training, and a completely different thing to face temptations or an enemy when they're most likely to emerge — when you're tired, angry, sick, heartbroken, or depressed.

As hard as it is, try to pay even more attention to your self-control when you aren't at your best. It's during those testing times that you can learn the most about your weaknesses, as well as your hidden strengths.

To better prepare yourself to handle such negative, unpredictable circumstances, periodically test your character while you're under the weather. For example, while writing these words, I'm pushing myself to complete two days' worth of work even though I've been having low spirits the past few days. Even though it's hard, I know that it will serve me well the next time I'll have to deal with a different sudden, unexpected trial.

# Day 214: On Fearing the Future

*The only thing we know about the future is that it is going to be different.*

—***Peter Drucker***[212]

A quick thought-provoking question for today: if you know for a fact that the future will be different, then what's the point of fearing it?

When people fear that they will fail or succeed (fear of success is a real thing: success can change your life in many ways, and not always in the ways you expected, which makes it scary), they're essentially fearing that their lives will be different, but it's a fact anyway.

No matter what you do, your life *will* be different and you'll have to deal with the aftermath of your life changing, no matter if you pursue your goals or not. If that's the case, both fears are unfounded because a change is guaranteed anyway.

And not only that — *not* taking action because you're afraid of the future is a worse choice, because when you pursue your goals, at least you have a certain amount of control over *how* your future will be different.

If you let fear overpower you, your future will still be different, but you won't be able to steer it or know (with at least some accuracy) how it's going to change.

For example, if you change your nutritional habits and start exercising more, you can predict with some accuracy that your health will most likely improve, or at least not get worse. Can you predict what kind of health deterioration you will go through if you don't make any changes?

What's scarier, the prospect that you'll become a different person through your new positive habits, or the prospect of not knowing if (and if so, what) disease, a health disorder, or another unpleasant thing will hit you?

# Day 215: On Self-Determination

*The most successful people, the evidence shows, often aren't directly pursuing conventional notions of success. They're working hard and persisting through difficulties because of their internal desire to control their lives, learn about their world, and accomplish something that endures.*

—*Daniel Pink*[213]

Take a cue from the most successful people and figure out how to link your goals with the desire to control your life, learn about the world or accomplish something that endures.

How can your desire to build a business play into your need for autonomy, learning, or contribution? Easy. A business will give you financial freedom and let you control your life to the fullest extent. Growing your business will help you discover the parts of you that you've never known existed. And finally, building a successful business will leave a mark on the world; even if it's a small one, it's still a big accomplishment to build an organization of any kind.

What about dieting? How can you link something as mundane as caring for your body to such high desires? It isn't that hard, either. Only a healthy person can control their life. A sickness can quickly remind you who's the boss. Self-discovery? Go on a diet, explore how you feel when temptations arise, and you'll get to know a lot about yourself. Accomplish something that endures? Change your body permanently and you'll not only build something that hopefully lasts for a long time, but also discover how powerful a physical change can be for your mental state.

Now, think of your own goals and go through the same thought process, which will increase their significance to you and boost your determination.

# Day 216: On Accounting for Flexibility in Your Plans

*Another drawback of daily plans is that they lack flexibility. They deprive the person of the chance to make choices along the way, so the person feels locked into a rigid and grinding sequence of tasks. Life rarely goes exactly according to plan, and so the daily plans can be demoralizing as soon as you fall off schedule. With a monthly plan, you can make adjustments. If a delay arises one day, your plan is still intact.*

—*Roy Baumeister*[214]

I'm a fan of daily routines: writing a specific number of words, sticking to the same number of consumed calories, or learning the same number of words in a foreign language every day.

However, at the same time, having experienced on more than a few occasions that life often doesn't go exactly according to the plan and disruptions are bound to happen, I account for some flexibility in my plan. This way, when I mess up one day, it doesn't have to affect my entire progress.

For example, whenever I'm tweaking my caloric intake, I try to focus more on what happens during an entire week or month than any specific day. This way, if I mess it up one day by eating too little or too much, it doesn't matter because I can make up for it the next day or a week later. Granted, it carries the risk of making regular exceptions and setting a precedent, so it's important to always plan exactly when you're going to adjust for a day of variance.

Recently I set for myself a goal to write 10 daily entries for this book for 10 days so that after the end of this sprint, I will have written entries for 100 days, or almost 30% of the book.

If I were to only count it as successful if I stuck to writing 10 entries every day, without allowing myself any kind of flexibility, I'd have failed on the eighth day, which I spent outdoors. However, knowing that such a disruption would happen, I wrote 14 entries the day before my trip and 6 in the early morning before my departure.

Thanks to accounting for flexibility, I avoided the demoralizing effect of dropping the ball, and after 10 days, I had also completed my goal of writing 100 entries in total.

When setting new routines and goals, allow yourself some flexibility, too. If you have a daily quota, don't immediately count it as a failure if you don't perform it for one day. Work a little more for the next several days and instead of falling off the bandwagon, you'll still achieve your original goal.

# Day 217: On Things Not Being Up to Us

*Some things are in our control and others not.*

—*Epictetus*[215]

Living according to the most fundamental principle of Roman Stoicism — acknowledging that some things are up to us and others aren't, and it's of no use to worry or complain about the latter — is an excellent way to strengthen your self-control.

At the moment I'm writing this, I'm in the process of launching a new book. Things went bad from the start. I had to wait over 36 hours before my book was published, something that normally takes a few hours. This in itself delayed my entire launch schedule.

Then it turned out that because of another error, some early reviewers couldn't post their review. Then I realized I forgot to upload my audiobook, which pushed back its release date. In the meantime, I had other fires to put out related to other aspects of the business.

I won't lie: I was frustrated. However, in the end it all proved to be a valuable exercise in self-control. By trying not to get overly frustrated or worry too much about something that I couldn't control, I became slightly better at handling such situations, which are bound to repeat in the future.

Whenever you're going through hardships that are beyond your control, look at them as an exercise in reining in your emotions.

There's nothing you can do to change the situation, so at least you can learn something from it.

# WEEK 32

# Day 218: On Protein in Your Diet

> *Potential beneficial outcomes associated with protein ingestion include the following: 1) increased satiety — protein generally increases satiety to a greater extent than carbohydrate or fat and may facilitate a reduction in energy consumption (...); 2) increased thermogenesis — higher-protein diets are associated with increased thermogenesis, which also influences satiety and augments energy expenditure (...); and 3) maintenance or accretion of fat-free mass — in some individuals, a moderately higher protein diet may provide a stimulatory effect on muscle protein anabolism, favoring the retention of lean muscle mass (...)*
>
> —*Douglas Paddon Jones*[216]

Research suggests that one of the simplest ways to improve your adherence to a diet is to increase the amount of protein in it.

Protein is a miraculous macronutrient. It's not only the body's important building block, but is also more satiating than carbohydrates or dietary fat. Moreover, when on a diet, consuming higher amounts of protein helps to retain muscle mass.

Foods rich in protein include meat, fish, eggs, cheese, milk, yogurt, beans, nuts and seeds.

Making sure that your diet is rich in protein will help you lose weight, but also to maintain a healthy weight later on, so if your diet is mostly carbohydrate- and fat-rich, make some adjustments to include more protein-rich foods.

However, be careful to not increase your overall calorie intake. When looking for potential high-protein foods, make sure that higher content of protein doesn't come with higher amounts of fat (it's a common combination).

# Day 219: On Dropping Unnecessary Tasks

*You can complete a project by dropping it.*

—*Arianna Huffington*[217]

I understand: there's certain allure in being busy all the time, always having a long list of things to do. And let's not forget, you're the only one who can perform all those tasks, right?

However, if you want to become more productive and still have energy for your other goals, when you look at your to-do-list, in addition to thinking about when and how to do a certain task, ask yourself if you can drop it.

For example, one of my contractors recently pointed out there was a small mistake in one of my old books. I'm not going to lie. At first, I added it to my to-do list. But then, the next day, I realized that the error was so inconsequential that it made no sense to spend time fixing it. I had more pressing things to attend to, and my readers would benefit more from another book of mine released on time than me wasting time fixing a thing nobody had ever noticed before.

Look at your to-do list and be honest with yourself: how many tasks are there on your list because you put them there automatically, without even asking yourself if they're important? How about dropping them to make more time for what matters?

# Day 220: On a Lack of Vision

*A lot of times when people come to us and they say, "Hey, I really struggle with self-discipline in this area or that area," what we almost always find is it's not that they struggle as much from a lack of discipline as they do from a lack of vision. The amount of our endurance is directly proportionate to the clarity of our vision.*

—*Rory Vaden*[218]

When you're staring at this delicious piece of cake, you might start wondering why you're taking such great pains to avoid it. Unless you have a clear, specific vision that acts as a mental picture reminding you why, it's easy to say "to hell with it!" After all, you aren't really sure why you're depriving yourself of such a pleasure, so why continue to do it?

I strongly suggest starting each day with a quick mental reminder of your goals. Imagine what you want to accomplish, how it will make you feel, and why it's so important that you want to reach it.

On my journey toward building a successful business, I regularly read a document that described (in detail) the future in which my goals are accomplished. It not only made it easier for me to stay productive and keep going despite hardships, but also made the prospect of achieving my goal more vivid and boosted my confidence that I would eventually reach it.

Write a few paragraphs that describe your own goals or create a vivid mental image and frequently review it to boost your resolve and enable you to stay away from temptations.

# Day 221: On Antimodels

*People focus on role models; it is more effective to find antimodels — people you don't want to resemble when you grow up.*

—*Nassim Taleb*[219]

A common piece of advice to inspire you to pursue your ideal lifestyle is to find successful people whom you'd like to emulate.

However, what sometimes works better than positive motivation is negative motivation. For example, you'll most likely run faster if you're running away from a psychopathic killer than if you're running in a race with monetary prizes.

In the same way, you might find more motivation in making a list of traits or describing the kind of a lifestyle you don't want to live, identifying people you don't want to resemble, and then using them as your antimodels.

Whenever you find yourself tempted to give up, cheat, or otherwise betray your values, remind yourself that each time you're doing it, you're getting closer to becoming your antimodel. If you've chosen your antimodels well, you'll do whatever you can to avoid their fate — and that's the power of negative motivation.

If you don't know any people who can serve as antimodels, imagine your future self as a person who did the opposite of what you want and is now stuck in living the worst kind of a lifestyle that you could ever imagine. Treat the undesirable "future you" as your antimodel.

# Day 222: On Your Depleting Willpower

> *Self-control is highest in the morning and steadily deteriorates over the course of the day.*
>
> —*Kelly McGonigal*[220]

Some scientists (like Kelly McGonigal and Roy Baumeister) believe that willpower is a depleting resource. You wake up with a specific amount of willpower and it steadily decreases during the day until (in the evening) you're supposedly no longer in control of your actions.

In their research, critics of this theory like Veronika Job and Carol S. Dweck pose that whether willpower is a resource or not largely depends on what you think about the issue.[221] If you believe that your self-control is something that you use up during the day, that will be the case. If you believe it's something that is with you whenever and wherever you want it, you won't notice a drop in self-control over the course of the day.

Instead of taking sides, I suggest being neutral about it. Even if your willpower is not a depleting resource, it's better to perform your habits in the morning — not because your self-control will run out later on, but because things tend to happen during the day that will capture your attention and possibly make you forget about what you vowed to do in the evening. You might also simply get tired and don't feel in the mood to push yourself once again.

At the same time, don't limit yourself by making an excuse that you've run out of self-control. Try to exercise your willpower muscle, whether it's in the morning or in the evening. The moment you can't lift a certain weight or continue running is largely in your head and you can often push it[222] — why that wouldn't be the case when it comes to self-control?

# Day 223: On Clear Cues and Rewards

> *People who have successfully started new exercise routines show they are more likely to stick with a workout plan if they choose a specific cue, such as running as soon as they get home from work, and a clear reward, such as a beer or an evening of guilt-free television.*
>
> —*Charles Duhigg*[223]

According to bestselling author Charles Duhigg, a habit consists of a cue (a signal to perform a habit), a routine (action), and a reward for engaging in the habit. This loop, when repeated over and over again, creates an automatic behavior.

When creating new habits, make sure that you have clear cues and rewards. This will help you introduce new routines with less resistance.

For example, if you want to start running every morning, keep your running shoes by your bed and before you leave, put your coffee mug on the table in the kitchen so that when you get back, coffee will serve as a reward for a job well done.

One thing to be aware of is that your reward can't undo the benefits of the habit. If you want to reward yourself for exercising by eating a giant pizza, you'll be taking one step forward and two steps back each time you engage in such a habit loop.

Instead, think of a healthier, less-caloric reward — a smoothie, some nuts, a piece of fruit — or something that has nothing to do with eating, such as an hour spent reading a book, watching your favorite TV series, or taking a long bath. Please note that in the beginning a new habit like jogging in the morning can be unpleasant, but with time the action itself can be a reward (a workout can produce a feel-good endorphin rush).

Some effective cues include: another habit (like engaging in a positive habit after you finish brushing your teeth), a certain place (like getting back home after work and immediately sitting down to work on your side business for an hour), or a certain time (each day at 6 p.m. you spend fifteen minutes stretching).

# Day 224: On Juggling Five Balls

*Imagine life is a game in which you are juggling five balls. The balls are called work, family, health, friends, and integrity. And you're keeping all of them in the air. But one day you finally come to understand that work is a rubber ball. If you drop it, it will bounce back. The other four balls... are made of glass. If you drop one of these, it will be irrevocably scuffed, nicked, perhaps even shattered.*

—*James Patterson*[224]

Self-discipline and your long-term goals are important, but throughout all of my books, I periodically emphasize that life isn't only about accomplishment. In fact, your well-being, living with integrity, and the relationships you have with your friends and family matter more than everything else.

What's the point of self-improvement if you can't share your successes and failures with others? Is being super-rich worth it if you've developed a reputation of a crook? Does it make sense to lose your health just to get a promotion at work?

When balancing between different aspects of your life, always prioritize the glass balls over the rubber one. You can always accomplish your goals later, but you can't always restore relationship with your family, revive your friendships, recover your health, or regain trust.

Spend five minutes today thinking whether you're careful enough when handling the glass balls in your life. How often do you ignore your health or family to focus on work? How can you work on your goals in a more sustainable way that would reduce the risk of losing your health, integrity, or relationships?

# WEEK 33

# Day 225: On Following Someone Else's Plan

*Ester asked why people are sad.*

*"That's simple," says the old man. "They are the prisoners of their personal history. Everyone believes that the main aim in life is to follow a plan. They never ask if that plan is theirs or if it was created by another person. They accumulate experiences, memories, things, other people's ideas, and it is more than they can possibly cope with. And that is why they forget their dreams."*

—*Paulo Coelho*[225]

I like to say that self-discipline can change a lot in your life, but it won't change much if you're following someone else's dreams.

For example, I went to college because my parents wanted me to do it. Graduating from college was, according to them, a necessity to succeed in life. I couldn't care less about formal education, but they did, and since I was young and inexperienced, I obeyed.

Despite being a self-disciplined and persistent person, I didn't last even two years. I dropped out, tired of constantly forcing myself to follow a plan that was not created by me. The day I decided to drop out was one of the happiest days of my life. It was also the moment when I finally embarked on my own journey, focused on my own goals.

If no matter what you're doing, you're finding it immensely difficult to pursue your goals, ask yourself if they're really your own goals. Are you studying because *you* want to study? Are you a lawyer because it was *your own* choice? Do you want to make money to buy a house in the suburbs because it's *your* idea of a perfect life or is it what society expects you to desire?

Don't forget your dreams. Discard any goal or idea that was forced upon you by somebody else that isn't aligned with your values and personality. Get to work on your own plans and then follow them instead.

# Day 226: On Waiting to Be Saved

*No one saves us but ourselves. No one can and no one may. We ourselves must walk the path.*

—*Gautama Buddha*[226]

It's easy to fall victim to the belief that you need to wait for someone or something to save you.

You won't start a business unless you find an investor or a mentor. How about starting your business on a shoestring and learning along the way?

You won't change your eating habits unless you find the right diet that was designed by a world-famous dietitian. How about eating more vegetables and fruits and eliminating unhealthy foods from your diet, one by one?

You won't start exercising unless you find the right coach. How about putting on your sneakers and going for a walk or dropping to the ground and doing a few pushups?

You won't start a long-term relationship unless the perfect, flawless person appears in your life. How about looking for a potential partner yourself, accepting that nobody is perfect, and committing to the other person as they are — with all of their positive traits and also their flaws?

Don't wait to be saved. You yourself must walk your own path. Use the resources offered by other people when you have access to them, but don't use them as crutches.

# Day 227: On Being Stuck in the Past

> *People are all over the world telling their one dramatic story and how their life has turned into getting over this one event. Now their lives are more about the past than their future.*
>
> —*Chuck Palahniuk*[227]

As a teenager, I was so insecure that I couldn't talk with women. I was bullied (fortunately, a stronger classmate stood up for me and the bullying quickly ceased), had terrible acne (and needed to take expensive medication to get rid of it), and exuded awkwardness that could earn me the starring role in the Revenge of the Nerds.

Yet, I somehow managed to overcome all those debilitations and I turned out okay. One of the keys was not letting my dramatic story define me. Yes, I struggled with all those things and plenty more, but so did many other people — and many of them struggled with issues that make my problems look like a joke.

If you're using a past story as an excuse for what your life is like today, ask yourself how this strategy has been serving you. Isn't constantly looking into the past reinforcing the belief that you're a victim? And if so, how does it affect your chances of succeeding in life?

Unless you turn the page and look to the future, you'll be forever stuck living in the past, reliving your dramatic story and never changing your identity to create the future you desire.

# Day 228: On Going Where Your Eyes Go

*In racing, they say that your car goes where your eyes go. The driver who cannot tear his eyes away from the wall as he spins out of control will meet that wall; the driver who looks down the track as he feels his tires break free will regain control of his vehicle.*

—*Garth Stein*[228]

When you face hardships and feel like you're about to crash, heed the advice of racing drivers: look at where you want your car to go, not at the wall you want to avoid hitting.

In practical terms, this means focusing on taking the next step to solve the difficult situation instead of busying your mind with worrying about what will happen if you don't manage to succeed. Doing the latter is not only a waste of energy, it also actively works against you by convincing your brain that the failure is inevitable, thereby making it less likely that you'll avoid it.

For example, I was once close to being forced to close my business because I didn't have sufficient money to keep it running. Instead of thinking about closing up shop and worrying about how it would affect my long-term goals, I focused on the next step I could take — doing whatever I could to secure some money to keep the business afloat. Instead of staring at the wall, I looked down the track and managed to avoid hitting the wall.

Adopt the same attitude when dealing with problems and setbacks. Obsessing about the imminent failure guarantees it, while holding the steering wheel tightly and looking down the track increases your chances of escaping such a fate.

# Day 229: On the Opportunity in Chaos

*In the midst of chaos, there is also opportunity.*

—*Sun Tzu*[229]

When everything goes wrong, you might be tempted to think that everything is already lost. You've already made a mistake, you can't go past the obstacles, the negative circumstances got the best of you.

There's no denying the fact that chaos doesn't make it easy to think logically. However, if you exert some willpower and force yourself to examine the situation without emotions clouding your judgment, you might discover new opportunities in the middle of chaos.

For example, if you're on a diet and somehow one cheat meal turned into a week-long binge, you can conclude that everything is lost and give up. It's the easy choice, but as we've already discussed on many occasions, easy choices are rarely the right ones.

The chaos that has ensued in your diet offers opportunities. For example, you can now jot down the thoughts you have when you gorge on unhealthy food after a long period of going without it. What makes you eat it? What's the underlying motive? How can you satisfy your need for junk food without actually eating it?

If you've been following a healthy diet for several weeks, you can probably also notice the difference in how you feel after eating crap. Whenever I spend a few days eating less healthily, I have a craving to return to my usual diet. Your mistake can then reinforce your will to part ways with junk food forever.

Treat chaos as an opportunity to learn, and you might benefit from it even more than if you had never found yourself in the middle of it.

# Day 230: On Laser-Focusing on Specific Aspects

> *Franklin identified the aspects of his performance that needed to be improved and found a way to stretch himself, the essential core of deliberate practice. Significantly, he did not try to become a better essay writer by sitting down and writing essays. Instead, like a top-ranked athlete or musician, he worked over and over on those specific aspects that needed improvement.*
>
> —*Geoff Colvin*[230]

Saying that you want to become more self-disciplined is too vague of a resolution. You need to be more specific about what areas of your life you want to improve and specifically how you're going to do it.

In what domains or situations are you lacking self-discipline? How does it manifest? What do the people who control their temptations in those situations do? How can you work over and over again on those specific things to improve yourself?

If you're not good at exhibiting patience around people who annoy you, that's a specific aspect you can focus on to improve your self-control. If you often overeat on French fries, that's a specific trigger that you can focus on to improve your self-control around food. If you struggle to wake up early, figure out how to specifically boost your self-discipline in the morning when you're still half-asleep.

This laser-focus approach will make you more effective at strengthening your willpower muscle, rather than merely trying to *become more disciplined*, as it's too difficult to define what that entails.

# Day 231: On Minimizing What You Need

*A man is rich in proportion to the number of things which he can afford to let alone.*

—*Henry David Thoreau*[231]

Thoreau was a big proponent of simplicity, particularly when it comes to material possessions. We can extend his maxim to living a successful life in general, namely that a human is strong in proportion to the number of things which he or she can let alone.

If you can still manage to achieve your goals despite not having the right resources, then ultimately you'll become a stronger and more capable person than an individual who has never gone without them.

Kenyan javelin-thrower Julius Yego won the gold medal at the World Championships in Beijing. There would be nothing particularly interesting in this story except that he learned how to perfect his technique without a coach, and instead learned from YouTube videos.[232] Achieving such a feat without all of the resources that world-class javelin-throwers usually have demonstrates how capable and determined Yego is as an athlete.

Does it mean that you should deliberately reject the resources you have at your disposal? Not really. Look at it more as encouragement that, even if you don't have the best tools available, you can still make it big.

In addition to that, practice your mental strength by sometimes deliberately going without something you need.

For example, I sometimes climb with a blindfold on. Without being able to see the next handhold or foothold, the sense of touch heightens, and it serves as a valuable exercise in improving precision when climbing.

You can apply it in many other areas of your life: sleep on the bare floor for a few days to discover that you can still get a good night's rest once you get used to it, exercise without any equipment whatsoever, or try to learn a new skill by figuring it out by yourself instead of immediately looking for a coach or teacher.

# WEEK 34
# Day 232: On Going All In

*I demolish the bridges behind me... Then there is no choice but to move forward.*

—*Fridtjof Nansen*

If working on your goals with a safety net makes you lazy and less likely to reach your goals, try the opposite approach: demolish the bridges behind you and go all in. You will either succeed or lose in a big way.

Obviously, before making such an extreme decision, take into account all of the risks. If you're the sole breadwinner of your family, quitting your job to work on a business might not be an entirely good idea.

However, in many cases you *do* have an option to cut all escape routes.

For example, if you want to start a diet, you can throw away all of the unhealthy food you have in your house, pay in advance for three months of a healthy meal delivered to your doorstep, announce to all of your friends and family that you're on a diet, and give your friend a substantial amount of money that he or she can spend as they like if you fall off the wagon.

If the only choices you have are a spectacular success or a spectacular failure, it often makes it easier to stick to your resolutions because the consequences of success and failure are balanced. If you have a safety net and failure isn't particularly hurtful, in a moment of doubt the temptation to back out can be too alluring to resist it.

# Day 233: On Obstacles as Filters

*The brick walls are there for a reason. The brick walls are not there to keep us out. The brick walls are there to give us a chance to show how badly we want something. Because the brick walls are there to stop the people who don't want it badly enough. They're there to stop the other people.*

—*Randy Pausch*[233]

If obstacles piss you off, ask yourself how would you enjoy reaching your goals if there were no difficulties and everyone would have been able to achieve their goals without breaking a sweat. How valuable would that success be? How sweet would it feel if you knew that you'd accomplished something that everyone else easily could?

Think of setbacks as filters: each problem reduces the number of people eligible to attain the ultimate prize. Are you going to be one of the also-rans or are you going to prove how badly you want your goal and stick to your resolutions for however long it takes?

# Day 234: On Forgiving

*To err is human, to forgive, divine.*

—*Alexander Pope*[234]

What is a quote about forgiving doing in a book about self-discipline and success? The answer is simple: holding a grudge is like instant gratification. It gives you a little reward today at the expense of your future. Meanwhile, forgiving requires some sacrifice today, but eventually brings bigger benefits.

This means that the act of forgiving can serve as a valuable exercise in improving your self-control, particularly emotional control.

Engaging in negative emotions by staying angry at somebody who hurt you can give you some pleasure by satisfying your need for "fairness" in the world; expressing your dislike or anger is like punishing the one who erred.

However, in the long run, holding a grudge poisons only one person, and that person is you. Choosing to forgive — which doesn't necessarily mean to *forget* — is therefore an act of freeing yourself from pain.

Instead of being stuck in a negative emotional loop, you choose the temporary discomfort of making peace in exchange for the substantial long-term benefits of improved well-being.

# Day 235: On Looking Only One Day Ahead

*When I face the desolate impossibility of writing five hundred pages, a sick sense of failure falls on me, and I know I can never do it. Then gradually, I write one page and then another. One day's work is all I can permit myself to contemplate.*

—*John Steinbeck*[235]

I share John Steinbeck's sentiment every time that I start writing a new book, particularly if it's such a big and difficult project as *365 Days With Self-Discipline*. The most effective strategy I've found to help me is precisely the same recommendation as Steinbeck's: I contemplate only one day's work.

Today, I need to write 10 more daily entries, and that's all that counts. Each time I catch myself calculating how many entries I have left and how much time it's still going to take, I demoralize myself, thus making it more difficult to keep going and more likely that I'll stumble.

While you're standing at the foot of the mountain and looking at its peak, it looks like it's impossible to scale it. But then, if you decide to climb it — step by step and minute by minute — you slowly advance and soon you're looking down, surprised at how high you are.

If you're facing a big project, embrace the same attitude. Don't look a year ahead; instead, focus on what you need to do *today* to get a little bit closer to your destination. Do it today, and then do it tomorrow, and then the day after tomorrow. Then continue week by week and month by month, until you make the impossible possible.

# Day 236: On Being a Normal Chap

*In response to the question, "So, Mr. Lamborghini, in short what type of man are you?":*

*A normal chap, a man who likes creating things. A good worker in the morning, and a man who likes enjoying himself in the afternoon.*

—*Ferruccio Lamborghini*

It's easy to put successful people on a pedestal and think that they're so exceptional that you'll never become even half as great as they are. In reality, world-class performers aren't that different from you or me.

Mr. Lamborghini, the creator of one of the most desired sports car brands in the world, described himself in simple terms that can apply equally to any other successful person: they like to create things (which comes down to never-ending self-improvement), they're good workers, and just like everybody else, they like enjoying themselves after work.

Thinking that successful people live on a different planet can hinder your personal growth. You might assume that their achievements are only within the reach of similar superhumans, but not you. In reality, while there are certain exceptions of people who were born with extraordinary talent, prior to their success, most people didn't differ much from others.

If you have a tendency to become star-struck, remember that beyond their successes, they're the same human beings as you or me.

They might be exceptional at one thing, but horrible at something else. The only reason why many of them have achieved success might be because of their persistence, and not because of any special abilities or resources that were available to them. Stick to your own resolutions and with enough dedication, nothing will prevent you from attaining their level of accomplishment.

# Day 237: On Shifting Responsibility to Others

> *Many seek to avoid the pain of their problems by saying, "This problem was caused me by other people, or by circumstances beyond my control, and therefore it is up to other people or society to solve this problem for me."*
>
> —*M. Scott Peck*[236]

I have a friend who's often late. When confronted about his tardiness, he says, "When I was a child, my parents were always late to pick me up at school, so I learned it from them."

This way, he conveniently shifts the responsibility for the problem to his parents. It's no longer *his* lack of self-discipline to leave ten minutes early: it's his *parents* who were late (decades ago), so now he's late for his appointments, too.

You can often notice similar sentiments among people looking for a job. It's not *their* job to find employment — it's the *government* that should do something about it, as if the government could create jobs out of thin air.

While those people wait for somebody else to fix their problems, other job seekers take additional training, volunteer, or start small businesses, knowing that even if the economic situation in the country is beyond their control, it's within *their* control to do something that can increase their chances of getting a job.

Do you have any problems in your life that you think were caused by other people and therefore you don't accept that it's your responsibility to fix them?

What do you think? What are your chances of ever solving them if you deny that it's within your control to do something about them?

# Day 238: On Dividing Your Life into 10-Minute Units

> *You can do so much in ten minutes' time. Ten minutes, once gone, are gone for good. Divide your life into 10-minute units and sacrifice as few of them as possible in meaningless activity.*
>
> —*Ingvar Kamprad*[237]

No, there's no need to divide your life into 10-minute units and behave like a robot for the rest of your life. However, Kamprad's suggestion can be a valuable exercise in discovering how productive you can be if you develop better control of your schedule.

Conduct an experiment: for one day, track every single activity you engage in and how much time you spend on it. Jot down everything, including how much time it takes you to get out of bed, commute, cook, eat, how much time you spend on social media, how much time you spend on each specific task at work, etc. For your electronic life, you can use RescueTime, which is time management software that shows you how you spend your time on your devices.

Just one day of tracking your activity can give you an incredibly valuable insight into how many 10-minute periods are gone, wasted on meaningless activities.

As an additional exercise, choose a task — any important task you need to perform — and set a timer for 10 minutes. For the next ten minutes, act as if a huge meteor were to hit Earth and destroy everything on it if you failed to maintain 100% concentration.

Even if you don't finish the task, you'll probably multiply your productivity by a factor of five or ten — and that will serve as a powerful reminder that you can push your limits if you're only more diligent about your use of time.

# WEEK 35

# Day 239: On Imagining the Process as a Litmus Test

*If we hate doing something, we imagine it as hard. We think of it as broken into many pain-in-the-ass steps.*

*If we love something, it seems easy. We imagine it as one fun step.*

—**Derek Sivers**[238]

When setting new goals, do you imagine them as hard, broken down into countless frustrating steps, or is the process clear to you, largely reliant on just one big action you need to take consistently to make your dream come true?

The way you imagine how the process will go can serve as a valuable litmus test that indicates whether you're pursuing the right goal, and if so, whether you're pursuing it in the right way.

For example, I wanted to improve my flexibility and reached out to a physical therapist to give me some pointers on the best exercises for my particular weaknesses.

I received a list with several different stretches I was told to perform at least two times a day (a *day*, not a week — this alone was completely unrealistic). I thought about the program as broken into many pain-in-the ass steps instead of a fun challenge. At first, I listened to the advice, despite having reservations about it. Just a few days later I started skipping some exercises and soon stopped following the program entirely.

I was still interested in reaching the goal of improving my flexibility, but I had to come up with my own, simpler plan that I would consider fun and easier to implement in my everyday life.

If you're currently following a plan that feels as inspiring as my original protocol for improving flexibility, perhaps it's time to reconsider how to structure it in a different way so that it will feel more like one fun step rather than a long-term arduous journey.

# Day 240: On Separating Yourself From the Pain

> *Elite runners feel pain and discomfort during their hard workouts, but they react differently. Rather than panicking, they have a calm conversation: "This is starting to hurt now. It should. I'm running hard. But I am separate from this pain. It is going to be okay." Like meditation, choose how to respond to the stress of a workout.*
>
> —*Brad Stulberg and Steve Magness*[239]

Pain isn't you, and you aren't your pain. Separating yourself from temporary pain is a crucial ability if you want to put yourself in uncomfortable situations for the sake of bigger and better rewards in the future.

Whether it's exercise, dieting, work, or virtually anything else requiring effort, pain is sometimes inevitable. Depending on how you react to it — with panic or a calm inner conversation — you'll either let it hinder your progress or you'll defeat it and progress further.

For example, when I'm climbing a particularly difficult route, my forearms burn like hell, I can barely breathe, and my grip is so weak that I'm mere milliseconds from falling. Whenever I'm able to do so, I try to disassociate myself from the pain and try to advance my position further, even if I fall right after grabbing the next handhold. This way, I get to train my mental toughness and strengthen my ability to perform despite pain.

Whenever you feel temporary pain or discomfort, remind yourself that you can make the pain partly fade into the background when you mentally refuse to associate yourself with it. Obviously, make sure that the pain you feel isn't a sign of an impending injury or that it can lead to an accident.

# Day 241: On Enabling the Future

*Your task is not to foresee the future, but to enable it.*

*—Antoine de Saint Exupéry[240]*

Let's perform a quick exercise…

Imagine your ideal future. To make it easier, for now focus on only one part of your life, say, your financial situation. You probably desire to have more money in the future. You want to be able to afford what you want and never have to worry about money again.

Now let's focus on the present. Think about your choices today, yesterday, and the entire past week. Are they enabling the future you desire or disabling it?

Think of it as traveling on a toll road that will eventually take you to your desired future. At each toll booth, you need to pay to continue your journey. If you make the right choice, one that favors your ideal future, the toll barrier will open. If not, you'll be stuck there, standing in front of the barrier until you can scrape something together — in this case, making the choices that enable the desired future.

Whenever you find yourself torn between instant and delayed gratification, think of sitting in a car in front of the toll booth. Do you want the barrier to open, so that you can continue your journey toward your goal, or are you fine with waiting and wasting your time?

# Day 242: On Selectivity

*Few people take objectives really seriously. They put average effort into too many things, rather than superior thought and effort into a few important things. People who achieve the most are selective as well as determined.*

—*Richard Koch*[241]

Selectivity is one of the key attributes for success. Nobody in the world is good at everything. Most are exceptional at one, two, or perhaps three things, okay at several others, and mediocre or horrible at a multitude of other things.

When setting goals, ask yourself what kind of performance you demand from yourself. Would becoming merely okay satisfy you or are you seeking excellence? Prioritize your objectives accordingly.

It's also important to determine the place each goal has in your life.

For example, I made a decision to become as good as I can in rock climbing, but not at the expense of my health. This meant that I had to forego certain other activities (such as tennis, in which I was horrible and had little hope for improvement), but it also meant that whenever I would find myself in a situation that was a potential risk to my health, I would back out.

Now I have an easy rule in climbing: if there's a substantial risk of injuring myself in any way, I don't push myself — and I don't feel guilty when giving up. I made a conscious decision about the role of rock climbing in my life, and I won't prioritize my performance in it over what I consider much, much more important: my health and well-being.

Such clarity is important to help you understand how you should approach your goals when they clash with other aspects of your life.

If you want to become a billionaire and run big businesses, are you so obsessed about this goal that you're fine with possibly not starting family for a long time?

If you want to become a world-class athlete, do you accept the fact that professional sports will put immense stress on you and take a toll on your health?

Be selective with your goals, and once you establish which ones are the most important, ensure that you know where they all stand in terms of their priority in relation to other aspects of your life.

# Day 243: On the Crime of Aiming Too Low

*I will commit not the terrible crime of aiming too low. I will do the work that a failure will not do. I will always let my reach exceed my grasp.*

—*Og Mandino*[242]

Aiming too low is in essence yet another manifestation of choosing immediate rewards over bigger rewards in the future.

You set your sights low, which ensures success and gives you some peace of mind from knowing that you'll probably make it. However, at the same time, you limit your accomplishments. You get some comfort today at the expense of possible bigger rewards in the future.

The alternative is to set ambitious goals that make you feel uncomfortable because they carry a higher risk of failure. You suffer some discomfort today, but in the long run stand to gain more.

Which choice is more aligned with a person who values self-discipline in life?

Please bear in mind that you shouldn't confuse aiming high with being unreasonable. If you have no idea what is possible and what is not, start slowly with a safe, easily attainable goal, and aim higher only when you understand the odds of making a more ambitious goal become a reality.

As a rule of thumb, if you've already been working on a particular area of your life for several months or years, you probably know what is easy to achieve, what is realistic and what might be beyond your reach. If you're new to something, it's unlikely that you can determine that right away without first gaining some experience.

For example, I know (from my experience in business) that, in a six-month timeframe, it's an easy goal to make $100 a month from an online business, a realistic goal to make $500 a month, and a "stretch" goal to cross $2000 a month.

At the opposite end of the spectrum is golfing. I don't know anything about it, so instead of setting an ambitious goal (something I can't do properly because I don't understand the odds), I can only focus on an easy, attainable goal (such as learning the basics of how to hit the ball properly), and only begin to aim higher after I have understood the fundamentals.

# Day 244: On the Fun in the Impossible

*It's kind of fun to do the impossible.*

—*Walt Disney*[243]

Continuing the topic of aiming high, there's another benefit of doing the impossible: it's more fun than being realistic, and since it's so much fun, the excitement it generates supercharges your motivation to make it a reality.

As we've already discussed, this obviously isn't about setting completely impossible goals. Becoming a billionaire in five years is unlikely if you're starting from zero, but becoming a millionaire — while also unlikely and impossible for most, isn't actually impossible.

While it isn't necessarily a good idea to set several impossible goals in your life, it's worth it to have one goal that borders on the line between what's possible and what's impossible.

For example, I set a goal to make enough money to build a countryside house for my parents while I had just a few pennies in my wallet. You could have said it was an impossible objective back then, and you'd be right — except that I *did* manage to accomplish it in the end, and I owe a lot of my personal drive to this bold, inspiring goal. I doubt that I would have had the same resolve if I had set a safer, more realistic goal.

If you want to test (on a smaller scale) the concept of impossible goals fueling your resolve, set a small goal with a short deadline. Write a full-length novel in two weeks. Learn a foreign language in three months. Make $5000 on the side in six weeks. It's a fun experiment, and if you treat it seriously, you might be surprised at what you can accomplish if you dream big.

# Day 245: On Following or Leaving a Path

*Anything is one of a million paths. Therefore you must always keep in mind that a path is only a path; if you feel you should not follow it, you must not stay with it under any conditions. To have such clarity you must lead a disciplined life. Only then will you know that any path is only a path and there is no affront, to oneself or to others, in dropping it if that is what your heart tells you to do. But your decision to keep on the path or to leave it must be free of fear or ambition. I warn you. Look at every path closely and deliberately. Try it as many times as you think necessary.*

—*Carlos Castañeda*[244]

A path is a tool, and it's only useful as long as it's getting you closer to your goals. When it stops serving you, don't feel obligated to follow it to the end or you might end up in the bushes, scratching your head while staring at your scraped knees.

The key to making an intelligent decision about whether to leave the path or continue following it is to make that decision when you're free of negative feelings. People often give up their paths when they're struggling, and while they're in pain, they fail to notice there's a reward waiting just around the corner.

Another danger is sticking to the same path out of ambition or ego. "I'll see it through to the end," an ambitious individual proclaims, while it's clear that they should have changed the path a long time ago. They refuse to give up out of the fear of others laughing at them, or in fear of themselves coming to feel as if they had betrayed themselves.

I suggest periodically reviewing your path, but only after first ensuring that you're in a neutral state of mind. Ask yourself if your strategy is still delivering results. Does it still feel right to you? Do you still see yourself following it for another month, quarter, or year? Paths, like any other tool, sometimes need to be changed.

# WEEK 36
# Day 246: On Learning the Big Ideas

*You have to learn all the big ideas in the key disciplines in a way that they're in a mental latticework in your head and you automatically use them for the rest of your life. If you do that, I solemnly promise you that one day you'll be walking down the street and you'll look to your right and left and you'll think "my heavenly days, I'm now one of the few competent people in my whole age cohort." If you don't do it, many of the brightest of you will live in the middle ranks or in the shallows.*

—*Charlie Munger*[245]

All human knowledge is interconnected on some level. The big ideas can often be applied to general life. For this reason, it pays to develop at least a basic understanding of the key concepts of some of the most important disciplines, such as mathematics, physics, biology, psychology, engineering, history, etc.

Let's take compound interest, one of the most important big ideas in investing. When the interest you earn each year is added to your principal, your returns each year grow at an ever increasing rate. It might sound boring on paper, but in the real world it's what has made many investors millionaires or billionaires.

This big idea can be applied to personal growth, too. You never want to grow at a fixed rate; if you constantly build on top of your new experiences (interest), you'll grow at an ever-increasing rate.

Your personal growth might be relatively slow the first year, but each succeeding year, you'll get better and better results more quickly.

Strive to educate yourself in a broad variety of fields and focus primarily on the fundamentals. Try to find a real-world application of those principles in your own life. Even if you don't always find it, self-education alone will be a valuable exercise in self-discipline.

# Day 247: On First-Order and Second-Order Consequences

> *First-order consequences often have opposite desirabilities from second-order consequences.*
>
> *First-order consequences of exercise are the pain and time spent. Second-order consequences are better health and more attractive appearance.*
>
> *Food that tastes good is often bad for you and vice versa.*
>
> —*Ray Dalio*[246]

When making a decision, resist the temptation to think of the immediate consequences alone. Take into account both the first-order and second-order consequences.

When the first-order consequences are unpleasant, second-order consequences will usually make up for them. If it's the other way around and something has good first-order consequences, it's possible it will be bad for you in the long run.

If you're about to take it easy for the rest of the day and skip a workout, the first-order consequence is that you get to relax and do something more pleasant. However, the second-order consequence is that you miss a day of exercise, which will potentially affect your routine and in the long haul, lead to your returning to your old, inactive and unfit self.

There's more to each decision — no matter how small — than just how it's going to make you feel immediately. If you fail to account for the second-order consequences, you'll never learn how to discern between ultimately meaningless immediate gratification and the power of delaying rewards for a better outcome in the future (or vice versa — you won't be able to see that the pain or discomfort today can lead to immense benefits in the future).

# Day 248: On Reducing Your Targets

> *Never reduce a target. Instead, increase actions. When you start rethinking your targets, making up excuses, and letting yourself off the hook, you are giving up on your dreams!*
>
> —*Grant Cardone*[247]

When you're struggling to make progress, there's a temptation to let yourself off the hook and reduce your targets.

Instead of learning 500 new words in a foreign language, you feel tempted to drop it down to 300. Or better yet, make it 250, just in case.

Instead of giving 10 speeches this quarter, you're thinking about reducing it to 7 or 5. It's still a lot of speeches, you're still getting better as a public speaker, so why not rethink your targets and make them a bit more manageable?

Instead of hitting your target weight when dieting, you cut yourself some slack and settle with a weight 10 pounds (or 5 kilos) higher than your desired goal.

I don't entirely agree with Grant Cardone. Sometimes rethinking your targets is the only intelligent thing you can do — particularly if you've set unrealistic targets and the alternative is to give up altogether.

If, however, your goals are within your reach and you're otherwise feeling fine, but still making up excuses so you can let yourself off the hook, it's time to tap into your willpower resources, resist the temptation to take it easy, and start taking even more action.

If you choose the easy way out, you'll set a precedent: each time you feel challenged, you'll simply reduce your goals, and thereby never explore where your limits actually are.

When in doubt, remember this rule of thumb: it's better to fall short of meeting your original goals than to succeed because you cut them by half.

# Day 249: On Working Backwards

*A trick that screenwriters use: work backwards. Begin at the finish. If you're writing a movie, solve the climax first. If you're opening a restaurant, begin with the experience you want the diner to have when she walks in and enjoys a meal.*

—*Steven Pressfield*[248]

When people set new goals, they often feel resistance because they find it hard to figure out the process needed to get to where they want to go.

If you feel like you are spinning your wheels, frustrated by the impossibility of discovering what the first step should be, start from the other direction.

Imagine yourself as a person who has achieved your goal. Now work backwards: what have you done to get to where you are? What have you avoided doing? What are you doing daily as the successful person who has accomplished this goal? What are your beliefs? How do you feel?

Break it down into small parts and now you have a list of all of the actions you need to take to get to your destination. Start with an action you think is within your reach and take it from there.

Let's go through a quick example to better describe this process. Let's imagine that you want to become a fit, healthy person.

What would this person certainly *not* do? Would he or she eat fast food daily? Would he or she stay at home the entire day or lead an active life? Think of any actions that such a person would certainly *not* do. Now you have a list of smaller and bigger habits you need to implement in your life.

How would this person feel about themselves and which beliefs would they embrace? Would you agree with me if I said that they would probably feel firmly in control of their destiny and that their primary belief would be that they're the masters of their own fate and they would never blame anyone else but themselves for not living up to their standards? Now you know where you need to start to change your identity.

An additional benefit of this exercise is that you get to visualize all of the actions that are necessary to achieve the change; unlike visualizing the outcome alone (which is generally ineffective), this type of visualization can be helpful in boosting your resolve.

# Day 250: On Fluctuating Energy

*Alternating periods of activity and rest is necessary to survive, let alone thrive. Capacity, interest, and mental endurance all wax and wane. Plan accordingly.*

—*Tim Ferriss*[249]

As great as it would be to always have the same high level of energy, unfortunately it fluctuates.

Sometimes you'll feel more determined, and sometimes less. Sometimes you'll feel deep interest in what you're pursuing, and sometimes you'll feel bored, ready to give up and try something else. Sometimes you'll be able to deliver in one day what you usually create in a week, while on other occasions you'll barely do 25% of your daily quota.

Plan according to your fluctuating levels of personal resources. One of the biggest lessons I've gained while on my own journey was the necessity of learning how to be flexible and self-compassionate.

If you feel like you're about to fall asleep because you've had a challenging week at work, there's no rule stating that you must still perform your usual workout routine. Of course, it would be ideal to do so, but realistically, we aren't infallible and invincible. If you're honest with yourself, you'll know when the exhaustion you feel is mostly an excuse and when it's a genuine signal from your body.

I consider myself a self-disciplined person, but sometimes I still skip workouts or reduce their intensity when I feel it's sensible to do so. I've learned to listen to my body and plan accordingly.

This doesn't apply to fitness alone. In virtually every other area of life, your energy will fluctuate. Don't be afraid to change your plans if your current mental state isn't conducive to certain actions and choices. Don't stick to a calorie deficit if you're sick. Stop working on your side business for a few days if you're dealing with other pressing personal challenges.

You won't always be able to carry the entire world on your shoulders. Tune in to your body and mental state and rest guilt-free whenever you *genuinely* feel you *need* it.

# Day 251: On Relaxing While Working

*We scowl when we concentrate. We hunch up our shoulders. We call on our muscles to make the motion of effort, which in no way assists our brain in its work.*

*Here is an astonishing and tragic truth: millions of people who wouldn't dream of wasting dollars go right on wasting and squandering their energy with the recklessness of seven drunken sailors in Singapore.*

*What is the answer to this nervous fatigue? Relax! Relax! Relax! Learn to relax while you are doing your work!*

—*Dale Carnegie*[250]

Many people have an erroneous belief that work — both in the literal sense as well as work on your personal goals — has to involve a lot of effort and struggle. Consequently, their bodies reflect their attitude. As Dale Carnegie points out, they scowl when they concentrate, hunch up their shoulders and tense their muscles.

In reality, tensing is counter-productive. A good example comes from my rock climbing experience: whenever I get too tense and rigid when climbing, my performance decreases, and by a big factor. I forget about proper technique, find myself unable to breathe, and just like that, I can no longer hold onto the wall and I'm falling.

The same goes with work. I do my best work not when I'm scowling and punching myself in the face, trying to bring out my creativity. I work best in the early morning when I'm sitting somewhere outside in sunny, warm weather, with a cup of tea or water by my side. The environment relaxes me, unleashes my creativity and my productivity shoots up.

Design your environment in such a way that it relaxes you instead of making you tense. Whenever you catch yourself too tense at work, relax. Make a conscious effort to work with poise. Flex and unflex your tense muscles a couple of times while breathing deeply and you should feel tension going away — and your performance going up.

# Day 252: On Getting Older

*The average person is in the habit of saying, "The older I get" and he thereby calls the attention of his mind to the idea that he is getting older. In brief, he compels his mind to believe that he is getting older and older, and thereby directs the mind to produce more and more age. The true expression in this connection is, "The longer I live." This expression calls the mind's attention to the length of life, which will, in turn, tend to increase the power of that process in you that can prolong life. When people reach the age of sixty or seventy, they usually speak of "the rest of my days," thus implying the idea that there are only a few more days remaining. The mind is thereby directed to finish life in a short period of time, and accordingly, all the forces of the mind will proceed to work for the speedy termination of personal existence. The correct expression is "from now on," as, that leads thought into the future indefinitely without impressing the mind with any end whatever.*

—*Christian D. Larson*[251]

One of the people I admire the most are the elderly who continue to live their lives to the fullest despite the ocean of old people nagging and complaining that it's too late to change.

I never understood it: how can you conclude that your life is over and give up simply because you're older? Is there some force of nature that is making you unable to think, act, and change or is it a deeply-held limiting belief of yours?

There are plenty of examples of people aged 60 or more doing incredible things. I myself know a rock climber who's in his sixties or seventies, and yet (even after a complicated surgery) he is still climbing, and doing so better than many young people.

Don't use the process of aging as a rationalization for why you can't reach your goals. It's true that getting older comes with a higher risk that your body won't function as well as it used to, but it doesn't mean that now you should retreat from life.

Do the best you can with what you have, surround yourself with people who are mentally young (regardless of their biological age), and there's no risk you'll ever turn into those bitter, cranky old people who are living their lives while waiting for physical death (because *mentally*, they've already passed away).

# WEEK 37

# Day 253: On the Invisible Prison Bars

*You don't see your prison because its bars are invisible. Part of my task is to point out your predicament, and I hope it is the most disillusioning experience of your life.*

—*Dan Millman*[252]

People like to lie to themselves, even when they try really hard to convince themselves that that's not the case. Self-denial is like a prison with invisible bars — everything looks fine, except it isn't.

For example, when I was overweight, I rejected the notion that I was too fat. I was Big Martin. I sure as heck wasn't Overweight Martin. What's wrong about being big? One day, I saw my predicament for what it was: a prison with bars that would only move closer to me, if I continued to delude myself that I wasn't actually overweight.

If you can't generate such an epiphany yourself, it might be worth it to expose yourself to some constructive criticism from a professional — a doctor, a fitness instructor, a business mentor, or a life coach — in order to see your blind spots, or rather, take your blinders off and stop lying to yourself.

Are there any aspects of your life about which you lie to yourself? Is there something that you think is generally considered bad but you think that it's okay in your case? What makes you think that you're different?

# Day 254: On Capitalizing on Your Talents

*Overcoming deficits is an essential part of the fabric of our culture. Our books, movies, and folklore are filled with stories of the underdog who beats one-in-a-million odds. And this leads us to celebrate those who triumph over their lack of natural ability even more than we recognize those who capitalize on their innate talents. As a result, millions of people see these heroes as being the epitome of the American Dream and set their sights on conquering major challenges. Unfortunately, this is taking the path of most resistance.*

—*Tom Rath*[253]

Beware of applying your self-discipline where it's least likely to make a positive impact. If something is your weakness and it's not a matter of life or death (like healthy nutritional habits or regular physical activity are), it might make more sense to give up than to try to conquer something in which ultimately you'll never be good.

For example, I'm a natural introvert. I don't use it as an excuse not to socialize or have poor communication skills, but I've accepted that I don't recharge when I'm in a large group of people.

Consequently, I don't strive to become the life of the party because it clashes with my personality. Instead of forcing myself to socialize as much as it's possible against my nature, I decided to focus on a different aspect of my communication skills: better communication in one-on-one conversations.

This way, I can still improve myself, but in a way that will bring better results than trying to triumph over something that isn't (and never will be) my natural ability.

In the case of working on your strengths or weaknesses, taking the path of *most* resistance is the wrong choice. Focus on your strengths, and become as good as you can in what naturally comes to you, as that's where you'll benefit most from increased self-discipline.

# Day 255: On Self-Image

*You always behave consistently with the picture that you hold of yourself on the inside.*

—*Brian Tracy*[254]

Your self-image directly affects your self-discipline and virtually everything else in your life.

If you think of yourself as a lazy person, how likely is it that you will engage in productive behaviors? The picture that you hold of yourself on the inside won't match your intended actions. Whenever people feel their actions aren't congruent with themselves, they stop engaging in them.

On the other hand, if you think that (deep down) you're productive, you'll feel good when you manifest that in the real world. At the same time, whenever you catch yourself being lazy, you'll feel that it clashes with your personality and subsequently, do whatever you can to avoid it.

Negative self-image keeps you away from making a change, while positive self-image creates a virtuous cycle. Whenever you're setting new goals, start with your self-image. What do you think of yourself in relation to the goal you want to pursue?

What if, instead of calling yourself a failure in business, you'd call yourself a person with many experiences to draw from?

What if, instead of thinking of yourself as a person with weak self-control, you'd call yourself a person deeply motivated to build self-discipline?

Change your opinion about yourself and it will be easier to stick to actions that would otherwise feel unnatural and clash with who you think you are, deep down.

# Day 256: On Taking a Real Decision

*A real decision is measured by the fact that you've taken a new action. If there's no action, you haven't truly decided.*

—*Tony Robbins*[255]

Here's a simple rule: don't conclude that a decision has been made until you've taken a real-world action that reflects it.

Examples:

If you decided to change your nutritional habits, no real decision has been made unless you physically get rid of junk food from your house and prepare a healthy meal.

If you decided to start saving money, you haven't really decided unless you have put some savings in a saving jar or wired some money to a separate savings account.

If you decided to start a business, the decision will only become real when you start physically working on your product or service or you get busy selling it.

Don't fall victim to the erroneous belief that making a decision is merely saying some words in your head. The decision only becomes real in the moment you take a real-world action and can no longer easily back out by pretending that you were just "thinking" about making a decision.

# Day 257: On Being Impeccable With Your Word

> *Be impeccable with your word. Speak with integrity. Say only what you mean. Avoid using the word to speak against yourself or to gossip about others. Use the power of your word in the direction of truth and love.*
>
> —*Miguel Ángel Ruiz*[256]

Self-control has a wide variety of applications, one of which is the control you have over your own words. Negative habits like gossip, harsh unconstructive self-criticism, telling half-truths or speaking without integrity are all manifestations of a weak-willed person.

A person who's in control of their speech, who makes sure that their words are used primarily to tell the truth or are motivated by love and other positive emotions, will spread positivity and respect. This, in turn, will make the other person feel better, too, and it all creates a positive chain reaction. Moreover, controlling your words and making sure that whenever you open your mouth, you bring value to the world, is in itself a powerful exercise in self-restraint.

On the other end of the spectrum, a vile person who constantly gossips about others, hides what they think, and uses their words to hurt others, will ultimately live a bitter, gloomy life.

Being impeccable with your word is a big challenge, and possibly a lifetime endeavor, but it's well worth the benefits. Start

now by developing more awareness of how you use your words —
and change them whenever your motives aren't positive.

# Day 258: On Helping, With No Strings Attached

> *Successful people are always looking for opportunities to help others. Unsuccessful people are always asking, "What's in it for me?"*
>
> —*Brian Tracy*[257]

You can help others in two ways: help with no expectation for getting anything in return but the pleasure of helping, or help in a calculated way, expecting a reward.

Obviously, some situations require scratching each other's back. It would be foolish to help someone without expecting a clear compensation in return if you're conducting a regular business transaction.

However, many trivial everyday situations are opportunities for learning to exhibit the other approach: offering help with no strings attached.

This type of help is a valuable exercise in learning self-discipline because when you make difficult choices, you won't always have a guarantee of a future reward. Helping for the sake of helping is a powerful exercise in learning that it's worth it to do something positive for the sake of doing it, and not necessarily for immediate compensation.

Nobody is going to jump out of the corner with a trumpet, clapping their hands and congratulating you for making the right choice when you skip dessert. However, just like when helping with no strings attached, doing it anyway (without others' congratulations or expressed approval) can help you learn to draw pleasure from the mere fact of doing something that you know is good for you.

In addition to that, looking for opportunities to help others will help you develop the mindset of a successful individual — a person who's constantly on the lookout to contribute more to the world.

# Day 259: On the Motivation to Get Up Early

> *It's like waking up on a cold, snowy day in a mountain cabin ready to go for a walk but knowing that first you have to get out of bed and make a fire. You'd rather stay in that cozy bed, but you jump out and make the fire because the brightness of the day in front of you is bigger than staying in bed.*
>
> —*Pema Chödrön*[258]

Without a doubt, one of the most difficult challenges for self-discipline is getting out of the warm, comfortable bed early in the morning, when you're still half-asleep, only partially able to think logically.

Curiously, in my personal experience, this rarely happens if I'm on a vacation. I might even jump out of bed, eager to start another exciting day.

I've found that if I don't have any particular expectations for the day in front of me, I struggle to get out of bed. Whether you're self-disciplined or not, a lack of something you're looking forward to during the day will make it hard to get out of bed.

Each evening, before going to sleep, think about a convincing reason to get out of bed early — or set an ambitious long-term goal on which you'll work daily that will ensure that each day you'll have a reason to get up.

Unless the reason is more exciting or pressing than sleeping in, you'll probably have a hard time getting out of bed. Note that nothing — including fancy clocks, tracking your sleep phases, or putting your alarm across the room — will be as helpful for your self-control in the morning as having a good reason to wake up.

# WEEK 38

# Day 260: On Courage

> *People who seem to act "courageously" usually have specific consequences in mind; they know the consequences both of acting and not acting. They've decided that the consequences of not acting are worse than the consequences of what we consider to be their courageous acts.*
>
> —*Harry Browne*[259]

Here's a little trick to inspire courage to make a change: prepare a list of the consequences of acting and not acting. List all the great things that will happen if you change and all the bad things that will happen (or keep on happening) if you decide not to act.

Aim to make the list of the consequences of not acting so terrifying that the only valid choice would be to act. In essence, that's what courageous people often do in a split second: they see something that fills them with fear and do it anyway because ultimately not facing their fears is an even scarier proposition.

For example, if you're afraid to change your job, imagine what will happen if you don't act. You'll have to continue working in a job you may even hate. Day by day, week by week, it will probably get even worse. The same faces, the same annoying tasks, the same frustrating boss. Isn't that prospect scarier than looking for a new job?

# Day 261: On Giving Up the Last Word

> *Consciously giving up the last word is a secret prayer because the you that wants the last word isn't really you at all... it's that dark spirit of one-upmanship, that dark spirit of combativeness.*
>
> —*Guy Finley*[260]

When having a verbal fight, it's tempting to argue your case until you convince your opponent to share your stance. Unfortunately, it rarely, if ever happens. He or she who has the last word doesn't succeed in anything except for making the other person feel worse.

Consequently, here's another challenge for your self-control: instead of always trying to one-up somebody else, give up having the last word. Don't try to prove that you're better (you aren't) or that your opinion is right (even if it is, you won't convince anybody by arguing with them). Agree to disagree and change the topic to something more pleasant.

Exercising self-restraint this way will not only improve your relationships with others, it will also help you improve your self-control by learning how to resist one of the strongest temptations: to continue to argue your case when you're convinced of your rightness.

# Day 262: On Fragility Caused by Comfort

*Diseases of civilization result from the attempt by humans to make life comfortable for ourselves against our own interest, since the comfortable is what fragilizes.*

—*Nassim Taleb*[261]

There's no doubt that modern comforts make our lives easier. However, while the benefits are clear, there are also disadvantages of living in so much comfort: we rarely get to experience the discomfort our ancestors had been dealing with on a daily basis, and consequently, we are less able to handle it when it manifests in our lives.

That's why I've mentioned more than several times throughout the book how important it is to voluntarily put yourself in uncomfortable situations. One additional thought that is related to this topic is to think of experiencing discomfort as a vaccine.

For example, I've fasted so many times on so many occasions that now whenever I find myself in a situation in which I'm forced to fast for some reason, I don't mind it. I've essentially immunized myself against the need to eat often, and this has made me a stronger person.

The immunization you get from practicing discomfort quickly adds up, making you more resilient in all areas of life. Think of the ways in which you make yourself fragile through always choosing comfort over discomfort, and every now and then temporarily forego that comfort, in order to toughen up.

# Day 263: On Thinking for Yourself

*You and you alone are the sole arbiter of the meaning in your life. The second you turn to someone and say, "What does life mean?" or, "What should my life mean?" you have slipped into a mind-set that courts inauthenticity and depression. The second you agree with someone simply because of her position or reputation, whether that someone is a guru, author, cleric, parent, politician, general, or elder, you fall from the path of personal meaning-maker.*

—*Eric Maisel*[262]

One of the things I emphasize in every book is that I'm not a guru nor do I wish to be one. I don't want you to take my advice at face value, assuming that it's right simply because I share it in my book.

Agreeing with somebody simply because of their position or reputation is dangerous, because you're essentially delegating your thinking process to this person. I make mistakes, you make mistakes, and even the world's most successful performers make mistakes.

Moreover, what works for one person doesn't necessarily work for another person. For example, I often take the extreme approach, which usually works out fine for me, but might hurt another person who isn't used to pushing their limits in such a way. Granted, you won't know which approach is good for you until you test it for yourself, but it's important to think before you act and to question any advice, including the tips you find in this book.

Finally, don't make the mistake of letting others decide the meaning of your life. You, and only you, can figure out how you want to live your life and what you want to get out of it. Following somebody else's recipe for an "ideal" life is a recipe for depression. Even if your dreams are considered weird by others, it doesn't make them incorrect. They're *your* dreams, and that's the only thing that counts for them to be valid.

# Day 264: On Being Honest With Yourself About Your Feelings

> *Always be honest with yourself about how you are feeling, no matter what kinds of emotions might be building up inside of you. (...) Pretending to ourselves that we are not feeling something does not make that emotion disappear.*
>
> —*Nigel Cumberland*[263]

Pretending to yourself that you aren't feeling a temptation to cheat on your diet, waste time instead of working, or vent your anger on somebody else doesn't make those urges disappear. If anything, there's a risk that those emotions will build up inside of you and explode one day. If there's one characteristic thing about explosions, it's that they're uncontrollable.

Instead of denying those emotions, observe them and seek a different outlet. Perhaps you could vent in a different way without hurting anyone. Maybe you need to schedule a cheat meal and indulge a little to avoid an unplanned cheat week. It's possible that you're overworking yourself and the temptation to take it easy is in reality your body's cry for help.

Be honest with yourself about your feelings, especially those that stand in direct opposition to what you want to achieve. Remain vigilant of them and manage them instead of denying that they exist, or one day those feelings might take control of you.

# Day 265: On Transformation Taking Place Now

*The present moment contains past and future. The secret of transformation is in the way we handle this very moment.*

—*Thich Nhat Hanh*[264]

The way you handle this very moment might mean nothing for you today, but in reality, each present moment is an opportunity to change your life. It all starts with one decision.

Maybe you're now reading this book and wondering if you could learn how to play the guitar. It's only in this present moment that you can decide to stop reading and head to a music store, buy a guitar and start learning.

In the very same moment you might glance at a bag of chips on your lap and instead of finishing it off, close it and put it in the trash.

When you're going about your day, each little choice subtly affects your future. Each repetition of a negative habit reinforces it, while each repetition of a positive habit makes it more likely you'll engage in it again in the future.

Personal transformation doesn't happen in the future — it's happening now. How are you making sure that you're transforming in the right direction?

# Day 266: On Temptations and Your Decision What to Do About Them

*An eye, when open, has no option but to see. The decision whether to look at a particular man's wife, however, and how, belongs to the will. And the determination whether to trust what someone says, and then, if we trust them, whether we should be angered by it — that also belongs to the will.*

—*Epictetus*[265]

When shopping, you'll undoubtedly find yourself surrounded by shelves filled with unhealthy food. However, the decision whether it lands in your shopping cart depends on you.

When taking a pause from learning for a difficult exam, you might receive a message from a friend asking you to hang out. The decision as to whether you hang out or finish your coffee and resume studying is yours to make.

When browsing online, looking for information to help you grow your business, you might stumble upon a cat meme or a funny video. It's within your control as to whether you waste your time on low-quality entertainment or continue your search for information.

It's tempting to shift the responsibility to the external factors, but does it benefit you in any way to claim that you cheated on your diet because you happened to go through the aisle with the potato chips? Is it a legitimate excuse to say that you didn't go for a jog because there was a comfortable sofa in your living room and it demanded your attention?

Do whatever you can to avoid situations that might tempt you to do something that will jeopardize your long-term goals, but if you happen to come upon them, remember that it's still your decision — and a test of your self-discipline — as to whether they will affect you negatively.

# WEEK 39

# Day 267: On Self-Monitoring

*The more carefully and frequently you monitor yourself, the better you'll control yourself.*

—*Roy Baumeister*[266]

People who monitor their weight regularly have a higher chance of maintaining weight loss permanently.

People monitoring their output at work have a higher chance of remaining productive in the long run.

People who monitor the hours when they go to sleep and wake up are more likely to become permanent early risers.

Self-monitoring is a crucial tool to help you keep track of your results and then, upon achieving your goal, maintaining them forever. I strongly suggest monitoring yourself at least weekly, and if possible, daily.

For example, to keep myself in check, even though I'm fit, I weigh myself daily and regularly monitor my physique in the mirror. No, I don't obsess about my appearance like a narcissist or feel my heart rate going up when I step on the scales. The only purpose of doing these things is to ensure that if I somehow fail to notice a slip-up in my habits, my body will communicate it to me and help me address it before it gets worse.

I follow the same approach in my business. I have a daily word count, but I also monitor my output compared to my output last year.

That way, I always know when I'm getting lazy and when I need to concentrate on strengthening my work ethic.

How often do you monitor yourself? Is it a part of your daily or weekly schedule? If not, it's time to make that happen.

# Day 268: On Taking Ownership for Your Ideas

> *Regardless of what we create — a toy box, a new source of electricity, a new mathematical theorem — much of what really matters to us is that it is our creation. As long as we create it, we tend to feel rather certain that it's more useful and important than similar ideas that other people come up with.*
>
> —*Dan Ariely*[267]

When people create something themselves — say, a birthday card for a friend — they value it more than something created by somebody else. Similarly, people take ownership of their ideas and feel they're more valuable simply because they're their own ideas.

You can use this phenomenon to improve your self-discipline. Instead of relying on *my* definition of self-discipline, come up with your own. Jot down what self-control means to you, when you feel it, how you feel it and why is it important to you. I can write all day long how important self-discipline is, but if you do it yourself and apply it to your personal situation, you'll immediately understand it on a deeper level.

In addition to reading the tips and tricks I share in this book, come up with your own ideas. You'll be more likely to act on your own ideas than on the ones that you learned from me or from any other person.

I usually give two or three applications for every piece of advice, but it's rarely limited to just those two or three uses. Think about how you can adapt the lessons to your own life or even test the opposite way of doing things — there's rarely, if ever, only one correct method. Discovering the right answer for your unique situation can deliver better results than reading even a hundred books about personal development.

# Day 269: On Stretching

> *The benefits of stretching are enormous. Stretching can increase your strength by 10%. It is a lot. The man [Russian Master of Sports Alexander Faleev] explains that "when you lift a weight your muscles contract. And after the workout the muscles remain contracted for some time. The following restoration of the muscles' length is what recovery is. Until the muscle has restored its length, it has not recovered. Hence he who does not stretch his muscles slows down the recuperation process and retards his gains." Besides, tension and relaxation are two sides of the same coin, "if the muscle forgets how to lengthen, it will contract more poorly. And that is stagnation of strength."*
>
> —**Pavel Tsatsouline**[268]

Here's your willpower exercise for the week: stretching. Stretching isn't only great for your physical health; since it's generally uncomfortable but provides long-term benefits, it's also great for your self-discipline.

I strongly suggest always beginning a workout with dynamic stretches (short stretches, usually with some kind of a dynamic motion) and concluding each training with static stretching (holding a stretch for a longer period of time, usually at least 15–30 seconds).

Static stretching is better for exercising your willpower because that's where you actually need to hold a stretch and keep at it, even though it's uncomfortable.

5-10 minutes of stretching a few times a week, focused particularly on the tightest areas (probably your hips, lower back and hamstrings) is a good target. If you don't know how to stretch, a quick search on YouTube will yield plenty of detailed video tutorials.

# Day 270: On Self-Reflection

*Socrates compared living without thinking systematically to practicing an activity like pottery or shoemaking without following or even knowing of technical procedures. One would never imagine that a good pot or shoe would result from intuition alone; why then assume that the more complex task of directing one's life could be undertaken without any sustained reflection on premises or goals?*

—*Alain de Botton*[269]

Set a timer for 15 minutes and do nothing else but sit or lie comfortably and think about your current problems or anything that's been on your mind recently.

It's incredible how much insight you can get by hitting the pause button for mere 15 minutes and simply thinking, without doing anything else.

When people are new to personal development, they tend to think more than act. They spend more time reading than actually implementing advice. Once you gain some experience and develop a habit of taking action, the opposite is often true: you take a lot of action, but rarely reflect on it.

The exercise for today can remedy this situation by reminding you that you get the best results not only when you act, but when you act *and* reflect on your actions to ensure the highest effectiveness.

# Day 271: On How to Use Books

*Books... are like lobster shells, we surround ourselves with 'em, then we grow out of 'em and leave 'em behind, as evidence of our earlier stages of development.*

—*Dorothy L. Sayers*[270]

When you're new to the world of personal development, you read whatever you can grab your hands on. Every single classic, every book recommended to you by somebody you respect, every new bestselling release. At first, it's a fine strategy: you get to expose yourself to different authors, learn the fundamentals, and look at personal development from different perspectives.

However, as time passes, you should leave some books behind and progress to more specific advice. For example, I used to read one general self-help book after another. Soon I found them all similar to each other. Each new title added little to my knowledge. I outgrew those books, and needed to find a new teacher.

I transitioned to reading books about a more specific topic than general personal development: how to change myself to become a successful entrepreneur (and how to actually start and run a profitable company), how to improve my communication skills, how to eat healthily, or how to develop focus.

Then I started reading more biographies and autobiographies, where the lessons usually aren't as clearly laid out as in a regular how-to book, but which are unique and more insightful, related to a specific problem the person portrayed in the biography had dealt with.

Recently I started expanding my horizons and seeking out books about specific problems I struggle with (for example, how to develop a better life philosophy) and reading books from other domains, so I could draw parallels from them and apply their principles to my own life.

Think of different categories of books as your development stages. When a given type of a book no longer serves you, find a new teacher.

# Day 272: On Extinguishing Bad Habits

*You can never truly extinguish bad habits. Rather, to change a habit, you must keep the old cue, and deliver the old reward, but insert a new routine. That's the rule: If you use the same cue, and provide the same reward, you can shift the routine and change the habit. Almost any behavior can be transformed if the cue and reward stay the same.*

—*Charles Duhigg*[271]

Some time ago we talked about the habit loop: a cue (a signal to perform a habit), a routine (action), and a reward for engaging in the habit. This loop, when repeated over and over again, creates an automatic behavior.

You can use this loop to create new habits, but you can also use it to replace bad habits with more empowering routines.

For example, instead of always eating a chocolate bar during a lunch break, eat a banana. Your cue is a lunch break and your reward is eating something sweet. Two parts of the habit loop remain the same, but are now satisfied by a healthier alternative.

Instead of always dealing with a stressful situation by emotional eating, head out for a quick run. Your cue is feeling stressed, and as a reward you get to reduce or eliminate the anxiety. Running can become an alternative, healthy way of satisfying your need for self-comfort.

If you have any bad habits you want to get rid of, think about how to keep your cue and reward the same while replacing the negative routine with something empowering. You'll reduce the risk of reverting to the old habit because it will only be the action in itself that changes — not your cue or the reward.

# Day 273: On Reprogramming Your Brain

*Given our human impulse to pick up the habits and energy of others, you can use that knowledge to literally program your brain the way you want. Simply find the people who most represent what you would like to become and spend as much time with them as you can without trespassing, kidnapping, or stalking. Their good habits and good energy will rub off on you.*

—*Scott Adams*[272]

Research shows that resisting peer pressure causes emotional discomfort.[273] Consequently, humans have a tendency to want to fit in, even when it means not thinking for themselves or doing things they would otherwise never do.

While it's not a positive phenomenon among college kids who all want to emulate the popular guy or gal who's into partying hard, it can be a beneficial tool for an adult who consciously chooses the group whose features he or she would like to acquire.

If there's any shortcut to building self-discipline, it's this: find a group of people who possess discipline and let the power of peer pressure change you.

For example, if you want to build self-discipline to exercise regularly, join a fitness group or hang out in the park with ripped guys who are into calisthenics.

If you want to become super productive and have enough self-discipline to wake up every single day at 5 in the morning to work on your start-up, join a local networking group of entrepreneurs or work in a co-working space.

If you want to stop spending so much money on unnecessary things, join a forum about frugality or follow bloggers in the personal finance niche.

Look at it from other perspective, too: if the groups you currently belong to don't exhibit the traits you'd like to acquire (or worse, exhibit the complete opposite of those traits), ask yourself whether you want to continue to let them influence your life.

# WEEK 40

# Day 274: On Constant Movement

*Well, I always know what I want. And when you know what you want — you go toward it. Sometimes you go very fast, and sometimes only an inch a year. Perhaps you feel happier when you go fast. I don't know. I've forgotten the difference long ago, because it really doesn't matter, so long as you move.*

—*Ayn Rand*[274]

Constant movement is the key to a successful life because humans are programmed to always be on the mission to improve their lives. The journey in itself can give life meaning, and obsessing about not being able to shorten it can only bring unnecessary frustration.

In addition to that, certain goals require years (or sometimes even decades) to achieve, and there's little, if anything, you can do to turn them into reality sooner. Complaining only breeds negativity, which does nothing to help you attain your goals.

You might think that it doesn't make sense to work on a goal if your progress is slow and you consequently feel tempted to give up.

But what's the alternative?

If you give up, you're guaranteed to not meet your objectives. What sense does it make to give up, frustrated by the slow progress, and then resort to wishing you could somehow magically turn your dream into reality?

# Day 275: On Staying a Champion

*You will never be entirely comfortable. This is the truth behind the champion — he is always fighting something. To do otherwise is to settle.*

—*Julien Smith*[275]

I'm sorry to break it to you, but if you expect that one day all discomfort will be gone from your life and you'll be able to enjoy the fruits of your hard labor for the rest of your days, you're wrong.

If you not only want to become a champion, but also *stay* a champion, by definition you'll always need to fight something: fight to reach a new goal, overcome hardships, expand your comfort zone, and continue improving yourself little by little.

For example, at the time I'm writing this, it's been two years since I started rock climbing. I used to be terrified of heights and taking falls. While my fear of heights and taking falls has greatly diminished, I'm still not free — and will never be free — from fear and discomfort when I'm climbing.

If you want to improve your climbing, you need to climb harder and harder routes. They will still make you uncomfortable and scared. Even the best rock climbers in the world still feel fear and experience discomfort — just like skydivers, public speakers, successful businesspeople, athletes, and any other top performers.

If you'd like to stay a champion, accept the fact that discomfort is here to stay. Embrace it as a teacher that will strengthen you and help you achieve ever greater feats, not as an annoying part of the process that you'd like to put behind as quickly as possible.

# Day 276: On the Price of Personal Growth

*Personal growth has its price, and she was paying it without complaint.*

—*Paulo Coelho*[276]

As we've discussed it in yesterday's entry, staying a champion means that you'll always need to put yourself in new, uncomfortable situations. It's the price you have to pay for excellence.

Personal growth in general has its price, too. From my personal experience, here are several things you should expect on your journey toward improving your life:

1. People being confused about your actions. Unless you're surrounding yourself solely with top performers, your immediate social circle will probably be puzzled why you're subjecting yourself to discomfort, prioritizing work over enjoying yourself, or rejecting pleasures today for the sake of tomorrow. The sooner you learn to ignore those voices, the better off you'll be.

2. Outgrowing certain people in your life. It's painful, but you'll probably outgrow some friends or loved ones. You'll find it harder to connect with them and they'll find it harder to connect with you. This doesn't necessarily have to happen in every situation and with everyone, but prepare yourself for the reality that some of your relationships will probably weaken or stop being as fulfilling as they used to be.

3. An incessant desire to improve everything. Once you start making positive changes in your life and experience in your own skin how powerful new habits and attitudes can be, you'll feel the desire to improve everything. This can be a source of frustration when you realize that certain people don't want to change or that certain social mores actually value mediocrity over excellence.

4. Self-guilt that you have it better than other people. As strange as it sounds, if you successfully introduce some important changes in your life — develop a healthy physique, form positive nutritional habits, set aside some savings and find meaningful work you enjoy or at least one that satisfies you financially — you might start feeling guilty that others have it worse.

Considering that most people are either obese, unhealthy, broke, or unhappy at work, chances are you that you will indeed live a better life than they are living. However, in the end you gained the right to enjoy the life you have now through your own efforts. Don't feel guilty because you made better choices. Other people could have done the same.

5. A difficulty to enjoy what you have. The more you achieve in your life, the more you'll want to achieve. When you notice that something is lacking in your life, you'll want to change it. This carries the risk that you'll never be able to enjoy what you have or unrealistically expect that everything and everyone needs to be perfect. Sooner or later (ideally sooner) you'll need to learn how to be grateful for what you have and be content with it.

# Day 277: On Making Things Convenient

*Nutritionally speaking, frozen veggies are similar to — and sometimes better than — fresh ones. This makes sense, considering that these veggies are usually flash-frozen (which suspends/pauses their "aging" and nutrient losses) immediately after being harvested. Frozen veggies are often picked in the peak of their season, too.*

*—Ronald B. Pegg*[277]

Here's the ultimate hack when it comes to eating more vegetables: eat ones that have been frozen. At least 50-60% of vegetables I eat have been frozen (the rest are canned and fresh). Research shows that nutrition-wise, frozen vegetables aren't worse — and might be even better — than fresh vegetables.

One of the biggest issues when it comes to improving your eating habits is a lack of time or being too lazy to prepare fresh vegetables. You can get rid of this excuse by buying a frozen vegetable mix. Steam it, sprinkle it with some good herbs and spices and voila! You're getting your veggies for the day with no need to go through the entire ordeal of peeling, washing, and cooking fresh vegetables (for which you might not have enough willpower).

Please note that this entry isn't merely about frozen vegetables; it's about making sure that your new positive habits are as convenient to stick to as possible.

The more convenient you make it to stick to a healthy diet, the more likely you'll be to stick to it. Even if one day scientists discover that frozen or canned vegetables aren't as healthy as the fresh ones, it's still better to eat them than not eat vegetables at all because it's too inconvenient for you to eat them fresh.

The same applies to other goals. Yes, it would be ideal if you found a fun outdoor activity, but if you really can't afford to do so, buying some basic equipment and exercising at home (to make it more convenient) is still better than not exercising at all.

When you're choosing between failing to stick to a positive habit because it's inconvenient or making it more convenient but perhaps a little bit less effective, choose the latter.

# Day 278: On the Rent Axiom

*The Rent Axiom says that success is never owned. Success is only rented and the rent is due every day.*

—*Rory Vaden*[278]

The Rent Axiom is a powerful way to look at success. Instead of thinking of success as something that is given to you, thus risking that you'll take it for granted and become complacent, you assume that you only rent it — and to keep it in your life, you need to pay the rent each and every day.

Another consequence of adopting this perspective is that you'll stop looking for shortcuts or temporary solutions. The rent is due every day, so it's not like you can take one magic pill and forever solve all of your problems.

It's an empowering outlook on life that will help you not only *reach* success, but also (which is even more important) to *maintain* it.

Thousands of people all over the world have successfully lost weight, started exercising more, built successful businesses, improved their relationships, learned new skills, wrote books, and achieved other goals. However, thousands of them also lost their success when they assumed it was there forever.

Spouses stopped putting in the effort. Businessmen let their competition crush them. Dieters reverted to their old habits and regained weight. If you don't want this to happen to you, remember to pay your rent every day and always make sure that your current actions confirm that you deserve the success you've achieved.

# Day 279: On Learning With Age

*It's very simple. As you grow, you learn more. If you stayed at twenty-two, you'd always be as ignorant as you were at twenty-two. Aging is not just decay, you know. It's growth. It's more than the negative that you're going to die; it's also the positive that you understand you're going to die, and that you live a better life because of it.*

—*Mitch Albom*[279]

As time passes, one might feel tempted to believe that their best years are behind them. Now decay commences, and things can only get worse. How about looking at it from a different point of view and embracing aging as the learning process?

I like to say that if in five years I'm the same person that I am today, then I'll have failed. Ideally, in five years I should feel slightly uncomfortable about the type of a person I was in the past.

Aging is not merely about your body's cells dividing and multiplying — it's also about your *knowledge*, which (if you make an effort to do so) constantly expands, gives you new perspectives and helps you live an ever better life.

You can look at aging in both ways: a process of deterioration or a process of improvement. Which attitude will bring more happiness and success in your life?

# Day 280: On Seeing Your Troubles from the Proper Perspective

*I try to see my troubles in their proper perspective. I say to myself: "Two months from now I shall not be worrying about this bad break, so why worry about it now? Why not assume now the same attitude that I will have two months from now?"*

—*William L. Phelps*[280]

At the moment I'm writing this, I'm questioning my ability to persevere for another two weeks before I finish this book. I've been working on it for a long time, and it's been my most difficult project so far.

The thought that helps me see my current troubles from the proper perspective is imagining myself two months from now, when the work is already done and the book is published.

In the grand scheme of things, what does two additional weeks of work mean? I'm almost done, so now I only need to push myself for a little while longer and the situation will resolve itself.

In the past, a friend helped me handle my financial troubles in a similar way. I was worried about the money I owed to the bank, but in the grand scheme of things it mattered little: my friend made me aware that my new business had been making money, it was quickly growing, and it would only be a matter of several months and I'd be debt-free.

If you're currently struggling or worrying about something, try to look at your troubles from the perspective of you in the future. If your situation will end in several days or weeks, then is it really such a big problem? Even if it's going to take at least several months, it's still a temporary condition and worrying about it excessively is counter-productive.

# WEEK 41

# Day 281: On the Hardships Writing Your Life Story

*You can recall everything you have worked hard and patiently for in your life, but how many things that you have attained with little or no effort can you remember?*

—*Thomas Sterner*[281]

When you're struggling with your goal and feel tempted to give up, remind yourself that ultimately, it's the hardships that write your life story and make it so exciting and memorable.

As Thomas Sterner points out, we don't remember things that we achieved easily — and often, they don't even make us particularly happy or we don't consider them significant.

Working hard and patiently to achieve an important but difficult goal isn't just an unpleasant thing that you need to do to get to your destination — it's life itself, a state a human being needs to feel fulfilled and inspired. A life without challenges is neither happy nor does it lead to you realizing your full potential.

See your current hardships for what they are — a powerful opportunity to embrace your human nature, grow as a person, and an awesome inspirational story you'll be able to share with others in the future.

# Day 282: On Analysis Paralysis

*The ten thousand questions are one question. If you cut through the one question, then the ten thousand questions disappear.*

—*Xinxin Ming*

Analysis paralysis happens when you overthink a situation to such an extent that you never take a decision.

For example, a person who wishes to lose weight will never commence a diet because they'll forever keep searching for the right diet or the ultimate answer to the question of which foods are healthy and which are not (hint: even scientists don't know the correct answer).

As a result, weeks and months pass by, and all you have is more and more unresolved questions and zero real-world results.

While it often pays to think deeply about your goal and how you want to approach it, if you have a tendency to over-analyze and overcomplicate things, give yourself just one day to figure out the answer to one key question — and instead of aiming for the perfect answer, aim for an answer that's *good enough*.

For example, if you want to start a diet and are unsure which one to follow, research the most common and most successful diets. Limit your choices to the few best options and then choose the one that feels like the best fit. Don't worry about getting it perfect — in the state of analysis paralysis you won't get any results, so even mediocre results are still an improvement.

Think of it as driving a car in foggy weather. Even though you can't see everything around you, you can still drive. It's the same with goals — even with limited knowledge, you can still work on your objectives.

# Day 283: On Being Hungry

*Stay hungry. Be hungry for success, hungry to make your mark, hungry to be seen and to be heard and to have an effect. And as you move up and become successful, make sure also to be hungry for helping others. Don't rest on your laurels.*

—*Arnold Schwarzenegger*[282]

One of the biggest dangers of success is that when people achieve it, they frequently lose the hunger that has led them to demonstrate the incredible amounts of willpower and determination it took to make their dreams come true. As a result, they run a huge risk of losing the success they've worked so hard to achieve.

If you don't want to be like those people, once you're done celebrating your success, find another source of hunger that will make you pursue new challenges and continue to grow. Set bigger goals, or find a deeper meaning behind your actions. Discover a new itch to scratch, to keep yourself always learning more.

Note that always searching for a new source of hunger doesn't mean that you can't ever be content with what you have. It's not about constantly chasing the carrot, dissatisfied with what you have. It's about making your life ever so much larger, while being appreciative and protective of what you have.

For example, I'm extremely grateful for my successes in the self-publishing world — and for people like you reading my books — and precisely because of that, I still push myself. I know that it's only through constant effort and through producing new works that I can reach even more people and achieve new goals. Writing new books protects my success and lets me grow as a writer, constantly taking things to the next level. Should my hunger for writing disappear one day, I'll find a new reason to be hungry in a different area.

Don't let comfort persuade you that challenges aren't important in life. When there's nothing difficult that you're striving to achieve, you will eventually lose your hard-earned achievements, habits, and traits — and along with it, the comfort that you're now enjoying.

# Day 284: On Habits as Handcuffs

*Don't let your habits become handcuffs.*

*—Elizabeth Berg*[283]

Few, if any, self-help authors would challenge the opinion that habits are of key importance to a person wishing to improve their life. Most would agree that good habits unlock success, while negative habits are destroying you.

Yet, sometimes even positive habits can act like handcuffs that limit your life and choices to a preselected set of routines that you've decided are most optimal for you.

Is waking up early generally a positive habit? It is. It can become like handcuffs, though, if you assume that now you need to wake up early every single day, even if there's a special occasion to celebrate the evening before, such as your spouse's birthday.

Is eating healthy a positive habit? Of course it is. However, it can act as shackles if you never let yourself lower your guard for a while and enjoy (preferably in great company) whatever food strikes your fancy.

Is being highly productive and always working on something new a good habit to have? It is — but if you never relax or get a little lazy, you'll miss out on some valuable experiences in life and eventually burn out.

Whenever forming new habits, establish rules as to when you'll allow yourself to temporarily forego them. Self-discipline and positive habits are important, but life isn't about living like a robot that always follows the same routines, no matter what.

# Day 285: On Small Efforts at Self-Control

*Committing to any small, consistent act of self-control — improving your posture, squeezing a handgrip every day to exhaustion, cutting back on sweets, and keeping track of your spending — can increase overall willpower.*

*—Kelly McGonigal*[284]

Don't discount the power of small efforts. They count, too. Little challenges that you can do throughout the day (with a small time investment) can help you improve your overall self-discipline.

In fact, some of those small things (such as reminding yourself to have a good posture or avoid cursing), when done repeatedly, can deliver immense personal changes because they force you to be more mindful of your everyday actions. By pausing yourself intermittently throughout the day to control your small behaviors, you develop more mindfulness, and consequently, more self-control.

Here are some little exercises you can consider adding to your everyday routine to improve your self-discipline, even when you're strapped for time:

- keep your back straight when working;
- every hour, stand up and do five bodyweight squats;
- pause for five seconds before you start cursing;
- keep a notebook with you and, each day, write down three new ideas to improve yourself;

- every day put one dollar into a savings jar — if you don't have money to spare, this means resisting a temptation to buy something you consume daily, like coffee or a bagel.

# Day 286: On Avoiding Problems

*Avoid what causes the opposite of what you want to achieve.*

—*Peter Bevelin*[285]

If you want to be safe, it's best not to attend dangerous venues. For example, one of the most common places where bad things happen are nightclubs and their immediate vicinity. If you don't go to nightclubs, your risk of getting into a brawl or being attacked by a drunk person is greatly decreased.

It's the same with self-control. Instead of exerting self-discipline, it's better to avoid problems that can cause the opposite of what you want to achieve.

If you want to be a frugal person, don't go to shopping centers if you don't have to, and don't hang out with people who love shopping.

If you want to become more productive, sell your TV set, video console, and any other thing a lazy person considers a must-have.

If you want to stop drinking alcohol, stop going to parties where alcohol is the primary source of entertainment, and don't spend time with people who live for the weekends.

Think about your goal, figure out what its opposite is, and then ask yourself which actions, people, and places can lead you to that opposite result and avoid them.

# Day 287: On Reducing Procrastination That Comes From Overwhelm

*The bigger and more overwhelming the project seems to you, the greater your tendency to procrastinate.*

—*Neil Fiore*[286]

A common reason why people procrastinate about something that they consider extremely important to them is exactly that — they consider it so crucial that it overwhelms them and paralyzes their actions.

When you think of something as your only big chance in life, you'll understandably try to tread as carefully as possible. This, however, can quickly convert into procrastination when your fear of ruining the opportunity will prevent you from taking action.

If you currently find yourself in such a situation, ask yourself what is the end result of putting off this big, once-in-a-lifetime chance in life. Isn't procrastinating about it going to lead to the exact same thing you're afraid of — losing the opportunity?

Whenever setting new resolutions, manage your attitude about them so that you aren't overwhelmed by them.

Think of it as having an opportunity to meet a famous person. You can hold them in high regard, but it doesn't mean that you have to act like a crazy fan around them. In fact, that's what will put them off, while a person who treats them as another human being will be a welcome difference.

It's the same with your goals. Yes, they might be so important that they will change your life. However, this will only happen if you keep a cool head about them. Otherwise you can let them overwhelm you to such an extent that you'll altogether fail to act.

# WEEK 42

# Day 288: On Routines and Relationships

> *People are offended when you repeatedly turn down their invitations. But, at that point, I felt that the indispensable relationship I should build in my life was not with a specific person but with an unspecified number of readers. My readers would welcome whatever life style I chose, as long as I made sure that each new work was an improvement over the last. And shouldn't that be my duty — and my top priority — as a novelist?*
>
> —*Haruki Murakami*[287]

Haruki Murakami's dedication to his readers is impressive, but you might wonder if it means that if you want to achieve your goals by adopting consistent routines, you'll lose friends and live the life of a social recluse. The answer is: partly yes, and partly no.

You often can't choose when you're the most effective. For me, it's mornings, between 5 and 9 a.m. This means that each day I need to go to sleep around 9 or 10 p.m. at the latest, in order to to have a good night's sleep and ensure maximum productivity the next morning.

Obviously, this affects my life. I rarely hang out with my friends in the evening. However — and here's where we get to the core of the issue — sometimes you need to make a choice between a routine and a relationship.

A person whose primary role is that of a parent will understandably adapt their routine to that of their child.

An entrepreneur will choose to not spend time with some of his or her friends, if that means that his or her business can grow more quickly.

A person who wants to banish negative emotions from their life will ensure that their day is constructed in a way that is most conducive to positive feelings.

Define your most important priorities and roles in life and adjust your life accordingly. Don't try to please everybody, because it simply can't happen.

# Day 289: On Accounting for Taxes

*Everything you do has a tax attached to it.*

*For example, the tax on traveling is all the waiting around.*

*Disagreements and occasional frustration are taxes placed on even the happiest of relationships.*

*Theft is a tax on abundance and having things that other people want.*

*Stress and problems are tariffs that come attached to success.*

*Simply pay the taxes in life, and enjoy the fruits of what you get to keep.*

—*Ryan Holiday*[288]

It's exciting to set new goals and imagine how your life will change when you achieve them. However, people often forget that everything in life has a tax attached to it. When they wake up to the reality that their goals aren't all roses and require some sacrifices on their part or generate problems, their excitement fades away and their odds of success decrease.

As Ryan Holiday notes, there are taxes on traveling, relationships, and financial success, but they aren't limited just to those areas.

If you want to become healthier, one of the taxes is that you'll have a harder time when you eat in a social setting.

If you want to get more fit, you'll most likely have to forego some other activities in order to make time for physical activities.

If you want to become a bestselling author or become virtually any kind of an expert, you'll undoubtedly attract critics.

Thinking about the dark side before you even start working on your goals doesn't sound like a good way to motivate yourself, but it's necessary to acknowledge it and be prepared for the fact that any change in life — including a positive one — will bring some new problems with it, and it's a price you have to pay to enjoy it.

# Day 290: On Letting Go of the Old Person

*You must be willing to let go of the old person in order to become the new person. You must be willing to stop doing certain things in order to start doing the things that are consistent with the new you.*

—*Brian Tracy*[289]

People want to get rid of their flaws and improve themselves, but at the same time they aren't willing to let go of their unfavorable behaviors and habits. They're slaves to their weaknesses, often equating them with who they are.

An overweight person will never change unless they stop thinking of themselves as an overweight person. If being obese is something that you use as your personal definition and (what's even worse) you feel fine referring to yourself in such a way, how do you expect to become a new person?

I was overweight as a teenager and in my early twenties. One day I realized that, in some twisted way, I enjoyed it. Upon discovering this fact and realizing that my future wouldn't be very bright if I were to stay faithful to this definition of myself, I decided to let go of this identity and lose weight. Today, I'm proud to define myself as a slim, fit person.

A person who defines themselves as a video gamer and wears it as a badge of honor will be unlikely to adopt new, more productive behaviors until they become willing to let go of their old identity of a gamer. True, there's nothing inherently wrong in being a gamer. However, if it stands in the way of accomplishing your goals, rethink whether it's an identity that serves you or if perhaps it's time to give it up so you can start doing other things that are more consistent with a new you.

Who's the old you and who's the new you? How often do you engage in the behaviors of the old you and how often do you manifest the traits of the new you? Shift the balance toward the new you and one by one, eradicate the undesirable old behaviors.

# Day 291: On the How Instead of the Outcome

> *Many people don't understand that how you climb a mountain is more important than reaching the top. (...) The goal of climbing big, dangerous mountains should be to attain some sort of spiritual and personal growth, but this won't happen if you compromise away the entire process.*
>
> —*Yvon Chouinard*[290]

All goals require you to go through a process to attain them. If you compromise away the process by cutting corners, you're missing out on what goal achievement is really about: personal growth, through making the journey.

When all is said and done, you aren't going to talk for hours about how you stood on top of the mountain, but about the ordeal you had to go through to reach the top.

You won't grow because you got to the peak — it's everything that happens prior to reaching it that results in growth, not the mere act of putting your foot one more step forward and achieving the summit. Whether you take that last step or not, it won't erase all that you've had to go through to get that far.

In the quote, Yvon Chouinard refers to the wealthy individuals with no climbing experience and skills — or any desire to develop them — who pay huge sums of money to reach the top of Mount Everest (with the help of the Sherpas who carry the equipment needed to make the ascent as easy as possible). Those rich men and women aren't after the personal growth — they're after the bragging rights of getting to the top of the tallest mountain the world at all costs. They reach the top, but they deprive themselves of the lessons the difficult process would offer them.

When chasing after your goals, don't be like those wannabe climbers. By all means, do whatever you can to achieve your dreams as quickly as possible, but don't cut corners, compromise your moral principles, cheat, or hurt anyone, just so you can brag that you accomplished your objective.

# Day 292: On Mental Resilience

*Do not grieve. Anything you lose comes round in another form.*

—*Jalaluddin Rumi*[291]

The essence of mental resilience is the belief that anything bad that happens to you will ultimately turn out to be good for you.

However, I wouldn't go so far as to say "don't grieve" after losing a loved one, so please note that today's entry is about being mentally resilient when it comes to less impactful negative events happening in your life.

When faced with heartbreaking losses such as a business going bankrupt, a lost job opportunity, a breakup, or even your new diet going south, it's hard to see it as a possible blessing in disguise. After all, you've just lost something — a business, a relationship, a job, or hope for improvement.

As an immediate reaction, it might be challenging to *not* feel bad about the situation. However, once you process that it *has* happened and accept that, one of the best ways to move on is to remind yourself that what you've just lost will come around again in a different form.

Maybe a breakup was necessary so that you can start over again and find a different, better partner. Maybe your business had to go bankrupt so you could free up your resources to focus on a better idea. Your diet went south, and maybe it happened because now you'll discover new nutritional habits that will be easier to maintain than your previous restrictive diet.

Each time something bad happens, try to find a lesson in it and the new opportunities it presents. I suggest that you start small, with less significant negative events, as it will take time and experience to learn to handle bigger difficulties with calm and dignity.

# Day 293: On Cutting Your Losses

*Cut your losses short and let your winners run.*

—*A Wall Street saying*

I once invested several thousand dollars in an extensive coaching course. I thought that since I was already an author, it wouldn't be that different to become a coach, too. I spent over a month learning from that course, and ultimately gave up with little to show for it.

After a month of studying, I didn't feel I knew that much more about coaching to be able to coach — and it didn't matter, because I knew that I wouldn't do it, anyway. My idea to become a coach was a mistake. I realized that my strengths lie in writing books, and not in giving personalized advice. Continuing my education would have been continuing to invest my time and energy into something that was destined to fail anyway. I cut my losses short and refocused on writing.

Due to loss aversion, people have a tendency to avoid losses over acquiring equivalent gains,[292] This means that you'd rather keep investing your time and energy into a failed project than cut it short and redirect your attention to something that can produce better results.

It's a dangerous trap for persistent people, because you might spend months (if not years) doing something that will ultimately lead you nowhere. If you're keeping at it only because of what you've already invested, ask yourself if it's the best use of your time. If it isn't, and there are better things you can do, accept the losses as a learning experience and move on.

# Day 294: On the All-or-Nothing Mentality

*Part of abandoning the all-or-nothing mentality is allowing yourself room for setbacks. We are bound to have lapses on the road to health and wellness, but it is critical that we learn how to handle small failures positively so that we can minimize their long-term destructive effects. One setback is one setback — it is not the end of the world, nor is it the end of your journey toward a better you.*

—*Jillian Michaels*

People often don't act on their goals because they don't see how they can make it big right away. For them, it's all or nothing.

It's either a sexy, firm, and beautiful body or nothing. It's either a glamorous start-up, backed by the biggest names from the Silicon Valley, or nothing. It's either being a perfect dancer or not learning how to dance at all.

It's easy to see that there's only one outcome of this mentality: you do nothing because no matter what you do, you won't get your perfect results right away. Even if you do start, one setback will discourage you from further efforts: after all, it's all or nothing and since you just suffered a failure, it's time to give up as you won't be perfect anymore.

Avoid developing such a mindset in yourself by acknowledging that everybody has to first be bad at something in order to become good at it. No world-class performer started out with incredible skills; they all fumbled and failed on their journey toward success. If you don't believe me, read some autobiographies.

If you managed to get past the all-or-nothing thinking and started working on your goals, but small slip-ups discourage you from further efforts, tell yourself that you only have to adhere to your resolutions in 90% of your efforts. The remaining 10% is your margin for mistakes.

That way, one slip-up won't destroy your entire progress: after all, you've already accounted for it, so it's not ruining your forecast result.

# WEEK 43

# Day 295: On Wandering Aimlessly

> *We are engineered as goal-seeking mechanisms. We are built that way. When we have no personal goal which we are interested in and which "means something" to us, we are apt to "go around in circles," feel "lost" and find life itself "aimless," and "purposeless." We are built to conquer environment, solve problems, achieve goals, and we find no real satisfaction or happiness in life without obstacles to conquer and goals to achieve. People who say that life is not worthwhile are really saying that they themselves have no personal goals which are worthwhile.*
>
> —*Maxwell Maltz*[293]

If you've been wandering aimlessly, asking yourself what's the point of life and feeling like you have no purpose, it's possibly because you don't have any important long-term goals to achieve.

Whenever I found myself in such a situation, it was always during a transitory period between finishing work on one important goal and looking for a new challenge.

When you reach an important long-term goal, by all means celebrate it, but don't give yourself more than a couple of weeks to set a new challenge. Failing to identify a new exciting target and living your life without any big goals eventually leads to depression.

I'm talking from my personal experience: if I don't have a guiding star in the form of a significant long-term goal, I lose motivation for everything, including my passions.

For this reason, I always have secondary goals. Whenever I accomplish my primary goal and don't immediately come up with a new primary goal, I promote one of the secondary goals to become my new objective.

I strongly suggest creating a "waiting list" of goals to achieve, so that when you find yourself without a goal, you'll be able to quickly refocus on a new challenge.

# Day 296: On Your Habitual Thoughts

> *Such as are thy habitual thoughts, such also will be the character of thy mind; for the soul is dyed by the thoughts.*
>
> —*Marcus Aurelius*[294]

The thoughts you entertain most often will have the biggest impact on who you are as a person. If you think about your business every day, you'll define yourself as an entrepreneur. If you have negative thoughts every day, your attitude will be negative. If every day you blame everything and everyone but you for your problems in life, you'll self-identify as a victim.

For this reason, it's a good exercise to periodically take stock of your most habitual thoughts and their potential impact on who you are as a person.

For example, I recently discovered that I had been engaging in too many negative thoughts. While those negative thoughts usually represent a small percentage of the thoughts I have, lately they had multiplied. Using Marcus Aurelius's words, I don't want to let them dye my soul black, so I've made a decision to focus on cultivating more positive thoughts and weeding out the negative ones.

Think of the most common thoughts you've been engaging in recently and ask yourself if they represent the kind of a person you want to be. If not, it's time to exert some self-discipline and regain control of your mind.

# Day 297: On the Best Time to Work

*I do my best thinking at night when everyone else is sleeping. No interruptions. No noise. I like the feeling of being awake when no one else is.*

*—Jennifer Niven*[295]

The best time to work — and by work, I mean work on your highest priorities, not necessarily your day job, with hours that you can't control — is a highly individual matter, but for most people there are only two choices for maximum productivity: early morning, when people aren't awake yet, or late at night, when everyone is already asleep. The common denominator is the lack of interruptions that can ruin your concentration in a matter of seconds.

Early mornings have the advantage of being easier to combine them with a normal everyday schedule. Even if you wake up at five in the morning, you can still lead a regular life: go to work or attend other obligations during the day with plenty of energy, spend time with family and friends during the afternoon, and every now and then stay up late and enjoy the evenings.

Unlike the way most self-help slogans go, staying up late doesn't mean that you'll never reach success, but in general it's more difficult to maintain this schedule when compared to waking up early.

For one, most humans don't handle night shifts well because we're programmed to sleep when it's dark and be active when there's light. Second, having to sleep during the day means missing out on many social events. Moreover, a typical employee can't afford to stay up late; they need to be at work at 9. In the long run, it's impossible to survive 8 hours of work after only a couple of hours of sleep.

For this reason, working at night is most suitable to people with flexible schedules. I used to follow such a routine — I worked until 3-4 a.m. and woke up around 1-2 p.m. In the end, I switched my routine and took the opposite approach. While I was generally productive while working at night, my mental health and energy levels visibly deteriorated, due to a deficiency of sunlight and a messed-up circadian clock.

Still, it's good to test both approaches and see which one is most suitable for you. The key is to find a period of time when you feel most productive and able to concentrate.

# Day 298: On the Suffocating Mantras

*The Yogic sages say that all the pain of a human life is caused by words, as is all the joy. We create words to define our experience and those words bring attendant emotions that jerk us around like dogs on a leash. We get seduced by our own mantras (I'm a failure... I'm lonely... I'm a failure... I'm lonely...) and we become monuments to them. To stop talking for a while, then, is to attempt to strip away the power of words, to stop choking ourselves with words, to liberate ourselves from our suffocating mantras.*

—*Elizabeth Gilbert*[296]

Self-talk can build you up or it can drag you down. If each day you repeat in your head the mantra that you're a failure or you're lonely, guess what you're going to get... Success and companionship? Think again. You exhibit actions congruent with your inner self-talk. If you consider yourself a failure and a lonely person, that's what you're going to get: more failure and loneliness.

Be aware of the suffocating mantras in your life. Liberate yourself from suffering by refusing the negative self-talk. Each time you tell yourself something negative, seek the proof of the opposite.

When you say to yourself, "I'm a failure," think of one — just one — situation in which you succeeded. How can you be a failure if you experience successes?

When you say, "I'm weak-willed," think of one — just one — instance in which you managed to overcome a temptation. You might not have the level of self-discipline you desire, but it doesn't mean that you're automatically too weak-willed to change.

Strip away the power of negative mantras by citing (in your head) the evidence against them. Repeat this evidence as a sort of a "counter-mantra" so that you can, instance by instance, weaken the grip of the negative mantra and eventually free yourself of it.

# Day 299: On Generalizations

*I often wonder why the whole world is so prone to generalise. Generalisations are seldom if ever true and are usually utterly inaccurate.*

—*Agatha Christie*[297]

Generalizations demonstrate lazy thinking, and lazy thinking is one trait that you most certainly don't want to have if you want to improve your self-discipline.

Resist the temptation to categorize everyone and everything. Acknowledge that — besides black and white — there are all kinds of shades of gray.

One of the most dangerous types of generalizations is assuming that a frequently repeated opinion is a fact. Examples include:

1. Every salesman is a liar wanting to make as much money as they can on every sale. If that's the generalization you believe, how effective will you be at selling your own services or yourself to a potential employer?

2. All men/women are horrible people. Good luck developing happy relationships with people if you categorize every member of the opposite sex as a horrible person.

3. All successful people got lucky. If that's what you believe, do you think it's possible you'll ever achieve success?

4. The only way to become properly educated is to go to college, and (what usually follows that generalization) your education ends

the moment you graduate. Without lifelong learning, achieving and maintaining success will be a tricky proposition.

5. You need to be white/wake up early/start a business/be rich/live in the United States/be male/fill in the blank to become successful. Be cautious not to equate success with a single trait or habit. Warren Buffet drinks five cans of Coke every day.[298] Does it mean that drinking Coke leads to success and longevity?

Catch yourself whenever you proclaim generalizations that masquerade as facts. Unless you can state beyond a reasonable doubt that everything or everyone is the way you describe it (and it takes only one thing or person to prove otherwise), you're only voicing an opinion.

# Day 300: On Walking

*All truly great thoughts are conceived while walking.*

*—Friedrich Nietzsche*[299]

Walking is not only a fantastic exercise that almost everybody can perform, but also a powerful way to awaken your creativity and boost your problem-solving skills.

I strongly suggest adding the habit of walking regularly — even if it's just 15 minutes — to your weekly schedule. For even better results, pick a route leading you through natural surroundings or at least away from the hustle and bustle of city living.

I like to take walks with a specific intention in my mind. For example, I think of a problem I've been struggling with recently and dedicate my entire walk to brainstorming potential solutions. I sometimes listen to important podcasts when walking because I know that if it weren't for the walk, I wouldn't listen to them with as much focus as they deserve.

Don't underestimate the power of this simple exercise to change your life. Walking gives you an opportunity to move your body, recharge, reflect, and potentially resolve difficult problems that you wouldn't otherwise be able to handle in your distracting, day-to-day life.

# Day 301: On the Power of Rituals

*A growing body of research suggests that as little as 5 percent of our behaviors are consciously self-directed. We are creatures of habit and as much as 95 percent of what we do occurs automatically or in reaction to a demand or an anxiety.*

—*Jim Loehr*[300]

If the vast majority of what we do is an automatic behavior, then what we need to focus on in the first place is making sure that our rituals are empowering. But first, we need to identify and assess our automatic behaviors.

Starting from when you wake up, make a list of all of the automatic behaviors you engage in throughout the day.

Do you immediately go to prepare coffee? When commuting to work, do you always swear at other drivers? When you arrive at work, do you automatically start gossiping with your colleagues? When shopping, do you automatically buy things you don't necessarily need if you see that they're discounted by 50%? When you're tired but there's still one more chore to attend to, do you routinely watch TV first and then take care of the chore (or forget about it entirely) or do you do it immediately, instead of giving in to the temptation to procrastinate?

This simple exercise will help you take stock of your rituals and decide which ones to keep and which ones to discard. Since automatic behaviors often take place without us being entirely aware of them, making such a list may help you discover your blind spots.

In addition to performing this exercise, pick one day during which you'll try to catch yourself whenever you're automatically engaging in disadvantageous behaviors. It's only with heightened self-awareness that you can identify some of the little everyday habits that negatively affect your willpower.

# WEEK 44

# Day 302: On Listening to Your Gut

> *You might find the idea of listening to your gut feelings odd or even ridiculous. Some people I coach, normally left-brain individuals who use logic and facts all day like engineers or accountants, are not used to following their intuition and feelings. Instead of asking themselves "What do I feel?", they are more comfortable asking "What do the facts tell me?"*
>
> —*Nigel Cumberland*[301]

Using logic and facts is essential in accomplishing your goals, but sometimes it's important to listen to your gut, instead of what you can determine through using a rational thinking process.

For example, I was once running a company in a profitable industry, with a good and proven business model. There were many possibilities for growth, clients enjoyed the service, and it was probable that (with enough persistence) I would get venture capital funding and expert coaching.

However, in my gut I felt that the business wasn't for me. It clashed with my personality, and no amount of rational thinking, facts, and logic would have persuaded me otherwise.

In the end, I sold the company and it proved to be the right decision, a decision that was based primarily on my intuition and feelings, not logic.

Don't ignore the usefulness of your gut feelings. It's fine to be self-disciplined and remain persistent no matter what, but if deep down you no longer care about your goal or it otherwise makes you feel uneasy, let your intuition make its case. It's highly probable that it's right.

# Day 303: On Buddha's Counsel

*The Buddha also counseled the monks and nuns to avoid wasting any precious time by engaging in idle conversation, oversleeping, pursuing fame and recognition, chasing after desires, spending time with people of poor character, and being satisfied with only a shallow understanding of the teaching.*

—***Thich Nhat Hanh**[302]*

Buddha's advice offers several interesting challenges you can dedicate yourself to in order to work on your self-discipline.

The first one is not engaging in idle conversation. Small talk might be useful to initiate a conversation, but the sooner you get to the business at hand, the more effective your communication will be. By "idle conversation," we can also include gossip, criticizing others, or complaining, all of which are *not* practices in which a disciplined person should engage.

The second suggestion is simple: avoid oversleeping. As long as you don't need more sleep to recover from a difficult workout, illness, or any other similar situation, sleeping too much doesn't deliver any benefits and, according to scientific research, might even hurt (in one study, sleeping too much was associated with psychiatric diseases and higher body mass index[303]).

The third suggestion advises against the pursuit of fame and recognition. Too often, people care too much about their status in other people's eyes and neglect other, more important aspects of their lives, which may only be visible to themselves. Focus on becoming better, but not necessarily with the expectation that somebody will reward you for it.

The fourth recommendation is not to chase after desires. There's not much to add here — this entire book is about learning how to control them and focus on something more important than your temporary urges.

The fifth piece of advice pertains to structuring your social life in a disciplined way. Spending time with people of poor character increases the risk that you'll develop a poor character, too.

Lastly, Buddha reminds us not to be satisfied with only a shallow understanding of what we're learning. This advice is particularly useful for students and virtually any person learning a new skill. Resist the temptation to learn just the bare minimum and only scratch the surface of the topic you're learning before you leave it altogether. Use your willpower to make sure that you thoroughly understand the fundamentals and then proceed to more advanced concepts, so that you deepen your understanding of what you are seeking to learn.

# Day 304: On the Unsexy Reality of Work

*How much time can you spare each day? For that interval, close the door and — short of a family emergency or the outbreak of World War III — don't let ANYBODY in. Keep working. Keep working. Keep working.*

—*Steven Pressfield*[304]

Some people believe that super-productive individuals have some kind of a secret or a natural inborn talent that allows them to produce so much output. However, the reality is unsexy: all they do is put themselves in front of their computers (or whatever else they need to do their job), close the door, and work.

There are no miraculous solutions, no pills, frameworks, or blueprints that the most productive people have to be able to produce more than you do. When reading his masterpieces, it's difficult to imagine Stephen King simply sitting in his room and tapping away on his keyboard, but that's how his day-to-day life looks.

If you're unsure whether you're doing it "right" because there's nothing attractive nor particularly outstanding in how you perform your daily work, stop worrying; everyone else — including world-class performers — works in the exact same way. The only difference between you and them is that they have spent a bit more time than you have, working on their craft, but there's a level playing field here that requires the same resources from every participant: self-discipline, persistence, and an unbreakable resolve.

# Day 305: On the Addiction to Electronics

*It is one of the unexpected disasters of the modern age that our new unparalleled access to information has come at the price of our capacity to concentrate on anything much. The deep, immersive thinking which produced many of civilization's most important achievements has come under unprecedented assault. We are almost never far from a machine that guarantees us a mesmerizing and libidinous escape from reality. The feelings and thoughts which we have omitted to experience while looking at our screens are left to find their revenge in involuntary twitches and our ever-decreasing ability to fall asleep when we should.*

—*Alain de Botton*[305]

There's no denying the fact that modern technology is a blessing. It allows us to learn, make money, connect with our loved ones and other people from all over the world, entertain ourselves, and with each passing year, do a whole lot more.

Yet, there exists a danger of becoming addicted to electronics. Smartphones reduce our attention spans, easy access to information makes us too lazy to learn, and since it's now so easy to get new things delivered to your doorstep, we're constantly looking for a new shiny thing that will be the ultimate magic pill and solution to all of our problems.

I don't believe that technology is our enemy, but I do believe that too much of it — as with excess in anything — leads to problems. Fortunately, where there's a problem, there's an opportunity to learn. You can dramatically improve your self-control by periodically reducing the amount of time spent using your phone or other devices.

For example, while you're on vacation, resist the temptation to take a picture and share it on Facebook. Instead, focus on the present moment and engrave it in your memories, not your social feed.

In the evening, at least every now and then, turn off all of the blue-light emitting devices and spend an hour reading a book. You'll have an easier time falling asleep, and it will be more recharging, too.

Whenever you catch yourself feeling anxious to check your phone or social media feeds, it's a sign that you're losing control. Reestablish it by periodically going on short technology fasts or deliberately checking your phone less often than usual.

# Day 306: On Ignorance

*There is nothing more frightful than ignorance in action.*

—*Johann Wolfgang von Goethe*[306]

Ignorance is a manifestation of laziness. Instead of actively choosing to expand your knowledge, you instead choose to willfully bypass the opportunity to educate yourself. A side effect of ignorance is the fostering of negligence and laxity, two traits that are the opposite of what a successful person should embrace in their life.

Disregarding important information and choosing to *not* know when you *do* have access to education is like willfully asking for trouble.

Being financially illiterate, for example, can lead to economic problems. Ignoring the needs of your partner — instead of learning about what they need from you — can destroy your relationship. Ignorance of the law can lead to prison. Ignoring new technologies and failing to learn about relevant modern inventions makes *you* less relevant in your professional life.

Choose to be prepared rather than ignorant. Know too much instead of too little. Practice your self-discipline by constantly expanding your knowledge — and don't discontinue your self-education when the truth is uncomfortable or leads to difficult questions.

# Day 307: On Breaking Your Rules

*Laws and principles are not for the times when there is no temptation: they are for such moments as this, when body and soul rise in mutiny against their rigour. (...) If at my convenience I might break them, what would be their worth?*

—*Charlotte Brontë[307]*

We've already talked about adopting principles you'll live by in order to make your decision-making process more efficient and make choices that are more aligned with your true desires.

It's important to note that those principles aren't for the times when everything goes smoothly. In fact, you don't necessarily need them when things are going well. It's primarily when there's a temptation to give up that you can experience the power of rules. You create them to prevent yourself from making the wrong choices, no matter what the circumstances are and which temptations you feel.

For example, I have a rule that growth happens outside my comfort zone. I don't always feel like subjecting myself to discomfort and fear. However, there's a reason why I adopted such a rule: without it, I know that I would back out more often, and thus miss out on those opportunities to grow.

Whenever you feel a temptation to break your rule, remind yourself that it's there for a reason. Breaking it means that the principle — and the reason why you chose it — isn't important to you. What does breaking your own rules say about your reliability?

Can you trust yourself if you fail to keep a promise that you made to yourself?

# Day 308: On Not Having Money

*"If only I had more money" is the easiest way to postpone the intense self-examination and decision-making necessary to create a life of enjoyment — now and not later.*

—*Tim Ferriss*[308]

It's easy to say that you don't have money and consider it the ultimate excuse as to why you aren't working on your goals.

I don't have money, so I won't start exercising because I can't afford fitness equipment.

I don't have money, so I won't start saving money because how can I save money if I don't have it?

I don't have money, so I won't start eating more healthily because healthy food is too expensive.

Is it really true that nobody has ever become fit without having loads of money? The marketing techniques of the fitness industry lead you to think that expensive gear is needed to get fit, but many do without it (often as their own choice), and are more than fine.

Are you really unable to save even one dollar a day, just to establish a new positive habit? Are you saying that your every single purchase is necessary and can't be reduced even by a small fraction?

Is healthy food really more expensive than junk food? Ask any person taking hypertension or diabetes medication — caused by their own bad dietary choices — whether they think that eating junk food was a more economical choice. You don't need to eat all organic or shop in expensive stores to eat healthily.

Using money as an excuse is taking the easy way out, defaulting to mental laziness rather than seeking a solution. True, it helps you avoid some effort and hard thinking today, but costs you future improvements in your life and leads to a victim mentality.

# WEEK 45

# Day 309: On the Matters of Right and Wrong

*Right is right even if no one is doing it; wrong is wrong even if everyone is doing it.*

—*Augustine of Hippo*

More than 70% of U.S. adults aged 20 and over are overweight or obese.[309] Does that mean that it's right to be obese?

On average, American adults are watching five hours and four minutes of television per day.[310] Does that mean that it's right to spend a third of your waking hours and well over a half of your leisure hours watching TV?

If you're after self-improvement, you need to acknowledge that the right thing is right even when few people are doing it — and that no matter how many people are doing the wrong thing, it's still wrong.

Don't comfort yourself by saying that your negative habits aren't *that* negative because so many people engage in them. Even if everybody exhibits such behaviors, it doesn't make them right.

Have the courage and self-discipline to resist the temptation to compare yourself to the majority. Instead, if you must compare yourself to anyone, compare yourself to the people you want to emulate, even if they're but a speck in an infinite crowd of people who don't care in the slightest about becoming better.

# Day 310: On Having Good Private Teachers

> *From my great-grandfather, [I learned] not to have frequented public schools, and to have had good teachers at home, and to know that on such things a man should spend liberally.*
>
> —*Marcus Aurelius*[311]

Here's one of the ultimate shortcuts for success: if you want to learn something or achieve a goal more quickly, find a good private teacher to guide you. Spend your money eagerly on one-on-one instruction, because expanding your knowledge and experience (unlike many other investments) is a sure-fire way to get a positive return.

Group classes are extremely ineffective teaching tools because the teacher's attention is spread over too many students. If you have an hour-long class with a teacher and there are 9 other students, on average you only get 10 minutes of the teacher's attention. Even if the teacher's fee for a private class is five times higher, it's still cheaper than a group class, considering how much more you'll learn.

Consider hiring a coach for any important endeavors or to kickstart a new change. For example, you can hire a nutrition expert to develop a meal plan for you or a fitness coach to design a workout plan for you. You don't necessarily have to keep paying them forever; the initial help can be sufficient to get you started and then all you have to do is continue to practice what you learned from them, until your needs change.

One additional benefit of hiring a private coach is that once you start paying to get professional help, you'll start taking your objectives more seriously. It's easier to back out if there's nobody to whom you need to give an explanation as to why you want to give up.

# Day 311: On Setting an Example

*Example has more followers than reason.*

—*Christian Nestell Bovee*[312]

Does it bother you that people laugh at your efforts, wonder why you're deliberately making your life so difficult, or feel otherwise puzzled about your recent efforts at making positive changes in your life?

Save your time and energy trying to reason with them — it won't work. Instead, focus on your goals and set an example. Soon, when you achieve some results, people will start following your example, understand why you're doing what you're doing, or at least shut up.

For example, people criticized me when I was on my diet, saying that I was already skinny and shouldn't lose more weight. However, I knew that I had to drop some additional pounds to uncover more muscle definition. Once I reached that goal and my muscles became more visible, it became clear that I had been right from the get-go.

No amount of reasoning will make people change their minds in the same way as an example standing right in front of them.

Similarly, don't try to persuade people to implement positive changes in their lives just because that's what you're doing. Leave them be, and if they notice your results, some will probably ask you for advice and try to achieve the same results themselves. Again, it's about setting the example, not expending empty words.

# Day 312: On Learning Without a Desire to Learn

> *Just as eating contrary to the inclination is injurious to the health, study without desire spoils the memory, and it retains nothing that it takes in.*
>
> —*Leonardo da Vinci*[313]

You can learn almost anything you want as long as you have a desire to learn. Without a good reason why you want to learn something — or worse, being forced to learn it with no interest whatsoever on your part, as is often the case with college students — you'll retain little of what you learn.

The reason is simple: the human brain needs to be picky about what it remembers and what doesn't, so if you consider a fly on the wall as more exciting than the subject of your study, you'll be more likely to remember the fly's position during the entire hour of the class than the topic of your lesson.

For example, I once took a few Russian classes to prepare myself for a trip to Kyrgyzstan, a rugged mountainous country in Central Asia.

However, unlike with Spanish, a language I speak fluently and am fond of, I couldn't develop an interest in Russian. My classes weren't particularly effective because, deep down, I had little desire to learn that language; there was no positive emotional connection with it.

That's why I so strongly emphasize that each endeavor — including the goal of learning a new skill — needs to start with a strong desire. If you don't have that, you'll be fighting an uphill battle.

If you're forced to learn something and are struggling, try to find something interesting about the subject. For example, you might find that Russian grammar is not particularly interesting, but perhaps trying to improve your accent in it is fun for you.

You can also use educational resources that teach in an entertaining way. YouTube videos can be a good source for that. When it comes to learning languages, I'm a big fan of watching TV series that are broadcast in that same language.

If you still can't find anything exciting in learning the topic itself, turn toward the reward it offers you, such as a promotion at work or being able to graduate from your learning program, and use *that* (the reward) as your sole motivation. Be careful, though: extrinsic motivators are weak motivators, and it's always better to combine them with internal rewards, like the enjoyment you get from learning or from the challenge it poses for you.

# Day 313: On What You Demand From Life

> *Remember, no more effort is required to aim high in life, to demand abundance and prosperity, than is required to accept misery and poverty.*
>
> —*Napoleon Hill*[314]

It all comes down to what you demand from life. Accept nothing less than abundance and prosperity, and if you combine it with diligent work, you'll eventually get it. Tolerate misery and poverty, come up with rationalizations about why you're miserable, and bad fortune will stay in your life.

It's important to understand that it takes virtually the same amount of effort to come up with excuses as it is to find reasons why you *can* accomplish something. You can direct your energy either way, but only one of them leads to success.

The next time you catch yourself thinking that you're destined to be unsuccessful and that you should accept your bad fortune, change your thoughts: remind yourself about how dissatisfied you are with your current circumstances and come up with reasons why you *will* be successful instead of continuing as you are.

For example, while I was trying to build a successful business and failed one time after another, I still kept reminding myself that I would never tolerate being an employee. Nothing would have stopped me from making my goal come true; I would never accept anything else than abundance and prosperity.

They may sound trite, but some self-help bromides are actually true: your attitude and expectations do impact your life in a big way.

# Day 314: On Neatness

> *People exert less self-control after seeing a messy desk than after seeing a clean desk.*
>
> —*Roy Baumeister*[315]

Here's an easy self-discipline hack for today: clean your immediate surroundings and benefit from improved self-control.

A messy desk — and the unpleasant thought in the back of your head reminding you that eventually you'll have to clean it — occupies precious mental space you could otherwise spend on something more useful. Chaotic immediate environments are also distracting, and thus lower your productivity.

In addition to taking up both physical and mental space, clutter can also affect how you feel about yourself.

People feel better when they take a shower, shave their faces, put on make-up or perform any other grooming habit — and they feel worse when their appearance is not up to their standards.

A messy room has a similar effect: it indicates that the person working there isn't organized or lacks the self-discipline to keep it tidy. Keeping your room neat and tidy demonstrates in a physical way that you *are* organized and self-disciplined — and that will subsequently affect your inner world, too, just like dressing for success gives a small boost to one's confidence.

# Day 315: On the Cost of Education and Ignorance

*If you think education is expensive — try ignorance.*

—*Ann Landers*[316]

One of the worst excuses you can use to rationalize that you can't educate yourself is to say that you don't have the money needed to do so.

For one, ignorance is more expensive than education. One valuable piece of advice from a book can recoup its price a thousand times or more, while committing one big mistake (that educating yourself might have prevented) can lead to devastating losses.

A person who has never taken the time to learn how to eat healthily — something a $15 book can rectify — can ultimately pay for it with their life, while a person new to fitness may pay for their ignorance with a painful injury — something they could have prevented by watching a few free videos on proper form.

Second, in today's world, education is available freely to anyone who has access to the Internet. While a private teacher can help you immensely, you can also learn a lot (on your own) from free videos, tutorials, articles, and books.

For example, I taught myself how to write (I've never taken any formal courses, yet I'm now a bestselling author), how to create and modify websites (I'm not a programmer, yet I can design a professional website, using available resources), or how to promote my books (even though I don't have a degree in marketing).

It's important to escape the paradigm of "education equals a college degree." You aren't educated merely because a piece of a paper says so. In fact, it's often the opposite. Many students treat college as an extension of their childhood instead of an opportunity to learn and gain experience. Meanwhile, those who skip going to college often gain valuable, real-world experience that they can build upon.

When hiring contractors to help me in my business, I never look at their formal education. All I care about is their reviews, portfolio, and proposal specifying how they can help me. It's what they can specifically do for me that counts, not mere words that may or may not confirm that they're educated.

If you aren't sure where to find high-quality education online for free or for a low price, check out Udemy, Coursera, Khan Academy, Stanford Online, Harvard Extension, Open Yale Courses, Codecademy, or simply look for the topic that interests you on YouTube, Amazon or in the iTunes store.

# WEEK 46

# Day 316: On Doing What You Love

*Every man loves what he is good at.*

—*Thomas Shadwell*[317]

If at first you don't fall in love with the process necessary to make your dream come true, don't despair. As long as you don't hate it, everything is fine. The love for the process comes along with consistent improvements. It's impossible, or at least unlikely, to eventually not fall in love with what you're becoming good at.

For example, many entrepreneurs think that they need to do what they love in order for their business to succeed. In reality, what matters most is that their business fulfills a certain need or solves a certain problem.

If I hire your company to clean my house, I don't care if you're passionate about it. All I care about is whether you can do it well, on time, and for a reasonable price. Initially, you might not *love* being in the cleaning business, but if your business starts doing well and you become good at running it, you'll probably enjoy doing it — and thanks to that, it will get even easier to grow it.

The same applies to any other goal. Get started, make sure that you feel at least neutral about it, and be patient, because once you start getting better at it, the process will become addictive and you won't want to stop.

# Day 317: On Thinking You're Able

*They are able because they think they are able.*

—*Virgil*[318]

It might be a trite reminder, but it's nonetheless frequently true: people often achieve impossible feats merely because they think they are able to do so. If you don't think that you're able, you either won't try at all, or if you try, it will be a half-hearted attempt that is almost guaranteed to fail.

In rock climbing, I sometimes deliberately try routes or single moves well above my ability. I've found that sometimes the mere belief in your abilities can lead you to climbing a difficult route that, without such a belief, would result in a spectacular failure.

In business, the companies that grow the fastest are led by entrepreneurs who don't set any limits for themselves. If they decide to sell their services to a Fortune 500 company, they'll start figuring out how to *do* it instead of wasting time pondering whether they're able to do so.

In sports, it's often not the training in itself that makes an athlete successful. It's what they tell themselves during the competition that makes the difference between winning or losing.

The next time you face a big, seemingly insurmountable challenge or find yourself in a situation with a low chance of emerging victoriously, assume that you're able to overcome it — and then act as if it were true. Life isn't a fairy tale, so it won't *always* work. However, if you assume that you aren't able — and that will manifest in your hesitant actions — you'll be always doing yourself a disservice.

# Day 318: On the Inconvenience of Change

*Change is not made without inconvenience, even from worse to better.*

—*Richard Hooker*[319]

If you want to remodel your house, you expect and accept the inconveniences it will cause.

There's no way to replace the old windows, tiles, doors, or kitchen cabinets without making a mess. Repainting your bedroom means that you have to move furniture to another room. Giving your bathroom a makeover means that you'll have to use a different bathroom or go to a friend's house to take a shower.

You accept the disturbance that remodeling causes in your life because you want your house to be nice and cozy. Likewise, if you want to change something in your life, in order for the old to go, there also must be some mess involved in the process of replacing it with the new.

You might feel cranky upon waking up earlier than usual. You might be exhausted after the first several workouts. You might despair while you are trying to figure out how to learn a new skill.

Whenever you feel this way and feel tempted to give up, frustrated by how inconvenient the process of change is for you, remember that to go from worse to better, some minor (and sometimes major) annoyances are par for the course. Get over it and get on with your life!

# Day 319: On Learning From Refusal

*One never knows a man till he has refused him something, and studied the effect of the refusal; one never knows himself till he has denied himself. The altar of sacrifice is the touchstone of character.*

—*Orrin Philip Gilford*[320]

Let's be clear: denying yourself nice things is neither easy nor fun. However, in addition to the incredible benefits it brings in the form of increased self-control, it's also a powerful test of your character and a self-discovery tool.

For one, self-refusal provides an opportunity to understand what you need in your life and what you only *think* you need in your life. Unless you stay away from what you consider your "necessities" for a period of time, you won't know whether they're really necessities, after all.

For example, on many of my adventures, I had to sleep in less than comfortable circumstances, such as in a car parked by the road or in a soaking wet tent with homeless dogs fighting outside.

I had always thought that I wouldn't be able to recharge in such circumstances, but often I was actually more recharged after several hours of such uncomfortable sleep than in my own bed. What I considered a necessity was in fact a luxury. This realization made me a stronger person. I expanded my comfort zone and now I know I can handle sleeping in a wide variety of weird places.

Second, refusing yourself pleasant things can show you the depth of your addiction for them. For example, I used to eat a few pieces of dark chocolate daily. I assumed it wasn't a big deal and I thought I could stop eating it whenever I wanted to. However, when I decided to take a break from eating all kinds of sweets, I felt immense cravings. Denying myself a few pieces of dark chocolate — an innocent pleasure — made me realize that I had been addicted to it.

Finally, while we were young, it was our parents or other caretakers who told us we couldn't get something. We fumed and protested, but there was nothing we could do about it. This way, unbeknownst to ourselves, we learned that we couldn't always get everything we wanted — and I daresay it was one of the most powerful lessons in self-discipline a child could receive.

Today, as adults, most of us don't have such gatekeepers. If you want to eat chocolate, you can go to the store and buy it; nobody will force you to eat broccoli instead. If you want to spend the entire Sunday in bed, nobody will kick you out of it and force you to go out and play with other kids.

This freedom feels good, but there's also danger in it — by spoiling ourselves this way, we eventually do ourselves the same disservice as parents who spoil their children. Self-refusal, in essence, can act as an emergency brake, stopping us from spiraling into overindulgence.

# Day 320: On Change as a Cold Bath

*A great change in life is like a cold bath in winter — we all hesitate at the first plunge.*

—*Letitia Elizabeth Landon*[321]

Hesitation is normal when you face a big change in life. After all, you're facing the unknown, and what's unknown is scary. In the end, though, the longer you stare into the abyss, the more frightening it appears, and the more difficult it is to jump into it.

For this reason, it might be useful to think of a great change as being similar to taking a cold bath — the less time you give yourself to worry about how cold it might be, the more likely you are to actually jump into it.

For example, instead of wondering how tiring and uncomfortable it will be to go running, just put on your sports shoes and get out of the house. The more time you spend meditating on how unpleasant it might possibly be, the more likely it is that hesitation will kill any remnants of willpower you still have inside of you.

When decluttering your house, the same strategy can help you resist the temptation to keep things out of sentiment. Some old items are indeed so valuable that it might be worth it to keep them, but more often than not, people who tend to accumulate things use this rationalization for every piece of junk. Give yourself three seconds.

During those three seconds, if you can't come up with any *powerful* memory that the item gives you, throw it away.

If you need to make a difficult phone call or have an uncomfortable conversation, hesitation will make it even scarier. By taking the plunge as quickly as possible, you'll prevent your anxiety from growing and probably resolve the situation more effectively than if you were to wait.

# Day 321: On Being the Creator of Your Circumstances

> *Man is not the creature of circumstances, circumstances are the creatures of men.*
>
> —*Benjamin Disraeli*[322]

It would be nice to blame our circumstances for everything bad that happens in our lives. Finally, there would be something else that is responsible for our deficiencies, inaction, lack of willpower, etc.

Unfortunately (or rather, fortunately), we're the creators of the circumstances in which we find ourselves today.

While you can't change where you were born, you can change where you live.

While you can't change who your parents were, you can choose your teachers and mentors.

While you can't change whether you were born blind, deaf, mute, or with a different physical disability, you can change how you think about it.

So many people accept their circumstances for what they are, instead of acknowledging that they always have *some* control over them — even if it's just the ability to change how you think about them.

If you don't like something about your circumstances, you can change them, accept them, or find power in them.

If you don't like where you live, you can move to a different place. If for some reason you can't do that, you can accept where you live and focus on other aspects of your life there. You can also find power in your environment and discover the hidden benefits of where you live (for example, a small town might not be great for job prospects, but your costs of living are lower).

Don't make yourself a victim by believing that you're a creature of circumstances or you might as well give up any hope for a better future.

# Day 322: On Subtraction

*We survive on too little sleep, wolf down fast foods on the run, fuel up with coffee and cool down with alcohol and sleeping pills. Faced with relentless demands at work, we become short-tempered and easily distracted. We return home from long days at work feeling exhausted and often experience our families not as a source of joy and renewal, but as one more demand in an already overburdened life.*

—*Jim Loehr*[323]

It makes me exhausted just to read this quote, let alone imagine that it's possible to achieve any kind of positive results while living such a life.

If you're overburdened and feel like you have no control over your life, it's time to change your life philosophy from the philosophy of *addition* to the philosophy of *subtraction*. Let me explain...

The philosophy of addition is thinking that more is better. It means that you're afraid to miss out on opportunities and that you say yes to everything, worried that saying no will make you unpopular or that you'll appear selfish or lazy.

You constantly add and add, thinking that it's through adding that your life gets better. Of course, in a certain way it does. The more you learn, the better you are. Generally speaking, the more money you have, the easier your life is.

However, this doesn't apply to obligations and your calendar. The more tasks you have in your schedule and the more duties you need to attend to, the more difficult it is to stop, reflect, and decide what deserves your attention and what doesn't.

For this reason, I suggest adopting the philosophy of subtraction. You believe that less is more. You think twice before you accept any new responsibilities. You constantly seek to simplify your life and free up your calendar instead of stacking one task on top of another. You feel proud of having leisure time instead of feeling guilty about it.

As an exercise for today, think of just one regular task in your schedule that you could eliminate, in order to make your life less of a burden.

Perhaps you can hire a maid to save time spent keeping the house clean.

Maybe you already have enough money, but not enough time, and it would make sense to reduce the number of hours spent at work and accept the trade-off for the sake of your well-being.

Maybe you can move closer to your workplace, or the opposite: start working at home.

Perhaps it would be a good investment to use the services of a home meal delivery company and save the time spent on cooking and grocery shopping.

Subtract the unessential from your life to increase your focus on what is essential, but doesn't get enough attention because of all the other, less-important obligations.

# WEEK 47

# Day 323: On Prolonged Sitting

*Because a dramatic reduction in energy expenditure was not accompanied by reduced appetite, prolonged sitting may promote excess energy intake, leading to weight gain in both men and women.*

—***Kirsten Granados**[324]*

Research shows that even though there's a dramatic reduction in energy expenditure when we sit, our appetites don't drop down accordingly. This means that the more time you spend sitting, the more of a caloric surplus you create, and you gain weight more easily.

This poses a big problem for self-discipline because no amount of self-control will help you lose weight if you don't expend much energy but your appetite behaves as if you did.

If you sit at work, consider standing up for at least a period of time when working. Stand-up desks are getting more and more popular, so it might be worth it to consider buying one or building it yourself. If it's not possible to work standing up, at least get up every now and then and perform some quick exercises to offset some of the negative consequences of sitting.

At home, one of the biggest offenders is mindlessly watching TV. You can greatly reduce the amount of time spent sitting by eliminating cable TV and only watching specific movies or TV shows. Channel-hopping puts you in a zombie-like state, which, when combined with snacking, can make it almost impossible to ever get in shape.

Think of sitting as a debt you need to repay. Fortunately, you can repay the debt not only with actual exercise, but also with little actions: standing up in the kitchen, performing household chores, taking the stairs instead of the elevator, parking a little bit farther away from the entrance to the supermarket.

Strive to move as much as you can, and you'll reduce the negative impact prolonged sitting has on your well-being and increase your chances of successfully shedding that belly fat.

# Day 324: On Ignoring the World When You're Down

*So long as the man with ambition is a failure, the world will tell him to let go of his ideal; but when his ambition is realized, the world will praise him for the persistence and the determination that he manifested during his dark hours, and everybody will point to his life as an example for coming generations. This is invariably the rule. Therefore pay no attention to what the world says when you are down. Be determined to get up, to reach the highest goal you have in view, and you will.*

—*Christian D. Larson*[325]

Larson's words were as true during his era (he wrote those words in 1912) as they are now. If you're ambitious — something that most people lack — you're already considered a little weird by society's standards.

People will try to persuade you to give up or take it easy because it's a threat to their own egos. If you — a person just like them — manages to turn his or her dreams into reality, what does it say about their capabilities?

This invariably changes when you reach success. While you were down, few people stopped to lend a helping hand or offer you words of support. When you're successful, suddenly everyone proclaims that they knew from the get-go that you would succeed.

If you're currently struggling and feeling down, make an effort to surround yourself with positive input as if you wanted to build a protective bubble around yourself. Keep away from negative people who would love to finish you off with their nasty remarks. Get up, try again, and keep going until you get there.

Take note of who was there for you while you were struggling and don't forget to reward them with your gratitude. As for the others? Forget them; fair-weather friends are no friends at all.

# Day 325: On Being the Child of Your Own Works

*Every one is the son of his own works.*

—*Miguel de Cervantes*[326]

Here's a fun metaphor for today: you're the parent of yourself, and hence, you're the child of your own decisions, habits, and beliefs.

Would you raise your children in the same way as you're raising yourself?

Are you being a good parent, ensuring that their child grows up with self-discipline, or are you lax, constantly cutting your child some slack and ultimately turning them into a weak-willed adult?

Are you understanding and supportive or critical and mean when your child makes errors while trying to fail their way to success?

Lastly, are you setting a good example? Do you expect one thing from your child and then do the opposite when they aren't looking?

# Day 326: On Your Deeds Determining You

*Our deeds determine us, as much as we determine our deeds.*

—*George Eliot*[327]

You control what actions you take or don't take, but in the long run, the actions that you take or don't take also control *you* because they determine who you are.

As confusing as it sounds, there's an important lesson hiding in there: when pondering what to do or not do, ask yourself what the person you'd like to become would or wouldn't do. We define people by actions they take, so if you change the actions you take, you'll also change your own definition of yourself.

For example, a person who runs often is a runner, while a person who constantly exposes themselves to danger for the fun of it is a daredevil. On the opposite end of the spectrum, a person who sits on the sofa the entire day is a slacker, while a person who never stands up for themselves is a doormat. The primary determinant of a runner, daredevil, slacker or doormat — rather than a specific adjective or trait — is what actions they take or don't take.

Each action of yours, just like each thought or habit you have, has an impact on the direction your personal change is going to take. Think beyond the immediate consequences and consider each deed as a building block of the new you. What actions are congruent with the person you desire to become and what deeds aren't?

When thinking of the person you want to become in the future, along with setting new goals, make a list of actions the desired "future you" will engage in regularly and the actions that person will refuse to perform.

For example, if you want to become a more positive person, some of the actions you'll engage in regularly include smiling, laughing, and expressing your gratitude, while some of the actions you'll refuse to perform would be complaining, brooding, and criticizing.

# Day 327: On the Biggest Person Standing in Your Way

*You might occasionally feel that some people are standing in the way and slowing your progress, but in reality the biggest person standing in your way is you. Others can stop you temporarily — you are the only one who can do it permanently.*

—Zig Ziglar[328]

When others sabotage your efforts to implement a positive change in your life, it's tempting to blame them for your lack of results. However, while they can affect your endeavors temporarily, in the end it's only you who can torpedo your dreams.

For one, ultimately it's you who makes a judgment of what the action of another person means to you and your goals. You can approach somebody's effort to sabotage your dreams as an excuse to give up, or you can treat it as an obstacle that is an inherent part of the process. A "friend" who taunts you about your lack of results when dieting might discourage you, or they might boost your resolve to show them what you're capable of.

Second, when other people try to limit your dreams, question your abilities, or tell you to stop having your head in the clouds, ultimately it's not their belief that counts; it's what you yourself think about the feasibility of your goals. Will you be bothered by people who doubt that you'll ever build a successful business? Of course you will. Will they make you doubt that you'll succeed? That would happen only if you let them, by valuing *their* words more than your own belief in your abilities.

Finally, when others are required to make your dreams come true and it seems as if they're actively against you (say, a gatekeeper who won't let you get through to the CEO of the company you'd like to sell your services to), yet again they are not the ones who can destroy your goal. It's still up to you; you can come up with a different way to reach the CEO or develop a completely different approach to sell your service and grow your business.

Others can slow your progress, but it doesn't mean that you're powerless. When somebody stands in your way, jump over them, crawl underneath them, go around them, or punch them in the face (just kidding with the last one).

# Day 328: On Anger

*If you don't want to be cantankerous, don't feed your temper, or multiply incidents of anger. Suppress the first impulse to be angry, then begin to count the days on which you don't get mad.*

—*Epictetus*[329]

Anger — or any other emotion that leads to impulsive decisions that you later regret — is an enemy of self-discipline. While it's not always possible to catch yourself feeling angry before it converts into a full-blown attack of rage, whenever you can, act quickly and suppress the anger instead of feeding it. Anger that compounds on itself will quickly take away any remnants of self-control that you may have.

For example, when I'm stuck in a traffic jam, annoyed at other drivers or at the traffic lights seeming to take hours to change, I try to redirect my growing anger into another emotion, stop myself from cursing, or at least try to curse in a humorous way that won't feed my frustration. That way, I prevent my anger from taking control of the situation. It's a simple technique, but don't let it fool you — it's one of the most effective strategies to overcome attacks of unnecessary anger.

If you want to eliminate frequent attacks of anger from your life, begin counting the days on which you successfully suppress the first impulse to be angry. After a 7-day winning streak, you won't want to lose all of your progress because of such a trivial thing as another driver driving too slowly or things temporarily not going your way.

Will this strategy always work? Obviously not. Everyone gets angry from time to time. However, if you make a conscious effort not to feed your temper, you'll reprogram your default behavior, greatly reduce the frequency of losing your temper, and gain better control over your emotional state.

# Day 329: On a Change in Beliefs

*All personal breakthroughs begin with a change in beliefs. So how do we change? The most effective way is to get your brain to associate massive pain to the old belief. You must feel deep in your gut that not only has this belief cost you pain in the past, but it's costing you in the present and, ultimately, can only bring you pain in the future.*

—*Tony Robbins*[330]

You won't change until you recognize your bad beliefs and habits as your enemies. The best way to change them is to associate them with the pain that they've been steadily delivering to you ever since you first adopted them.

For example, I overcame my habit of staying up late and waking up at 1-2 p.m. largely because of associating it with the depression I felt each winter because of a lack of sunlight.

Upon realizing that my habit and belief that I was a night owl had cost me so much and would bring me so much more pain in the future, I switched my routine. Today I can hardly think of a better feeling than getting up early and being super productive from beginning my day in the early morning.

What are your habits and beliefs costing you? You need to recognize all the different kinds of costs they have generated, are generating, and will continue to generate in the future if you don't make some changes in your life. You will only be ready to change when you feel deep down in your gut how detrimental they are to you and your life.

# WEEK 48

# Day 330: On Turning Back Right at the Very End

*Don't turn back when you are just at the goal.*

—*Publius Syrus*[331]

Many people have a tendency to back out right at the end of the journey, mere steps from accomplishing their long-term goal. If they knew that success was around the corner, they would find it in themselves to keep going. However, since it's so difficult to diagnose whether success is right around the corner or still a long way off, it happens that many throw in the towel mere seconds from their opponent falling to the ground.

To prevent such an unfortunate situation from happening, from now on assume that if you've been working on a given goal for a long period of time and you're down on your knees, ready to accept defeat, it's the last test. Stand up, brush yourself off and take a few more steps. Give yourself a week or two more and make the last effort.

If your situation doesn't change and there's still no success around the corner, accept a (temporary) defeat and step away to recover. If it does change and you meet success, you'll be glad you'd used the last remnants of energy to keep going.

# Day 331: On Finding an Easier Way

*Once you figure out what it is you really want, ask yourself if there's a better way to get it than to go down the path you're planning on going down. Maybe you want to be rich so that you can travel all of the time. But do you really need to be rich to do that, or is there any easier way? For example, I wanted to be rich to buy an island, but then figured out how to do it without going through the hassle of getting rich first.*

—*Tynan*[332]

There's nothing wrong or dishonorable in finding an easier way to accomplish your goals. If you can make it easier for yourself to make your dreams come true — given that it's legal and moral to do so — do it. Anything that reduces the amount of self-discipline and mental energy you need to reach your goals is a good thing.

For example, if you want to travel all of the time but you currently don't have a million or two in the bank, it doesn't mean that now you need to dedicate a decade of your life to making millions. You could achieve this same goal by doing such things as finding a location-independent job, getting a flexible job, working on a cruise ship or as a flight attendant, starting an online business, or working on short-term contracts in different countries.

If you want to become fit, you can take fitness classes at your local gym and hate it every time you go there, or you can find a type of a physical activity you actually and genuinely enjoy.

If you want to lose weight, you can go on a restrictive diet that makes you feel miserable, or you can adopt lifestyle changes and embrace nutritional habits that give you some leeway while still helping you get thinner.

Oh, and for the curious: Tynan managed to buy an island without getting rich first by buying the island together with a few friends.

# Day 332: On a Lack of Variety

*Routine releases us from the work and willpower required for choice.*

—*Mark Sisson*[333]

When you ask several people for their first thought about what "a lack of variety" means, you'll probably get answers with negative connotations. To them, a lack of variety means boredom or being stuck in a rut. While routine can indeed be bad for you and your goals, it can also be a good thing.

For example, in dieting, eating the same meals over and over again (but changing them every several weeks or so when you get bored of them) simplifies the entire process. You no longer have to carefully calculate every macronutrient of a different food because you always eat the same things and can easily eyeball their caloric content.

In fitness, dedicating yourself to one sport or type of physical activity makes it easier to establish a habit of regular exercise. You don't have to be watchful about how much you move every given week because you have workouts scheduled on the same days, lasting the same amount of time, each probably with the same intensity.

In managing your productivity, waking up and going to sleep at the same time ensures that the structure of your day is always the same, which allows you to maximize your productivity and reduce the amount of time spent figuring out when to attend to each task.

There can be more freedom in a lack of variety than in living your life without such a restriction. For a period of time (say, a week), test this approach by limiting your choices and letting your routine make your decisions for you.

# Day 333: On Happiness as a Duty

*It is our duty to be happy.*

*Why? Because our moods and happiness or unhappiness are catching. They inevitably infect other people. When we are happy we make other people happy, especially the people closest to us, physically, at home, at work, socially; and even people we speak to on the phone, online, or by email.*

*And, vitally important, there is the multiplier effect. I am happy, I make you happier, you make them happier, they make yet other people — whom you may never know — happier. The effect is incalculable, and it is always large. The same is true in reverse when you are miserable.*

*So time spent being miserable is antisocial. Stop it now! Relax, change your mood, be happy, and make the world hum rather than shudder.*

—*Richard Koch*[334]

Just like you need self-discipline to become fitter, save money, learn a foreign language, or keep your house clean, so you need it to become and remain happy.

As we've already discussed, in some ways, being a negative person is being a lazy person. It takes more work to think positive thoughts, so we choose to feel unhappy because it's an easier state to access; we could just as well invest some energy and feel good.

Whether you're happy or not wouldn't mean much for your goals if it weren't for the fact that a positive attitude is one of the keys to accomplishment. It makes you believe that you can achieve the impossible, boosts your courage, and keeps you going when you're hit with one difficulty after another.

Consequently, you need to work on happiness, just like on any other important aspect of a self-disciplined life. If you find it challenging to put yourself in a good mood, think of happiness as a moral duty. You owe it to your loved ones and strangers to be happy because your mood — to a smaller or a larger extent — will infect them.

When you have the flu, you don't deliberately go to crowded places or sneeze near your loved ones; you try your best not to infect them. Why would happiness be any different? Exert some self-discipline to think happy thoughts and eradicate the bad mood. It's within your control to feel great or miserable.

Strive to infect others with happiness, not sadness. A great side effect is that the happier you make other people, the easier it will be to remain happy yourself.

# Day 334: On Self-Criticism

*Self-criticism is consistently associated with less motivation and worse self-control.*

—*Kelly McGonigal*[335]

Berating yourself for your failures simply doesn't work. Instead of motivating you to do better next time, it only brings you down, causing you to be even less likely to exert your willpower. In fact, being too harsh towards yourself can turn one slip-up into a full-blown crisis or even into giving up on your goals because you become convinced that you're too weak to change your life.

Instead of self-criticism, give yourself self-compassion. Whenever you fail to meet your standards, remind yourself that you were probably doing your best, but this time it simply didn't work. Human beings aren't perfect, so don't assume that you'll have 100% adherence to a diet, a workout program, or any other resolution you have.

Then, instead of looking for reasons why you suck because you failed, look for lessons in your slip-up and vow to do better next time, being careful to not repeat the same mistakes. Being kind to yourself will ultimately motivate you more to try again than poisoning yourself with your critical voice ever could.

# Day 335: On Wishing

*When people say "I wish," they don't really believe it. "I wish I could save money" or "I wish I could lose weight" means "...but I don't believe it's possible."*

—*Brian Tracy*[336]

One effective (and at first glance, perhaps a bit naïve) strategy to help you develop success-friendly habits, traits, and behaviors is to change your language.

The words that you use have a direct impact on *you*. If you tell yourself that you *wish* you could be different, you're essentially telling the world that it's not within your control to change.

How likely are you to change yourself if the words like "I wish" come out of your mouth so frequently? How much confidence will you have in your ability to reach your goals if you don't believe it's possible that you can achieve them?

Set a simple challenge: for the next seven days, whenever you catch yourself saying you *wish* you could do something, stop and rethink it.

Is it really something that you will never be able to accomplish (such as become younger), or is it just your brain serving you your own limiting beliefs? If it's the latter, make a list of immediate actions you can take to transform "I wish" into "Here's how I'm going to do it."

# Day 336: On Remembering That Your Time Is Limited

> *Thinking that we have ample time to do things later is the greatest myth, the greatest hang-up, and the greatest poison. If we knew that tonight we were going to go blind, we would take a longing, last real look at every blade of grass, every cloud formation. If we knew that we were going to be deaf tomorrow, we would treasure every single sound.*
>
> —*Pema Chödrön*[337]

Death can be the ultimate motivator. In a 2007 movie, *The Bucket List*, it's their impending death that motivates two terminally-ill men to embark on a road trip with a wish list of things they want to do before their illnesses claim their lives.

From time to time I like to imagine that I have a few months of life left. I ask myself if I would die fulfilled or if there would be something I would deeply regret not having done. Taking a few minutes to imagine such a scenario is a helpful exercise in discovering your true priorities and serves as a powerful boost of motivation to act now.

Thinking about death is morbid, but ultimately can also act as an inspiring experience that can shake you out of inaction. Imagine your last hours and think that you'll never be able to do the things that you've wanted to do your entire life, but never acted upon. The only thing left is regret that when you could have done them, you chose to put those things off and now you can only imagine how it would feel to accomplish them.

Now realize that you're still here, still alive and kicking, and there's still a possibility of making your dreams come true. Why on earth are you still putting off those important goals, knowing that one day you'll no longer be able to pursue them?

# WEEK 49

# Day 337: On a Coin Flip

*When you are undecided on a difficult decision, flip a coin.*

*Why?*

*Because when the coin is in the air, you suddenly know which side you really want.*

—*Nathan Barry*[338]

This simple trick is one of the most powerful decision-making tools. Whenever you're hesitant, let fate decide for you and you'll immediately realize which option you prefer to take.

If you don't have a coin, name your options A, B, C, etc. and ask your friend to randomly pick one letter. If there's nobody around you and you need to make a quick decision, randomly pick one of the options and ask yourself how you feel now that you've decided on it.

We often know in our gut which option is better, but we get stuck in the decision-making process out of a fear of missing out on something that another option might offer us. Turning the final decision over to something that is outside of your control amplifies your inner voice and leads to better decisions.

# Day 338: On "I Don't" vs. "I Can't"

*"I don't" is experienced as a choice, so it feels empowering. It's an affirmation of your determination and willpower. "I can't" isn't a choice — it's a restriction, it's being imposed upon you. So thinking "I can't" undermines your sense of power and personal agency.*

—***Heidi Grant Halvorson**[339]*

Be careful not to say "I can't" whenever you're working on implementing a new positive change in your life that requires you to give up something (such as going on a diet).

Thinking of your decision in terms of a restriction ("I *can't* do it") inevitably leads to discontent and approaching your change as a short-term solution. Admitting that a change is your *choice* by saying "I *don't* do it" lends itself to treating it as a permanent identity shift.

A related technique you can use to give up something that's bad for you is to associate it with the discomfort it leads to and deciding that you no longer want to suffer from it. You aren't saying that you *can't* do this thing any longer and thereby think of it as a restriction. You're saying that you *don't* do this thing because it's your own choice, dictated by your wish to avoid the unpleasant consequences.

For example, I was once a big lover of potatoes and they greatly contributed to me being overweight. When testing how certain foods affected me, I realized that potatoes made me bloated, tired, and led to digestive issues. Just like that, I stopped eating potatoes that I had been previously eating in copious amounts at least three times a week. I'm sure that if it weren't for uncovering my food intolerance and a conscious decision not to eat potatoes anymore, I would still be eating them. A restriction in the form of "I can't eat potatoes" wouldn't work.

Catch yourself whenever you say "I can't" and replace it with "I don't" or "I choose not to do it." It's a small change in your vocabulary, but the way you think about your changes can impact whether they become permanent or are only short-lived.

# Day 339: On Appreciating Your Body

> *When all is said and done, the most important thing is to respect and appreciate the body you have. It's great to strive for physical perfection, but the journey matters more than the destination.*
>
> —*Al Kavadlo*[340]

If you have a car, you probably regularly take it to the carwash. You drive it carefully in order not to scratch it or ding it. You respect it and appreciate it because it's *your* vehicle.

Sadly, while most people take great pains to keep their cars pristine, they don't think about their bodies in the same way. They fail to notice that while a car is replaceable, their body is the only body they're ever going to get.

If you're constantly failing to introduce healthy habits, think of it as an expression of respect toward your body. I know, it sounds cheesy, but ultimately many people fail to care for their bodies because they never adopt a good, empowering metaphor to help them in their efforts.

Make exercise primarily about self-respect and appreciation for your body, and not an obsession to build a perfect body (which often leads to so much pressure that people completely give up). It doesn't matter if you're obese, if you can't run for more than a minute, or if you can't perform a single push-up. What matters right here and right now is to learn to start caring for your body in the same way as you care for your other prized possessions.

Once healthy living becomes a habit (just like taking your car to the carwash or cleaning your house), then you can set more specific fitness goals to further strengthen your body. For now, your only preoccupation should be to change your actions so that they manifest your respect toward the only body you have.

# Day 340: On Better Learning

*Research shows that people who follow strategy B [read ten pages at once, then close the book and write a one page summary] remember 50 percent more material over the long term than people who follow strategy A [read ten pages four times in a row and try to memorize them].*

—Daniel Coyle[341]

Books can change your life, but only if you read them with the intention to learn.

Merely reading a book from cover to cover, closing it, and immediately finding another book to learn from might work as entertainment when reading fiction. However, it doesn't work with non-fiction. In order to learn, you need to exert a bit more self-discipline and read the book, along with noticing and remembering its key points. You can highlight important parts, make notes, or write short summaries.

What might be an even better idea than highlighting, making notes, or writing summaries is to make a bullet-point list of its practical applications in your life. A summary can be helpful if you need to memorize the information in itself, but a bullet-point list of practical implications will be more valuable if you're after a real education — changing your life through what you read.

Start today with *this* book. Grab a notepad or open a new document and make a list of at several practical applications of the advice you've discovered in this book. We're on day 340, so I'm pretty sure you can make a list of at least 10, if not 100, possible changes you can introduce in your life to instill more self-discipline.

# Day 341: On When Not to Make Important Decisions

*I've found that it's a good rule to never make an important decision when your emotions are in control. I try to program myself in advance to remember this rule when I need it. When I'm in an emotional state (either positive or negative), I try to keep just enough intellect working to tell me one thing: don't decide now. I wait until I've relaxed and can think more clearly.*

—*Harry Browne*[342]

If you want to greatly increase the chances of making a bad decision, make it when you're "under the influence" of strong emotions (either negative or positive). The same is true in reverse: to make a *good* decision, only do so when you're in a neutral emotional state, relaxed enough to think clearly and weigh all the pros and cons.

For example, I have a rule to never agree to make any big purchases over the phone or in person without giving myself at least a day to think it over. That way, I can think objectively about whether I really need to make such a purchase, and if so, research whether I was given a good offer.

Establish a similar rule in your life and always wait before making any big decisions. This also applies to setting big new goals. It's better to set them when you're in a neutral state of mind than when you're pumped up, because if you do so while being influenced by a temporary strong rush of endorphins, you'll probably overestimate your abilities and set goals that are beyond your reach.

# Day 342: On Doing the Best You Can With What You Have

*Success means doing the best we can with what we have. Success is the doing, not the getting — in the trying, not the triumph. Success is a personal standard — reaching for the highest that is in us — becoming all that we can be. If we do our best, we are a success. Success is the maximum utilization of the ability that you have.*

—*Zig Ziglar*

One of the best ways to destroy your resolve is to associate success with results alone. If you fail to generate any results for a long time (as is often the case when working on difficult, long-term goals), the belief that you're only doing well if you're getting immediate results will discourage you from continuing.

The proper approach is to espouse the belief that success means doing the best you can with what you have. Regardless of the outcome, as long as you're doing your best, you're keeping yourself to the highest standard and that's what matters the most. The results might come today, tomorrow, six months from now, or even a decade later.

Obviously, it's not like you're pursuing your goals for the sake of pursuing them — you want to get something for your efforts. However, it will be hard to make your dreams come true if you only obsess about the end result and forget to focus on the current process. After all, ultimately it's the journey itself that will shape you to become the person deserving the goal you're after.

A successful businessman isn't successful because he runs a successful business. He's successful because he stuck to his business, despite difficulties, failures, and the seemingly hopeless situations in which he found himself. He wouldn't have built a successful business if he had only defined himself by the results (which are rarely anything to brag about anyway, at least in the first several years of running a business).

A successful athlete isn't successful because she has received a medal. She's successful because she's been training harder than her competitors and kept going despite pain, exhaustion, and discomfort. She would have failed to become a successful athlete if she had obsessed solely about the prizes, and not on the act of bettering her performance.

Embrace success as holding yourself to a high personal standard and focus on the process of consistently becoming better. As long as you do your best with what you have, the results will show up eventually.

# Day 343: On Turning Intentions into Actions

> *I always wrote down my goals. It wasn't sufficient just to tell myself "lose twenty pounds and learn better English and read a little bit more." No. That was only a start. Now I had to make it very specific so that all those fine intentions were not just floating around. I would take out index cards and write that I was going to:* • *get twelve more units in college;* • *earn enough money to save $5,000;* • *work out five hours a day;* • *gain seven pounds of solid muscle weight; and* • *find an apartment building to buy and move into.*
>
> —*Arnold Schwarzenegger*[343]

The more vague your plans are, the more likely they are to remain in the realm of intentions instead of real-world actions. You need to make your plans specific, quantifiable, and (ideally) repeatable in some way so that each day brings you closer to accomplishing your goals.

"I'm going to write a book" is a good start, but it isn't going to lead to any accomplishments unless you make it more specific by listing the specific actions that you're going to take, such as: "Plot my story in 2000 words," "Write the first chapter," and later on, as the sole daily action that is required to reach your goal, "Write 1000 words every day."

With goals that make it difficult to tell whether or when you've accomplished them, such as Arnold's "I'm going to learn better English," it's crucial to set specific, quantifiable sub-goals, such as

"Master 100 common words related to medicine" or "Read ten history books in English," so that you can objectively say that because of the effort you've exerted, you've indeed improved your abilities and have evidence that supports that view.

Note that the real work doesn't begin until you take the first action designed to get you closer to your goals. Even the most specific and well-designed goal is still a dream until you figure out what concrete actions you need to take — and then take them — to convert it into a true goal with chances for success.

# WEEK 50

# Day 344: On the Desire for Safety

*The desire for safety stands against every great and noble enterprise.*

—*Tacitus*[344]

When setting any new goals, the desire for safety will fight against the desire for growth. Choosing safety is choosing instant gratification, while going for growth might be uncomfortable now, but will eventually deliver bigger and better rewards.

Learn how to overcome the desire for safety by regularly expanding your comfort zone and reaping the rewards of doing so. It's hard to imagine how beneficial temporarily giving up safety can be unless you actually do it. No words of mine will persuade you more than you actually venturing out, testing it for yourself, and feeling more powerful, thanks to facing your fears.

You can also follow the strategy of alternating between periods of safety and growth: after each big step forward that required courage and put you in an uncomfortable situation, give yourself a few days to enjoy safety. Then, when you feel secure and recharged, expose yourself to danger and growth again. That way, you'll consistently stretch yourself in a sustainable way, without ever completely exhausting your mental energy.

That's what I often do during my rock climbing workouts: on some workouts I favor technical routes that require little courage but lots of focus and then on other workouts, I climb difficult, mental routes where a fear of falling enters into the equation.

Thanks to this approach, I rarely don't feel like climbing; whenever I don't feel mentally ready to give up the feeling of security, I can simply do something else and then expand my comfort zone the next time, when I'll have recovered.

Stretch your comfort zone frequently, but do it in a sustainable way: ensure that you regularly get to enjoy at least a short period of security to gather energy for another expedition that will take you beyond your comfort zone.

# Day 345: On Injecting Adventure in Your Routines

*Writing interests me more than anything else. If I made a chore of it, my enthusiasm would die. I make it an adventure every day. I get more entertainment from it than any I could buy.*

—*Willa Cather*[345]

A daily routine sounds boring, but it doesn't need to be. If you inject some fun and adventure in it, you'll find it will be easier and more pleasant to stick to it.

For example, if you're on a diet, there's no rule stating that you can't cook exotic healthy meals or try foods you've never tasted before. Starting a diet can be a good opportunity to introduce more variety in your nutritional habits.

If you want to become more financially disciplined, turn it into a game. Set a challenge to save as much money as you can. Find better deals for the items you need to buy regularly. Come up with ways to make some money on the side.

If you want to become more productive, challenge yourself to get as much work done as possible in a short period of time. Experiment by working in different places. Try new ways of getting things done.

If your resolutions don't feel like chores, but more like opportunities to have some small adventures and entertain yourself, you'll be more likely to stick to them than if you looked at them as boring obligations.

# Day 346: On Surpassing Yourself

*A man's life is interesting primarily when he has failed — I well know. For it's a sign that he tried to surpass himself.*

—*Georges Clemenceau*[346]

One interesting and empowering way to look at failure is to consider it a sign that you're trying to surpass yourself. After all, you can't fail if you're doing something that is well within your abilities. You fail when you're doing something that is difficult for you, in order to grow. Hence, if you aren't failing, you're probably not stretching yourself enough.

If you've been going a long time without any failures, it's time to think bigger. Not experiencing any failures is a clear sign that you're setting your aims too low and it's time to seek a more challenging environment or establish new, more difficult goals.

Success is obviously a positive thing, but bear in mind that if you're constantly succeeding, it comes with the risk of getting too cocky and assuming that you're invincible. Setting goals with a high risk of failure will help you stay humble and ultimately aid you in keeping success in your life.

# Day 347: On Enduring Your Tyrants

*Power concedes nothing without a demand. It never did and it never will. Find out just what any people will quietly submit to, and you have found out the exact amount of injustice and wrong which will be imposed upon them; and these will continue till they are resisted with either words or blows, or with both. The limits of tyrants are prescribed by the endurance of those whom they oppress.*

—*Frederick Douglass*[347]

Likewise, the limits of problems in your life are determined by your tolerance of them. If you have a slight pain in your little toe, you probably aren't going to go see the doctor, but multiply the pain by a factor of five and you'll be at the doctor's office in a split second!

Think in the same way about your bad habits or any other harmful actions of yours. If the perceived pain (negative consequences) is weak, you'll most likely continue to tolerate it for as long as it doesn't increase. Intensify the pain, and you'll start looking for solutions.

There are two ways to inspire you to give up negative behaviors:

1. The pain caused by your negative behaviors intensifies by itself. One day you realize that the problem has grown to such proportions that you *must* do something about it. For example, your negative nutritional habits lead to a heart attack or failing to improve your self-confidence makes you a loner without any friends.

This is *not* a good way to deal with negative behaviors, because you're letting the problem grow uncontrollably until it poses a big risk in your life.

2. Intensifying the pain by making yourself aware of how deep the pain goes. Instead of ignoring the pain and keeping it running in the background, you tune in to it and focus on all of its consequences. Make them bigger and assume they will get soon get worse. Use the negative visualization to inspire the change.

For example, once you notice you're gasping for air after climbing a set of stairs, assume that it's the first sign of an incoming rapid deterioration of health. New symptoms will soon follow, and each will be stronger than the previous one. The slight discomfort you have now is only the beginning. Amplify its message and act now while you still can. Don't ignore it by thinking that you can forget about it for now and you will address it later if it gets worse.

Unless you can convince yourself how far-reaching and dangerous the consequences of your behaviors can be in the long term, you won't act. Think of any negative behaviors of yours as tyrants: to what extreme measures must they go before you stop enduring their oppression?

# Day 348: On Using Your Strength

*Greatness lies not in being strong, but in the using of strength.*

—*Henry Ward Beecher*[348]

I've never understood the point of going to the gym, lifting weights and then heading back home, sitting on your butt for the rest of the week and avoiding any kind of physical movement — never actually using your strength for anything besides lifting weights. Doesn't one find the purpose for getting strong by actually *using* it for something besides training?

Throughout the book, I've listed numerous exercises you can use to boost your willpower and become a more self-disciplined person. Those exercises aren't there for entertainment purposes; I'm sharing them with you so you can actually perform them and then apply the lessons and improvements that you gained through them to your goals.

There's little point in practicing self-control for the sake of practicing self-control. Of course, nothing prevents you from taking cold showers just because you'd like to test yourself or controlling your thoughts just because you'd like to get better at controlling your thoughts. However, remember that ultimately the intention of those exercises is to build strength, which you then *use* to make your life better.

# Day 349: On Managing Energy

*Energy, not time, is the fundamental currency of high performance.*

—*Jim Loehr[349]*

You can have all the time in the world, but if you don't have energy, it won't mean anything. Your energy is your primary resource needed to change your life for the better; if you lack it, your chances of attaining your goals drop to zero.

For this reason, it's vital to learn how to manage your energy. That's why I'm so adamant about the importance of healthy habits like getting enough sleep, eating healthily, and exercising regularly. If you don't have such habits, your energy levels are compromised and you're less likely to achieve your goals.

In addition to healthy habits, consider making a list of things, places, and people who energize you and a second list of those that rob you of energy. Now that you have both lists in front of you, think about how you can restructure your life to spend as much time as possible in an energizing environment with energizing people, and as little time as possible in situations that rob your energy.

For example, large crowds exhaust me, so you'll almost never find me in one. On the other end of the spectrum, spending time in nature recharges me, so I strive to be outdoors at least a few times a week.

Energy management is one of the key skills you need to perform well in both your professional and personal life. Let me assure you that no matter how disciplined you are, if you routinely exhaust yourself, one day you'll burn out. Wouldn't it be better to learn how to manage your energy today, so that you can avoid this unpleasant problem altogether?

# Day 350: On Doing Things Deliberately

*Working slowly in today's world goes against every thought system. You can only work slowly if you do it deliberately. Being deliberate requires you to stay in the process, to work in the present moment.*

—*Thomas Sterner*[350]

In rock climbing, when you're clipping the rope into a quickdraw and you rush it, your movements will be imprecise. In the end, with rapid movements it will take you more time to clip in the rope than if you were to do it slowly.

Working deliberately, particularly when the stakes are high, takes a lot of self-control. You need to battle against the temptation to rush things and maintain your concentration when stress threatens to consume you.

Doing things fast — but not necessarily well — isn't a particularly good strategy for achievement. In fact, it's usually the slow, deliberate, poised movements that lead to great outcomes, and not rushed, nervous, or impulsive actions.

Identify when your behaviors are hasty and unfocused and take advantage of such opportunities to exercise your willpower by doing things slowly and with precision.

# WEEK 51

# Day 351: On Admitting You're Struggling

> *To cut out every negative root would simultaneously mean choking off positive elements that might arise from it further up the stem of the plant. We should not feel embarrassed by our difficulties, only by our failure to grow anything beautiful from them.*
>
> —*Alain de Botton*[351]

I often talk about my failures in my books because I want my readers to understand that hardships are an inherent part of the process. If somebody claims they're successful but they've never failed, you can be sure they're lying.

Whenever you're dealing with problems and struggling to stick to your goals, don't be afraid to share your troubles with others and reach out for help. You might feel tempted to protect your ego and demonstrate that you're infallible, but doing so is counterproductive.

Denying that you have problems — or denying that you could use help or support — doesn't make you better than a person who publicly admits that things aren't going well and is looking for assistance.

In the end, there's nothing to be ashamed of when you're struggling. The only shame is in failing to recognize your problems because that's when you miss out on some of the most valuable opportunities to grow.

# Day 352: On the Empowerment in Trade-Offs

> *Essentialists see trade-offs as an inherent part of life, not as an inherently negative part of life. Instead of asking, "What do I have to give up?" they ask, "What do I want to go big on?"*
>
> —*Greg McKeown*[352]

We've discussed that it's essential to replace "I can't do it" with "I don't do it" in order not to think of your resolutions as punishments. This entry is about taking that even further: instead of asking yourself what you have to give up, think of something more important that you want to gain. In other words, frame your perception of giving up a harmful behavior as an act of empowerment, not an act of sacrifice.

For example, if you want to start saving money, it's not a question of what you won't be able to buy anymore. The right question is what will saving more money let you "go big on"? How about improving your peace of mind, spending less time shopping, treating your family to a nice vacation, or (ultimately) perhaps even retiring early? In the grand scheme of things, what does giving up some purchases mean in comparison to *that*?

Approach each trade-off in the same way: ensure that you understand deep down that it's an act of choosing to get more of something you consider important, and not an act of sacrificing something to get something else.

# Day 353: On Glancing at Your Smartphone

*If every moment of potential boredom is relieved with a quick glance at your smartphone, then your brain has likely been rewired to a point where it's not ready for deep work — even if you regularly schedule time to practice this concentration.*

—*Cal Newport*[353]

If you have a tendency to glance at your smartphone every few minutes or the thought of leaving your smartphone in another room for a few minutes gives you an anxiety attack, it's time to embrace your self-control to defeat this habit.

It sounds like a little insignificant thing, but in fact it's a sign of a deeper issue: your brain has been rewired in such a way that you physically *cannot* resist the urge to periodically check your phone. Consequently, you can't maintain focus for more than a few minutes, and I don't think I need to explain why this ruins your productivity.

Start slowly. Instead of checking your phone every five minutes, wait for ten minutes. Then, when it gets easier, try twenty. Thirty. Forty. One hour.

Again, it's a tiny bad habit, but working on it presents a valuable exercise in growing your willpower. It will also eventually improve your ability to engage in deep work that you'd otherwise keep interrupting by checking your phone every few minutes.

# Day 354: On Focusing on the Good Things

*I think it's almost an indulgence to focus on the dark side of things. And as you get older, you want to focus on the positive.*

—*Rob Brydon*[354]

On several occasions, we have talked about cultivating positive emotions when things go bad. I argued that focusing on the bad things is an act of mental laziness because they're easier to access than the positive ones. Today I'd like to talk about this topic yet again, this time by looking at it as a new habit to instill.

As people get older, they tend to focus more on the dark side of things. Perhaps it's because they've experienced more things, suffered more failures, or were let down by more people. Whatever the reason, if you want to remain a happy and successful person, grumbling is not the way to go.

If by default you focus on the dark side, it's time to develop a new habit: whenever you catch yourself focusing on the dark side of things, come up with one good thing about the situation and focus on that thought instead. Keep your mouth shut if you want to voice a complaint.

For example, if you're out enjoying a walk with a friend and it's starting to rain, resist the temptation to complain about the bad weather. Instead, say (for example) that it's nice to take a walk despite the rain because there are fewer people around, or redirect your attention to something else, such as your friend's recent success.

Exhibiting a positive attitude takes work, but it's work that is well worth the effort. Strive to focus on the positive and train yourself to always find something good, even in the worst circumstances. You'll get better at controlling your thoughts and become more optimistic and resilient.

# Day 355: On Luxuries

*The taste for luxuries increases with marvelous rapidity under indulgence.*

—*George Payne Rainsford James*[355]

The more luxuries you consume and surround yourself with, the more you'll become accustomed to them — and the harder it will be for you to tolerate something less than perfect.

While there's nothing wrong in enjoying the fruits of your labor and making your life a little bit more convenient, be cautious to not overindulge in luxuries. They can spoil you and make you less resilient and capable of dealing with difficult situations.

Not being able to accept something less than perfect is ultimately a big weakness. A disciplined person will be able to train in every gym or even without any equipment, eat healthily even if there are no Whole Foods markets available where they are, and stay productive even without a proper work desk.

Periodically go with something of a lower quality to remind yourself that things don't have to be world-class in order to still serve their function. Forego some conveniences to improve your tolerance of the hardships. Don't indulge yourself after a success, in order to remind yourself that ultimately the most valuable reward is the process you had to go through to achieve the final outcome.

Doing all of those things will increase your appreciation of what you *have*, and remind you that discomfort is always just a step away

— and yes, there's always the risk that one day it will be you who will have to tolerate it again.

# Day 356: On Taking the Initiative

*I've trained myself to propose solutions instead of ask for them, to elicit responses instead of react, and to be assertive without burning bridges. To have an uncommon lifestyle, you need to develop the uncommon habit of making decisions, both for yourself and for others.*

—*Tim Ferriss*[356]

You need a lot of self-discipline to take the initiative instead of taking the easy way out and waiting for somebody else to act. It's easier to present a problem and ask for solutions than to suggest some yourself. It's easier to delegate the responsibility for the decision to someone else, essentially freeing yourself of the discomfort of having to make a decision in exchange for losing control over the situation.

To obtain better results in all kinds of endeavors, become the person who takes the initiative.

If you're dealing with a problem that affects others, instead of only *presenting* the problem to the group, propose several solutions. Resist the temptation to be lazy by relying on others' ideas and come up with your own.

I used to work with a few business partners and I can tell you that there's nothing better than an associate who doesn't merely wait for the solutions, but offers them himself or herself. And the reverse is also true: there's nothing worse than a collaborator who only brings you problems and expects you to solve them all.

In addition, become proactive and react as quickly as you can. Yes, it's uncomfortable to stand out and take the initiative while everybody else is looking at you and judging you. However, ultimately, he or she who acts first is the leader; immediately reacting to situations also trains you to overcome hesitation and to develop a habit of taking action.

For example, if you're walking down the street and somebody looks like they're about to faint, overcome your social fears and ask them if they're fine. Such a small decision of yours might mean the difference between life and death for that stranger.

I was once on a bike ride with a friend when we noticed a man lying down in the middle of the sidewalk, blood dripping out of his ear. Nobody stopped to help him, and yet he was a stone's throw away from a church packed with people.

Who knows? Maybe nobody offered to help because they were afraid to take action or thought that somebody else would take the initiative. Fortunately, we attended to the man and the ambulance arrived quickly to take him to the hospital. What if nobody had stopped to help him for several hours?

Taking the initiative is often uncomfortable, but that's just one more reason to do it. Don't *react* — act. Don't present *problems*, present *solutions*. Don't shrug it off by saying "whatever"; choose an option if nobody else is willing to do it.

# Day 357: On the Rare Indulgence

*Rare indulgence produces greater pleasure.*

—*Juvenal*[357]

Here's a simple trick to postpone acting on a temporary urge: tell yourself that you'll engage in it later, and your reward for postponing it will be the greater pleasure it will give you.

I know, it sounds like an overly simplistic tip, but try it out.

I regularly tell myself that I'll reward myself with something that I crave right now, but only after I finish my work or any other important (or uncomfortable) task that I have to perform.

That way, I stop obsessing about getting the reward right now and I actually *want* to get it later, because I know that it will taste so much better than giving in to it now.

# WEEK 52

# Day 358: On Acting Differently From Others

*Unless you think that the majority of people are living successful lives, chances are that at some point you will have to act differently from those around you. Success can take many forms and it is often about standing out from the crowd or being above average, spotting when the crowd moves one way and making sure that you move the other.*

—*Nigel Cumberland*[358]

It takes guts to stand out from the crowd and move the other way when, deep down, you know that it's you who's right and not everyone else. Even if you're a self-disciplined, mentally tough person, it's still hard to go against the crowd.

For this reason, one of the most powerful exercises you can do to improve your chances of acting differently from others when you know that you're right is to practice holding your ground. If somebody tells you to do something in a given way but you don't understand why, ask them to explain their request. If the explanation isn't sufficient, suggest a different way of doing things that you think might be better.

Note that this isn't about confrontation for the sake of confrontation. It's an exercise in questioning doing things in a given way just because "that's how they've been done until now," but nobody knows why.

This way, you get to learn (on a small scale) how it feels when you're opposing the current, and this experience will help you hold your ground when the stakes are higher.

# Day 359: On Treats vs. Rewards

*A treat is different from a reward, which must be justified or earned. A treat is a small pleasure or indulgence that we give to ourselves just because we want it.*

*Treats give us greater vitality, which boosts self-control, which helps us maintain our healthy habits. When we give ourselves treats, we feel energized, cared for, and contented, which in turn boosts self-command. When we don't get any treats, we feel depleted, resentful, and angry, and we feel justified in self-indulgence. We start to crave comfort — and grab that comfort wherever we can, even if it means breaking good habits.*

—*Gretchen Rubin*[359]

Trying to totally do without treats and rewards is a posture that is destined to fail. I don't know of a single person, no matter how self-disciplined, who doesn't treat themselves to a small pleasure or indulgence every now and then and who doesn't use rewards as a motivational tool. Treats and rewards serve an important role: they help you to recover and to face future discomforts with a more positive outlook.

Don't make the mistake of assuming that you're so disciplined that you don't need rewards or treats in order to work on your goals. There's only one outcome from making such a dangerous assumption: after a period of doing well, you'll start craving comfort. Since you'll deny yourself the needed comfort, the desire to indulge will build up, eventually explode, and destroy any remnants of self-discipline that remained.

Set rewards for accomplishments and don't be afraid to indulge in small pleasures from time to time — as long as they're small and don't compromise your long-term goals. Self-care reinforces self-command, while self-denial depletes it.

# Day 360: On Self-Myofascial Release

*Self-myofascial release is a fancy term for self-massage to release muscle tightness or trigger points. This method can be performed with a foam roller, lacrosse ball, Theracane, or your own hands. By applying pressure to specific points on your body you are able to aid in the recovery of muscles and assist in returning them to normal function. Normal function means your muscles are elastic, healthy, and ready to perform at a moment's notice.*

—*Jeff Kuhland*[360]

As the quote explains, self-myofascial release is a term for self-massage. You focus on trigger points in your body to release tension and bring back the previous elasticity of your muscles.

What does it have to do with self-discipline? Here are three ways that it applies:.

First, it's difficult to be on top of your game if your body is constantly tense. I find it hard to focus on work if I suffer from back pain. When I spend a few minutes massaging the tightest spots, the mental tension goes away along with the physical tension.

Second, one common reason why people skip workouts or avoid putting themselves in uncomfortable situations is because they're in pain. A lot of that pain comes from your body being tight like a bowstring. Several weeks spent addressing your most painful trigger points can work miracles when it comes to eliminating chronic pain.

Finally, self-myofascial release (such as using a foam roller) isn't a particularly comfortable thing to do. In fact, it can be immensely painful. And that's precisely why self-massage can be a valuable exercise for your self-discipline.

Just like in any other exercise, you suffer some temporary pain or discomfort but eventually get a bigger reward. With self-massage, you experience the temporary pain of applying pressure to your trigger points, but then benefit from increased mobility and free yourself from the chronic pain of tight muscles.

Buying an inexpensive lacrosse ball or a foam roller can be one of your best investments. Greatly reduced (or even eliminated) pain, increased mobility, and improved self-discipline are more than worth the twenty or thirty bucks spent on a self-massage tool.

# Day 361: On Smiling

*If in our daily life we can smile, if we can be peaceful and happy, not only we, but everyone will profit from it. If we really know how to live, what better way to start the day than with a smile? Our smile affirms our awareness and determination to live in peace and joy. The source of a true smile is an awakened mind.*

—*Thich Nhat Hanh*[361]

Smiling is one of the easiest, and one of the hardest things to do. It's natural to smile when you're happy and feel good, and almost impossible when you're in pain or feeling unwell.

With increased self-control, your ability to do things in spite of what you *feel* like doing increases. Smiling can be an excellent exercise in this practice.

I don't want to downplay the negative things that may be happening in your or anyone else's life. However, the truth is that we often resort to scowling, crying, worrying, and radiating negativity when we experience negative emotions, just because this state is easier to access than the positive one.

When you think about it logically, it makes no sense to further ruin your mood after experiencing something negative. If you have a cold, you don't go out naked in the middle of the winter to catch pneumonia, too. Yet, that's pretty much what we're doing anytime we decide to humor negative emotions instead of smiling despite them, or at least trying to lift our spirits a little.

Obviously, it's easy to say that. Some negative events are such that they can destroy a person from the inside out, and telling them to smile would be ridiculous. Apply this advice primarily to the small everyday struggles you encounter, where your negative reaction isn't necessary.

For the next week, try to handle every difficulty with a smile on your face. It doesn't matter if your smile isn't entirely genuine. The point is to make an effort in overcoming your default reaction of feeling negative and replace it with a more positive attitude.

Even if you fail to maintain a better mood for more than a couple of minutes, the exercise in itself will help you better control your impulses and might even lift your spirits slightly. And if you repeat it often enough, your brain's pathways will change and make you more capable of feeling positive, even when bad things happen — and that's not a bad ability to have, is it?

# Day 362: On Professionalism

*Amateurs think that if they were inspired all the time, they could be professionals. Professionals know that if they relied on inspiration, they'd be amateurs.*

—*Philip Pullman*[362]

Inspiration is important to get you to start working on your goals, but you can't rely on it alone if you want to pursue excellence and become a high performer. The keys to professionalism are:

**1. Routine.** Don't wait for inspiration to strike you. In an ideal world you'd be inspired all the time, always pumped up to work. In the real world, you're probably going to be uninspired more often than you'll be inspired. Yet, if you want to become professional, you need to deliver on both good and bad days.

Establish a routine of what you need to produce each day (whether it's 1000 words of a book, playing the guitar for an hour, making 50 sales calls, or learning 20 new words in a foreign language) and stick to it, regardless of your mood.

**2. Reliability.** If you give a promise, you fulfill it — and that includes any promise you make to yourself. This also means sticking to deadlines and resisting the temptation to extend them just because they're difficult to meet.

**3. Constant improvement.** Amateurs dabble, while professionals constantly improve their craft. Always seek new ways to improve your performance and avoid the laziness of rejecting new, possibly better methods, just because they can disrupt your current way of doing things.

# Day 363: On Relying Upon Yourself

> *It always makes more sense to concentrate on the direct alternatives — the things you do control. What others do is up to them, but there's always a great deal you can do. Choose from the alternatives that require only your decision — not from among the many hopes that someone will be something other than what he is. To rely on your rights or on your ability to change others is far less promising than to rely upon yourself.*
>
> —Harry Browne[363]

One dangerous pitfall to be aware of when setting goals is to avoid tying them to the performance or willingness of other people.

For example, I believe that the best business partner is yourself and nobody else. If you have a goal to build a successful business so you can eventually dedicate yourself to your children and your business partner doesn't have such a strong motivation, it will be a source of conflict forever. You'll need his or her approval for any business decision, and 50% of the success of your business will depend on the other person. Losing full control over the decision-making process means lowering your chances of success.

In exercise, you might feel tempted to wait before you buy a gym pass until you persuade your friend to start exercising with you. Yes, working out with a partner is more effective, but if you're relying on this person to establish a positive change in your life, you've already failed. And what if your friend drops out? Will you drop out, too?

Don't wait for another person to change your life. You can hope that their desires will be in line with yours, but it's a better strategy to rely on yourself by choosing alternatives that require your decision alone.

# Day 364: On Books, Part Two

*Books are the treasured wealth of the world and the fit inheritance of generations and nations. Books, the oldest and the best, stand naturally and rightfully on the shelves of every cottage. They have no cause of their own to plead, but while they enlighten and sustain the reader his common sense will not refuse them. Their authors are a natural and irresistible aristocracy in every society, and, more than kings or emperors, exert an influence on mankind.*

—*Henry David Thoreau*[364]

On day 79 I shared with you three inspirational books and then, on day 158, I suggested some biographies to read. Today, now that we're at the end of this book, I'd like give you some additional recommendations that you might find it valuable to read after you finish *365 Days With Self-Discipline*. Here they are:

1. *Make It BIG! 49 Secrets for Building a Life of Extreme Success,* by Frank McKinney. Brilliantly inspiring and practical book written by a fascinating entrepreneur and philanthropist.

2 and 3. *Unlimited Power* and *Awaken the Giant Within,* by Tony Robbins. Two self-help classics that everyone should read.

4. *Essentialism,* by Greg McKeown. If you're struggling to identify your priorities and focus on what matters most, this book will help you.

5. *The Obstacle Is the Way,* by Ryan Holiday. An excellent book, loosely based on the Roman philosophy of stoicism, that teaches you how to succeed in spite of hardships.

6. *How Not to Die,* by Michael Greger. If you want to learn more about the why and how of healthy eating habits, this book is for you. Understanding on a deeper level how your unhealthy choices can affect your life can boost your resolve to finally make a change.

# WEEK 53

# Day 365: On Sweeping the Floor

> *My friend the philosopher and martial artist Daniele Bolelli once gave me a helpful metaphor. He explained that training was like sweeping the floor. Just because we've done it once, doesn't mean the floor is clean forever. Every day the dust comes back. Every day we must sweep.*
>
> —***Ryan Holiday**[365]*

As we're about to part ways, I'd like you leave you with an important reminder: cultivating self-discipline, like training or sweeping the floor, is something that must be done daily.

As incredible as it would be to build self-discipline just once and then enjoy it for the rest of your life, it requires constant work to maintain it so that it can aid you in your objectives.

The moment you put instant gratification back on the pedestal is the moment you start losing your self-control.

The moment you decide that it's time to embrace the easy life and stay away from the challenges is the moment your life starts getting harder.

The moment you decide that you're already strong enough and nothing can break your spirit is the moment you start losing mental resilience.

We've spent 365 days together, but your journey toward self-discipline doesn't end here. Grab the broomstick and start sweeping!

# Epilogue

Our journey has come to an end and I don't want to keep you here for long. I hope that you've gathered so many different ideas to apply in your life that you'll be busy implementing them for a long time to come!

As a quick final reminder, please remember that accumulating knowledge without applying it in real life is like reading cookbooks without ever actually following any of the recipes. What's the point? Put on your chef's uniform and get cooking; you have 365 different recipes to try!

Finally, please note that I wrote this book to give you inspiration and offer various tips that apply to different aspects of self-discipline. I prioritized brief, universal suggestions over detailed how-to advice.

If you want to get more specific, in-depth lessons about self-discipline please refer to my other books about self-discipline, which address areas like dieting (*Self-Disciplined Dieter*), exercise (*How to Build Self-Discipline to Exercise*), entrepreneurship (*Self-Discipline for Entrepreneurs*), impulse control (*How to Build Self-Discipline*), and long-term habits (*Daily Self-Discipline*).

# Download Another Book for Free

I want to thank you for buying my book and offer you another book (just as valuable as this one): *Grit: How to Keep Going When You Want to Give Up*, completely free.

Visit the link below to receive it:

http://www.profoundselfimprovement.com/365

In *Grit*, I'll tell you exactly how to stick to your goals, using proven methods from peak performers and science.

In addition to getting *Grit*, you'll also have an opportunity to get my new books for free, enter giveaways, and receive other valuable emails from me.

Again, here's the link to sign up:

http://www.profoundselfimprovement.com/365

# Could You Help?

I'd love to hear your opinion about my book. In the world of book publishing, there are few things more valuable than honest reviews from a wide variety of readers.

Your review will help other readers find out whether my book is for them. It will also help me reach more readers by increasing the visibility of my book.

# About Martin Meadows

Martin Meadows is the pen name of an author who has dedicated his life to personal growth. He constantly reinvents himself by making drastic changes in his life.

Over the years, he has regularly fasted for over 40 hours, taught himself two foreign languages, lost over 30 pounds in 12 weeks, run several businesses in various industries, took ice-cold showers and baths, lived on a small tropical island in a foreign country for several months, and wrote a 400-page novel's worth of short stories in one month.

But self-torture is not his passion. Martin likes to test his boundaries to discover how far his comfort zone goes.

His findings (based both on his personal experience and on scientific studies) help him improve his life. If you're interested in pushing your limits and learning how to become the best version of yourself, you'll love Martin's works.

You can read his books here:

http://www.amazon.com/author/martinmeadows.

© Copyright 2017 by Meadows Publishing. All rights reserved. Edited by Sara Zibrat.

Reproduction in whole or in part of this publication without express written consent is strictly prohibited. The author greatly appreciates you taking the time to read his work. Please consider leaving a review wherever you bought the book, or telling your friends about it, to help us spread the word. Thank you for supporting our work.

Efforts have been made to ensure that the information in this book is accurate and complete. However, the author and the publisher do not warrant the accuracy of the information, text, and graphics contained within the book due to the rapidly changing nature of science, research, known and unknown facts, and the Internet. The author and the publisher do not accept any responsibility for errors, omissions or contrary interpretation of the subject matter herein. This book is presented solely for motivational and informational purposes only.

---

[1] Kekich Credo. https://geniusnetwork.com/kekich/main.php
[2] DeMarco, MJ (2011). *The Millionaire Fastlane: Crack the Code to Wealth and Live Rich for a Lifetime.* Viperion Publishing.
[3] Henley, J. (2012, February 7). Why willpower matters — and how to get it. Retrieved September 13, 2017 from
https://www.theguardian.com/lifeandstyle/2012/feb/07/why-willpower-matters.
[4] Kurson, K. (2013, April 2). Surrender to Tim Ferriss: The Dynamo Behind the '4-hour' Books Should Run Your Life (And Maybe Our City). Retrieved September 13, 2017 from http://observer.com/2013/04/surrender-to-tim-ferriss-the-dynamo-behind-the-4-hour-books-should-run-your-life-and-maybe-our-city/.
[5] Allen, J. (1907). *The Path of Prosperity.*
[6] SCVHA (2011, October 6). From the Documentary Film Steve Jobs: Secrets of Life. Retrieved September 20, 2017 from
https://www.youtube.com/watch?v=kYfNvmF0Bqw.

[7] Kristof, N. (2015, June 13). It's Not Just About Bad Choices. Retrieved September 22, 2017 from https://www.nytimes.com/2015/06/14/opinion/sunday/nicholas-kristof-its-not-just-about-bad-choices.html?mcubz=0.

[8] Irvine, William B. (2008). *A Guide to the Good Life: The Ancient Art of Stoic Joy.* Oxford University Press.

[9] Hershfield, H. E., Goldstein, D. G., Sharpe, W. F., Fox, J., Yeykelis, L., Carstensen, L. L., & Bailenson, J. N. (2011). Increasing Saving Behavior Through Age-Progressed Renderings of the Future Self. *Journal of Marketing Research*, 48: S23-S37.

[10] King, S. (2010). *On Writing.* Hodder & Stoughton.

[11] Harris, J. S. (1982). *Pieces of Eight.* Houghton Mifflin.

[12] Allen, J. (1902). *As A Man Thinketh.*

[13] Robbins, T. (2015, August 5). In order to succeed, you must have a long-term focus. Most of the challenges in our lives come from a short-term focus. [Tweet] Retrieved September 24, 2017 from https://twitter.com/tonyrobbins/status/629064818603855872.

[14] Drucker, P. F. (2010). *The Drucker Lectures*, McGraw Hill.

[15] Aurelius, M. (167 A.D.). *The Meditations.* Translated by George Long.

[16] Seneca the Younger (c. 65 A.D.). *Letters from a Stoic: Epistulae Morales Ad Lucilium.* Translated by Robin Campbell.

[17] Beecher, H. W. (1864). *Sermons by Henry Ward Beecher, No. 1 - Strength According to the Days.*

[18] Dixon, P. L. (1984). *The Olympian.* Roundtable Pub.

[19] Epictetus (c. 108 A.D.). *Discourses of Epictetus.* Translated by Thomas Wentworth Higginson.

[20] Keller, G., & Papasan, J. (2013). *The ONE Thing: The Surprisingly Simple Truth Behind Extraordinary Results.* John Murray.

[21] Lally P., van Jaarsveld C. H. M., Potts H. W. W., & Wardle J. (2010). How are habits formed: Modelling habit formation in the real world. *European Journal of Social Psychology*, 40(6): 998–1009. doi: 10.1002/ejsp.674.

[22] Dorfman, H. A. (2001). *The Mental ABC's of Pitching: A Handbook for Performance Enhancement.* Diamond Communications.

[23] Crowley, A. (1989). *The Confessions of Aleister Crowley.*

[24] Lasikiewicz, N., Myrissa, K., Hoyland, A., & Lawton, C. L. (2014). Psychological benefits of weight loss following behavioural and/or dietary weight loss interventions. A systematic research review. *Appetite*, 72: 123–137.

[25] Kennedy, E. D. (2011, January 17). Turning Vacations into Adventures — Part II. Retrieved September 30, 2017 from http://www.artofmanliness.com/2011/01/17/turning-vacations-into-adventures-part-ii/.

[26] Sivers, D. (2000, September 7). *If this is draining your energy, please stop!* Retrieved September 29, 2017 from https://sivers.org/drain.
[27] Maslow, A. (1965). *Self-Actualization and Beyond.*
[28] Rippetoe, M. (2007, November 1). *Be Alive. Be Very Alive.* Retrieved September 30, 2017 from http://journal.crossfit.com/2007/11/be-alive-be-very-alive-by-mark.tpl.
[29] Waldschmidt, D. (2014, January 13). *You Have To Do The Hard Things.* Retrieved September 30, 2017 from https://www.danwaldschmidt.com/articles/2014/01/business/hard-things.
[30] Jung, C. G. (2014). *Collected Works of C.G. Jung, Volume 16: Practice of Psychotherapy: Practice of Psychotherapy.* (Adler, G. & Hull, R. F. C. Trans.) Princeton University Press.
[31] As quoted in Gilbert, J. H. (1895). *Dictionary Of Burning Words Of Brilliant Writers: A Cyclopaedia Of Quotations, From The Literature Of All Ages.*
[32] Brooks, F. (1995). *The Mythical Man-Month: Essays on Software Engineering. Anniversary Edition.*
[33] Paine, T. (1776–1783). *The American Crisis.*
[34] Finerman, W., Tisch, S., & Starkey, S. (Producers) (1994). Zemeckis, R. (Director). *Forrest Gump* [Motion Picture]. United States: Paramount Pictures.
[35] da Vinci, L. (1888). *The Notebooks of Leonardo Da Vinci.* Translated by Jean Paul Richter.
[36] Gautama Buddha, *Dhammacakkappavattana Sutta.*
[37] As quoted in Morris, B. (2014). *Simply Transcribed. Quotations from Writings by Fausto Cercignani.*
[38] Gollwitzer, P. M., Sheeran, P., Michalski, V., & Seifert, A. E. (2009). When Intentions Go Public. Does Social Reality Widen the Intention-Behavior Gap? *Psychological Science,* 20(5): 612–618. doi: 10.1111/j.1467-9280.2009.02336.x.
[39] Aurelius, M. (167 A.D.). *The Meditations.* Translated by George Long.
[40] Nordgren L. F., van Harreveld F., & van der Pligt J. (2009). The restraint bias: how the illusion of self-restraint promotes impulsive behavior. *Psychological Science,* 20(12): 1523–1528. doi: 10.1111/j.1467-9280.2009.02468.x.
[41] Musashi, M. (c. 1645), *The Book of Five Rings.*
[42] As quoted from Electrical Review (c. 1895) without further attribution in Baldwin, E. B. (1896), *The Search for the North Pole.*
[43] Keller, H. (1903). *Optimism.*
[44] Washington, G. (28 August 1788). Letter to Alexander Hamilton.
[45] Roosevelt, E. (1960). *You Learn by Living: Eleven Keys for a More Fulfilling Life.*
[46] As quoted in Morris, B. (2014). *Simply Transcribed. Quotations from Writings by Fausto Cercignani.*
[47] Epictetus (c. 108 A.D.). *Discourses of Epictetus.* Translated by Thomas Wentworth Higginson.

[48] Laertius, D. (1925). Lives of the Eminent Philosophers. Translated by Robert Drew Hicks.
[49] Williams, B. (2006, May 25). Steve Jobs: Iconoclast and Salesman. Retrieved September 20, 2017 from http://www.nbcnews.com/id/12974884/#.WcH6k9FpFPY.
[50] Tynan (2013, March 2). Isn't it Convenient. Retrieved October 1, 2017 from http://tynan.com/convenient.
[51] Gates, B. (1995). *The Road Ahead*. Viking Press.
[52] Aurelius, M. (167 A.D.). *The Meditations*. Translated by George Long.
[53] Wintle, W. D. (1905). *Thinking*.
[54] University of California - Los Angeles. (2013, July 29). Be happy: Your genes may thank you for it. ScienceDaily. Retrieved October 3, 2017 from www.sciencedaily.com/releases/2013/07/130729192548.htm.
[55] Xenophon, *Memorabilia*.
[56] de La Bruyère, J. (1885). *Characters*. Translated by Henri van Laun.
[57] Sivers, D. (2000, August 30). Extreme results = extreme actions. Retrieved September 29, 2017 from https://sivers.org/extremex.
[58] John F. Kennedy, Address at Rice University on the Nation's Space Effort, Houston, TX (12 September 1962).
[59] As quoted in Maxwell, J. C. (2007). *Talent Is Never Enough: Discover the Choices That Will Take You Beyond Your Talent*.
[60] Fox News (2013, April 11). Oregon man pinned under 3,000-pound tractor saved by teen daughters. Retrieved October 12, 2017 from http://www.foxnews.com/us/2013/04/11/oregon-man-pinned-under-3000-pound-tractor-saved-by-two-teen-daughters.html.
[61] Carson, B., & Murphey, C. (1992). *Gifted Hands: The Ben Carson Story*.
[62] The Pew Charitable Trusts (2015, November 18). Pew Finds American Families Ill-Equipped for Financial Emergencies. Retrieved October 12, 2017 from http://www.pewtrusts.org/en/about/news-room/press-releases/2015/11/18/pew-finds-american-families-ill-equipped-for-financial-emergencies.
[63] Epictetus (c. 108 A.D.). *Discourses of Epictetus*. Translated by Thomas Wentworth Higginson.
[64] From his interview with Louis Gannon for Live magazine, The Mail on Sunday (UK) newspaper (25 October 2009).
[65] Shakespeare, W. (c. 1613). *Henry VIII*.
[66] Parkinson, C. N. (1955, November 19). Parkinson's Law. Retrieved September 1, 2017 from http://www.economist.com/node/14116121.
[67] Roberts, N. (2011). *Nora Roberts's The Gallaghers of Ardmore Trilogy*.
[68] As quoted in Chang, L. (2006). *Wisdom for the Soul*.
[69] Branson, R. (1998). *Losing My Virginity*.
[70] Koch, R. (2004). *Living the 80/20 Way: Work Less, Worry Less, Succeed More, Enjoy More*.

[71] Kurtz, G. (Producer), Kershner, I. (Director). (1980). *The Empire Strikes Back* [Motion Picture]. United States: 20th Century Fox.
[72] As quoted in Samuelson, P. (1986). *The Collected Scientific Papers of Paul Samuelson, Volume 5.*
[73] Aurelius, M. (167 A.D.). *The Meditations.* Translated by George Long.
[74] Pope, T. P. (2010, December 21). Postings | Recent Entries From Our Blogs. Retrieved October 13, 2017 from http://query.nytimes.com/gst/fullpage.html?res=9505E5D81130F932A15751C1A9669D8B63.
[75] Eliot, C. W. (1895). *The Happy Life.*
[76] Epictetus (135 A.D.). *The Enchiridion.* Translated by Elizabeth Carter.
[77] Vivekananda, S., & Ranade, E. (Editor). (1963). *Swami Vivekananda's Rousing Call to Hindu Nation.*
[78] McKinney, F. (2002). *Make It BIG!*
[79] Holiday, R. (2016). *Ego Is the Enemy.*
[80] Sivers, D. (2000, April 14). This is only a test. See what happens. Retrieved September 29, 2017 from https://sivers.org/tvtest.
[81] Adams, A. (2013). *How to Fail at Almost Everything and Still Win Big.*
[82] K. C., Diwas, Staats, B. R., & Gino, F. (2013). Learning From My Success and From Others' Failure: Evidence from Minimally Invasive Cardiac Surgery. *Management Science*, 59(11): 2435–2449. doi: http://pubsonline.informs.org/doi/abs/10.1287/mnsc.2013.1720.
[83] Kekich Credo. https://geniusnetwork.com/kekich/main.php
[84] Waldschmidt, D. (2014, January 13). You Have To Do The Hard Things. Retrieved September 30, 2017 from https://www.danwaldschmidt.com/articles/2014/01/business/hard-things.
[85] Godin, S. (2007). *The Dip.*
[86] Pressfield, S. (2002). *The War of Art.*
[87] Epictetus (135 A.D.). *The Enchiridion.* Translated by Elizabeth Carter.
[88] Jobs, S. (2005, June 12). Stanford University commencement address.
[89] Manson, M. (2016). *The Subtle Art of Not Giving a F*ck.*
[90] Schwarzenegger, A. (2012). *Total Recall.*
[91] McKay, K. & B. (2015, October 26). The Sioux Guide to Mental and Physical Toughness. Retrieved October 16 2017 from http://www.artofmanliness.com/2015/10/26/the-sioux-guide-to-mental-and-physical-toughness/.
[92] Livingston, G. (2004). *Too Soon Old, Too Late Smart: Thirty True Things You Need to Know Now.*
[93] Strauss, N. (2015). *The Truth: An Uncomfortable Book About Relationships.*
[94] Hardy, D. (2014). *The Entrepreneur Roller Coaster.*
[95] Musashi, M. (c. 1645), *The Book of Five Rings.*
[96] Tzu, S. (5th century B.C.). *The Art of War.*

[97] Chödrön, P. (1996). *When Things Fall Apart*.
[98] Taleb, N. (2012). *Antifragile*.
[99] McGraw, P. (2001). *Self Matters*.
[100] McGonigal, K. (2011). *The Willpower Instinct*
[101] Aurelius, M. (167 A.D.). *The Meditations*. Translated by George Long.
[102] Pressfield, S. (2011). *Turning Pro*.
[103] Secrest, M. (1966, November 13).Writing Is Workaday For Herman Wouk: Inspiration Strikes at Nine Every Morning. Washington Post.
[104] Wansink, B., & Kim, J. (2005). Bad popcorn in big buckets: portion size can influence intake as much as taste. *Journal of Nutrition Education and Behavior*, 37(5): 242–245. doi: 10.1016/S1499-4046(06)60278-9.
[105] Heath, C., & Heath, D. (2010). *Switch*.
[106] Epictetus (c. 108 A.D.). *Discourses of Epictetus*. Translated by Thomas Wentworth Higginson.
[107] Merritt, A., Effron, D. A., & Monin, B. (2010). Moral Self-Licensing: When Being Good Frees Us to Be Bad. *Social and Personality Psychology Compass*, 4(5): 344–357. doi: 10.1111/j.1751-9004.2010.00263.x.
[108] Vanderkam, L. (2012, February 22). Are You As Busy As You Think? Retrieved October 19, 2017 from https://www.wsj.com/articles/SB10001424052970203358704577237603853394654.
[109] Holiday, R. (2016). *Ego Is the Enemy*.
[110] Thoreau, H. D. (1856). *Walden*.
[111] Pink, D. (2009). *Drive*.
[112] Duhigg, C. (2012). *The Power of Habit*.
[113] Ariely, D. (2008). *Predictably Irrational*.
[114] Abraham Lincoln, White House speech 11 April 1865.
[115] Tynan (2014). *Superhuman by Habit*.
[116] Dweck, C. S. (2006). *Mindset*.
[117] Baumeister, R., & Tierney, J. (2011). *Willpower*.
[118] Hiney, T., & MacShane, F. (Eds.) (2002). *The Raymond Chandler Papers: Selected Letters and Nonfiction 1909–1959*.
[119] As quoted in Grinnell, G. (2016, April 14). Gratitude—'A vaccine against impulsiveness'. Retrieved October 21, 2017 from https://medicalxpress.com/news/2016-04-gratitudea-vaccine-impulsiveness.html.
[120] Loehr, J., & Schwartz, T. (2003). *The Power of Full Engagement*.
[121] Runyon, J. (2012, March 30). Cold Shower Therapy. Retrieved October 22, 2017 from https://impossiblehq.com/cold-shower-therapy/.
[122] Dalio, R. (2017). *Principles*.
[123] Sterner, T. (2012). *The Practicing Mind*.
[124] Koch, R. (2004). *Living the 80/20 Way*.
[125] Bevelin, P. (2004). *Seeking Wisdom*.

[126] Coyle, D. (2009). *The Talent Code.*
[127] Peck, M. S. (1978). *The Road Less Traveled.*
[128] Epictetus (135 A.D.). *The Enchiridion.* Translated by Elizabeth Carter.
[129] Duckworth, A. (2016). *Grit.*
[130] Jordan, P. (1972, July 24). Tom Terrific and His Mystic Talent. Retrieved October 23, 2017 from https://www.si.com/vault/1972/07/24/612578/tom-terrific-and-his-mystic-talent.
[131] McGonigal, K. (2011). *The Willpower Instinct.*
[132] Berman, M. G., Jonides, J., & Kaplan, S. (2008). The Cognitive Benefits of Interacting With Nature. *Psychological Science*, 19(12): 1207–1212. doi: 10.1111/j.1467-9280.2008.02225.x.
[133] Newport, C. (2016). *Deep Work.*
[134] Livingston, G. (2004). *Too Soon Old, Too Late Smart.*
[135] Kennedy, D. (1996). *No B.S. Time Management for Entrepreneurs.*
[136] Duhigg, C. (2012). *The Power of Habit.*
[137] Fitzgerald, F. S. (1925). *The Great Gatsby.*
[138] Aurelius, M. (167 A.D.). *The Meditations.* Translated by George Long.
[139] Sahlgren, G. H. (2013). Work Longer, Live Healthier. IEA Discussion Paper No. 46. Retrieved October 15, 2017 from http://iea.org.uk/sites/default/files/publications/files/Work%20Longer,%20Live_Healthier.pdf.
[140] Ferriss, T. (2010). *The 4-Hour Body.*
[141] Plath, S. (1963). *The Bell Jar.*
[142] Dunwoody, A. (2015). *A Higher Standard.*
[143] Schwartz, D. (1959). *The Magic of Thinking Big.*
[144] Jordan, W. G. (1907). *Self Control — Its Kingship and Majesty.*
[145] As quoted in McKay, K. & B. (2015, July 23). Podcast #124: Self-Discipline & Personal Effectiveness With Rory Vaden. Retrieved October 24, 2017 from http://www.artofmanliness.com/2015/07/23/podcast-124-self-discipline-personal-effectiveness-with-rory-vaden/.
[146] Brooks, D. (2015). *The Road to Character.*
[147] Hardy, D. (2014). *The Entrepreneur Roller Coaster.*
[148] As quoted in Whitney, D. S. (1991). *Spiritual Disciplines for the Christian Life.*
[149] Seton, E. T. (1923). *The Woodcraft Manual for Boys.*
[150] London, J. (October 1899) On the Writer's Philosophy of Life. *The Editor.*
[151] Irvine, William B. (2008). *A Guide to the Good Life.*
[152] Jobs, S. (2005, June 12). Stanford University commencement address.
[153] Roosevelt, T. (1903, May 7). Address at San Bernardino, California.
[154] Kekich Credo. https://geniusnetwork.com/kekich/main.php
[155] Colvin, G. (2008). *Talent Is Overrated.*
[156] Eliot, J. (2015). *Overachievement.*
[157] Tracy, B. (1993). *Maximum Achievement.*

[158] Sanders, B. (2011). *Warrior Wisdom: Ageless Wisdom for the Modern Warrior.*
[159] Khan, H. I. (1978). *Mastery Through Accomplishment.*
[160] Keller, H. (1903). *The Story of My Life.*
[161] Roberts, R. (2014). *How Adam Smith Can Change Your Life.*
[162] Epictetus (c. 108 A.D.). *Discourses and Selected Writings.* Translated by Robert F. Dobbin.
[163] Currey, M. (2013). *Daily Rituals.*
[164] James, W. (1899). *Talks to Teachers on Psychology.*
[165] Hemingway, E. (1935, October). Monologue to the Maestro: A High Seas Letter. *Esquire.*
[166] Sivers, D. (2009, June 24). Doing the opposite of everyone is valuable. Retrieved September 29, 2017 from https://sivers.org/contrarian.
[167] McGonigal, K. (2011). *The Willpower Instinct*
[168] Fiore, N. (1988). *The Now Habit.*
[169] de Castro, J. M. (2000). Eating Behavior: Lessons From the Real World of Humans. *Nutrition*, 16(10): 800–813. doi: 10.1016/S0899-9007(00)00414-7.
[170] Brindal, E., Wilson, C., Mohr, P, & Wittert, G. (2011). Does meal duration predict amount consumed in lone diners? An evaluation of the time-extension hypothesis. *Appetite*, 57(1): 77–79. doi: 10.1016/j.appet.2011.03.013.
[171] Coelho, P. (1990). *Brida.*
[172] Denson T. F., DeWall, N., & Finkel, E. J. (2012). Self-Control and Aggression. *Current Directions in Psychological Science*, 21(1): 20–25. doi: 10.1177/0963721411429451.
[173] Pilcher, J. J., Morris, D. M., Donnelly, J., & Feigl, H. B. (2015). Interactions between sleep habits and self-control. *Frontiers in Human Neuroscience*, 9: 284. doi: 10.3389/fnhum.2015.00284.
[174] The Ideal Temperature for Sleep. Retrieved November 1, 2017 from https://sleep.org/articles/temperature-for-sleep/.
[175] Caffeine. Retrieved November 1, 2017 from https://www.drugbank.ca/drugs/DB00201.
[176] Babauta, L. (2008). *The Power of Less.*
[177] Ariely, D. (2010). *The Upside of Irrationality.*
[178] Browne, H. (1973). *How I Found Freedom in an Unfree World.*
[179] McKeown, G. (2012, August 8). The Disciplined Pursuit of Less. Retrieved November 13, 2017 from https://hbr.org/2012/08/the-disciplined-pursuit-of-less.
[180] Altucher, J., Altucher, C. (2014). *The Power of No.*
[181] McDougall, C. (2009). *Born to Run.*
[182] Bogle, J. C. (2010). *Enough.*
[183] Stulberg, B., & Magness, S. (2017). *Peak Performance.*
[184] Sull, D. (2015). *Simple Rules.*
[185] Nisbett, R. (2015). *Mindware.*
[186] Sophocles (c. 441 B. C.) *Antigone.*

[187] Krakauer, J. (1996). *Into the Wild*.
[188] Strauss, N. (2015). *The Truth*.
[189] Aurelius, M. (167 A.D.). *The Meditations*. Translated by George Long.
[190] Coyle, D. (2009). *The Talent Code*.
[191] Abercrombie, J. (2008). *Last Argument of Kings*.
[192] Armstrong, L., & Jenkins, S. (2003). *Every Second Counts*.
[193] Taleb, N. (2012). *Antifragile*.
[194] Ziglar, Z. (1985). *Raising Positive Kids in a Negative World*.
[195] Hill, N. (1937). *Think and Grow Rich*.
[196] de Clapiers, L. (1746). *Réflexions*.
[197] Pressfield, S. (2002). *The War of Art*.
[198] Carnegie, D. (1948). *How to Stop Worrying and Start Living*.
[199] Tracy, B. (1993). *Maximum Achievement*.
[200] Yutang, L. (1937). *The Importance of Living*.
[201] Holiday, R. (2016). *Ego Is the Enemy*.
[202] Schwarzenegger, A. (2012). *Total Recall*.
[203] As quoted in Carnegie, D. (1948). *How to Stop Worrying and Start Living*.
[204] Hardy, D. (2014). *The Entrepreneur Roller Coaster*.
[205] Duckworth, A. (2016). *Grit*.
[206] As quoted in Carnegie, D. (1948). *How to Stop Worrying and Start Living*.
[207] As quoted in Carnegie, D. (1948). *How to Stop Worrying and Start Living*.
[208] Maltz, M. (1960). *Psycho-Cybernetics*.
[209] Ferriss, T. (2010). *The 4-Hour Body*.
[210] As quoted in Jodorowsky, A. (2008). *The Spiritual Journey of Alejandro Jodorowsky*.
[211] Aurelius, M. (167 A.D.). *The Meditations*. Translated by George Long.
[212] Drucker, P. (1973). *Management: Tasks, Responsibilities, Practices*.
[213] Pink, D. (2009). *Drive*.
[214] Baumeister, R., & Tierney, J. (2011). *Willpower*.
[215] Epictetus (135 A.D.). *The Enchiridion*. Translated by Elizabeth Carter.
[216] Paddon-Jones, D., Westman, E., Mattes, R. D., Wolfe, R. R., Astrup, A., & Westerterp-Plantenga, M. (2008). Protein, weight management, and satiety. *The American Journal of Clinical Nutrition*, 87(5): 1558S–1561S.
[217] Sibonney, C. (2013, September 11). Arianna Huffington On The Third Metric: You Can Complete A Project By Dropping It. Retrieved November 4, 2017, from http://www.huffingtonpost.ca/2013/09/11/arianna-huffington-third-metric_n_3901302.html.
[218] As quoted in McKay, K. & B. (2015, July 23). Podcast #124: Self-Discipline & Personal Effectiveness With Rory Vaden. Retrieved October 24, 2017 from http://www.artofmanliness.com/2015/07/23/podcast-124-self-discipline-personal-effectiveness-with-rory-vaden/.
[219] Taleb, N. (2010). *The Bed of Procrustes*.

[220] McGonigal, K. (2011). *The Willpower Instinct*

[221] Job, V., Dweck, C. S., & Walton, G. M. (2010). Ego Depletion—Is It All in Your Head? *Psychological Science*, 21(11): 1686–93. doi: 10.1177/0956797610384745.

[222] Ross, E., Goodall, S., Stevens, A., & Harris, I. (2010. Time Course of Neuromuscular Changes during Running in Well-Trained Subjects. *Medicine & Science in Sports & Exercise*, 42(6): 1184–1190. doi: 10.1249/MSS.0b013e3181c91f4e.

[223] Duhigg, C. (2012). *The Power of Habit*.

[224] Patterson J. (2001). *Suzanne's Diary for Nicholas*.

[225] Coelho, P. (2005). *The Zahir*.

[226] As translated in Carus, P. (1896). *The Dharma, or The Religion of Enlightenment; An Exposition of Buddhism*.

[227] Palahniuk, C. (1999). *Invisible Monsters*.

[228] Stein, G. (2006). *The Art of Racing in the Rain*.

[229] Tzu, S. (5th century B.C.). *The Art of War*.

[230] Colvin, G. (2008). *Talent Is Overrated*.

[231] Thoreau, H. D. (1856). *Walden*.

[232] Bonesteel, M. (2015, August 26). YouTube-taught javelin thrower Julius Yego wins gold at world championships. Retrieved November 5, 2017 from https://www.washingtonpost.com/news/early-lead/wp/2015/08/26/youtube-taught-javelin-thrower-julius-yego-wins-gold-at-world-championships/?utm_term=.ddfa7289112f.

[233] Pausch, R. (2008). *The Last Lecture*.

[234] Pope, A. (1711). *An Essay on Criticism*.

[235] Steinbeck, J. (1962). *Travels with Charley: In Search of America*.

[236] Peck, M. S. (1978). *The Road Less Traveled*.

[237] As quoted in the October 2017 issue of Men's Health magazine, page 41.

[238] Sivers, D. (2009, September 12). Imagining lots of tedious steps? Or one fun step? Retrieved September 29, 2017 from https://sivers.org/steps.

[239] Stulberg, B., & Magness, S. (2017). *Peak Performance*.

[240] de Saint Exupéry, A. (1948). *Citadelle or The Wisdom of the Sands*.

[241] Koch, R. (1999). *The 80/20 Principle*.

[242] Mandino, O. (1968). *The Greatest Salesman in the World*.

[243] As quoted in Walker, D. (1982). *Animated Architecture*.

[244] Castañeda, C. (1968). *The Teachings of Don Juan: A Yaqui Way of Knowledge*.

[245] Charlie Munger. USC Law School Commencement Speech. 2007, May 13.

[246] Dalio, R. (2017). *Principles*.

[247] Cardone, G. (2011). *The 10X Rule*.

[248] Pressfield, S. (2011). *Do the Work*.

[249] Ferriss, T. (2007). *The 4-Hour Workweek*.

[250] Carnegie, D. (1948). *How to Stop Worrying and Start Living*.

[251] Larson, C. D. (1912). *Your Forces and How to Use Them.*
[252] Millman, D. (1980). *Way of the Peaceful Warrior.*
[253] Rath, T. (2007). *StrengthsFinder 2.0.*
[254] Tracy, B. (1993). *Maximum Achievement.*
[255] Robbins, T. (1992). *Awaken the Giant Within.*
[256] Ruiz, M. A. (1997). *The Four Agreements.*
[257] As quoted in Waite, R. (2004). *The Lost Art of General Management.*
[258] Chödrön, P. (1996). *When Things Fall Apart.*
[259] Browne, H. (1973). *How I Found Freedom in an Unfree World.*
[260] Finley, G. (1998). *The Lost Secrets of Prayer.*
[261] Taleb, N. (2012). *Antifragile.*
[262] Maisel, E. (2009). *The Atheist's Way.*
[263] Cumberland, N. (2014). *Secrets of Success at Work.*
[264] Hanh, T. N. (2006). *Understanding Our Mind.*
[265] Epictetus (c. 108 A.D.). *Discourses of Epictetus.* Translated by Thomas Wentworth Higginson.
[266] Baumeister, R., & Tierney, J. (2011). *Willpower.*
[267] Ariely, D. (2010). *The Upside of Irrationality.*
[268] Tsatsouline, P. (2008, December 18). Pavel: 80/20 Powerlifting and How to Add 110 Pounds to Your Lifts. Retrieved November 8, 2017, from http://www.fourhourworkweek.com/blog/2008/12/18/pavel-8020-powerlifting-and-how-to-add-110-pounds-to-your-lifts/.
[269] de Botton, A. (2000). *The Consolations of Philosophy.*
[270] Sayers, D. L. (1928). *The Unpleasantness at the Bellona Club.*
[271] Duhigg, C. (2012). *The Power of Habit.*
[272] Adams, A. (2013). *How to Fail at Almost Everything and Still Win Big.*
[273] Berns, G. S., Chappelow, J., Zink, C. F., Pagnoni, G., Martin-Skurski, M. E., & Richards, J. (2005). Neurobiological correlates of social conformity and independence during mental rotation. *Biological Psychiatry*, 58(3): 245–253. doi: 10.1016/j.biopsych.2005.04.012.
[274] Rand, A. (1936). *We the Living.*
[275] Smith, J. (2011). The *Flinch.*
[276] Coelho, P. (1998). *Veronika Decides to Die.*
[277] Pegg, R. B. (2014). Taking a fresh look at frozen. Retrieved November 4, 2017 from https://pbhfoundation.org/pdfs/pub_sec/webinars/Pegg_Webinar_April_2014_FINAL.pdf.
[278] As quoted in McKay, K. & B. (2015, July 23). Podcast #124: Self-Discipline & Personal Effectiveness With Rory Vaden. Retrieved October 24, 2017 from http://www.artofmanliness.com/2015/07/23/podcast-124-self-discipline-personal-effectiveness-with-rory-vaden/.
[279] Albom, M. (1997). *Tuesdays with Morrie.*

[280] As quoted in Carnegie, D. (1948). *How to Stop Worrying and Start Living*.
[281] Sterner, T. (2012). *The Practicing Mind*.
[282] Schwarzenegger, A. (2012). *Total Recall*.
[283] Berg, E. (2005). *The Year of Pleasures*.
[284] McGonigal, K. (2011). *The Willpower Instinct*
[285] Bevelin, P. (2004). *Seeking Wisdom*.
[286] Fiore, N. (1988). *The Now Habit*.
[287] Murakami, H. (2008, June 9 & 16). The Running Novelist. Retrieved October 27, 2017 from https://www.newyorker.com/magazine/2008/06/09/the-running-novelist.
[288] Holiday, R., & Hanselman, S. (2016). *The Daily Stoic*.
[289] Tracy, B. (1993). *Maximum Achievement*.
[290] Chouinard, Y. (2005). *Let My People Go Surfing*.
[291] Rumi, (1995). *The Essential Rumi*. Translated by Coleman Barks with John Moyne, A. J. Arberry and Reynold Nicholson.
[292] Kahneman, D. & Tversky, A. (1984). Choices, Values, and Frames. *American Psychologist*, 39(4): 341–350. doi: 10.1037/0003-066x.39.4.341.
[293] Maltz, M. (1960). *Psycho-Cybernetics*.
[294] Aurelius, M. (167 A.D.). *The Meditations*. Translated by George Long.
[295] Niven, J. (2015). *All the Bright Places*.
[296] Gilbert, E. (2006). *Eat, Pray, Love*.
[297] Christie, A. (1930). *Murder at the Vicarage*.
[298] Sellers, P. (2015, February 25). Warren Buffett's Secret to Staying Young: "I Eat Like a Six-year-old." Retrieved November 10, 2017 from http://fortune.com/2015/02/25/warren-buffett-diet-coke/
[299] Nietzsche, F. (1889). *Twilight of the Idols*.
[300] Loehr, J., & Schwartz, T. (2003). *The Power of Full Engagement*.
[301] Cumberland, N. (2016). *100 Things Successful People Do*.
[302] Hanh, T. N. (1991). *Old Path White Clouds*.
[303] Léger, D., Beck, F., Richard, J-B., Sauvet, F., & Faraut, B. (2014). The Risks of Sleeping "Too Much". Survey of a National Representative Sample of 24671 Adults (INPES Health Barometer). PLOS One, 9(9): e106950. doi: 10.1371/journal.pone.0106950.
[304] Pressfield, S. (2011). *Do the Work*.
[305] de Botton, A. (2011). *Religion for Atheists: A Non-Believer's Guide to the Uses of Religion*.
[306] von Goethe, J. W. (1964). *Collected Works*.
[307] Brontë, C. (1847). *Jane Eyre*.
[308] Ferriss, T. (2007). *The 4-Hour Workweek*.
[309] Centers for Disease Control and Prevention. Obesity and Overweight. Retrieved November 10, 2017, from https://www.cdc.gov/nchs/fastats/obesity-overweight.htm.

[310] Koblin, J. (2016, June 30). How Much Do We Love TV? Let Us Count the Ways. Retrieved November 10, 2017, from https://www.nytimes.com/2016/07/01/business/media/nielsen-survey-media-viewing.html.
[311] Aurelius, M. (167 A.D.). *The Meditations*. Translated by George Long.
[312] Bovee, C. N. (1862). *Intuitions and Summaries of Thought*.
[313] da Vinci, L. (1908). Leonardo da Vinci's note-books. Translated by Edward McCurdy.
[314] Hill, N. (1937). *Think and Grow Rich*.
[315] Baumeister, R., & Tierney, J. (2011). *Willpower*.
[316] Landers, A. (1975, October 4). Things You Always Wanted to Know About Belly Buttons. *The Dispatch*.
[317] Shadwell, T. (1679). *A True Widow*.
[318] Virgil. (29-19 BC). *Aeneid*.
[319] As quoted in the preface of Samuel Johnson's Dictionary of the English Language (1755).
[320] As quoted in Gilbert, J. H. (1895). *Dictionary Of Burning Words Of Brilliant Writers: A Cyclopaedia Of Quotations, From The Literature Of All Ages*.
[321] Landon, L. E. (1831). *Romance and Reality*.
[322] Disraeli, B. (1826). *Vivian Grey*.
[323] Loehr, J., & Schwartz, T. (2003). *The Power of Full Engagement*.
[324] Granados, K., Stephens, B. R., Malin, S. K., Zderic, T. W., Hamilton, M. T., & Braun, B. (2012). *Appetite regulation in response to sitting and energy imbalance. Applied Physiology, Nutrition, and Metabolism*, 37(2): 323–333. doi: 10.1139/h2012-002.
[325] Larson, C. D. (1912). *Your Forces and How to Use Them*.
[326] de Cervantes, M. (1605). *Don Quixote*.
[327] Eliot, G. (1859). *Adam Bede*.
[328] Ziglar, Z. (1975). *See You at the Top*.
[329] Epictetus (c. 108 A.D.). *Discourses of Epictetus*. Translated by Thomas Wentworth Higginson.
[330] Robbins, T. (1992). *Awaken the Giant Within*.
[331] Syrus, P. (1856). *The Moral Sayings of Publius Syrus, a Roman Slave*. Translated by Darius Lyman.
[332] Tynan (2017, November 11). The Most Important Daily Task. Retrieved November 12, 2017 from http://tynan.com/the-most-important-daily-task.
[333] Sisson, M. (2016, July 21). Boring May Be Better: Why Routine May Be Best for Certain Health Goals. Retrieved November 12, 2017 from https://www.marksdailyapple.com/boring-may-be-better-why-routine-may-be-best-for-certain-health-goals/#axzz4F3sF3f4a.

[334] Koch, R. (2016, December 20). On the Folly of Ever Feeling Blue. Retrieved November 12, 2017 from richardkoch.net/2016/12/on-the-folly-of-ever-feeling-blue/.
[335] McGonigal, K. (2011). *The Willpower Instinct*
[336] Tracy, B. (1993). *Maximum Achievement*.
[337] Chödrön, P. (1996). *When Things Fall Apart*.
[338] Barry, N. (2012, May 1). Coin Flip. Retrieved November 12, 2017 from http://nathanbarry.com/coin-flip/.
[339] Halvorson, H. G. (2013, March 14). The Amazing Power of 'I Don't' vs. 'I Can't'. Retrieved November 12, 2017 from https://www.forbes.com/sites/heidigranthalvorson/2013/03/14/the-amazing-power-of-i-dont-vs-i-cant/#163acebfd037.
[340] Kavadlo, A. (2013, October 29). Building Strength Without Mass. Retrieved November 12, 2017 from https://pccblog.dragondoor.com/building-strength-without-mass/?apid=4e8cb1ea167b0.
[341] Coyle, D. (2012). *The Little Book of Talent*.
[342] Browne, H. (1973). *How I Found Freedom in an Unfree World*.
[343] Schwarzenegger, A. (2012). *Total Recall*.
[344] Tacitus (1904). *The Annals of Tacitus*. Translated by George Gilbert Ramsay.
[345] Cather, W., & Bohlke, L. B. (1990). *Willa Cather in Person: Interviews, Speeches, and Letters*.
[346] Clemenceau, G., & Martet, J. (1930). *Clemenceau, The Events of His Life as Told by Himself to His Former Secretary Jean Martet*. Translated by Milton Waldman.
[347] Frederick Douglas. An address on West India Emancipation (3 August 1857).
[348] As quoted in Gilbert, J. H. (1895). *Dictionary of Burning Words of Brilliant Writers*.
[349] Loehr, J., & Schwartz, T. (2003). *The Power of Full Engagement*.
[350] Sterner, T. (2012). *The Practicing Mind*.
[351] de Botton, A. (2000). *The Consolations of Philosophy*.
[352] McKeown, G. (2014). *Essentialism*.
[353] Newport, C. (2016). *Deep Work*.
[354] As quoted in Preston, J. (2012, September 17). How Rob Brydon learnt to play nice. Retrieved November 13, 2017 from http://www.telegraph.co.uk/culture/9539089/How-Rob-Brydon-learnt-to-play-nice.html.
[355] As quoted in Alden, H. M. (Ed.) (1854). *Harper's New Monthly Magazine*, Volume 9, p. 806.
[356] Ferriss, T. (2007). *The 4-Hour Workweek*.
[357] As quoted in Douglas, C. N. (1917). *Forty Thousand Quotations: Prose and Poetical*.
[358] Cumberland, N. (2016). *100 Things Successful People Do*.

[359] Rubin, G. (2014, March 24). What Are Your Treats? Do You Have Any That Don't Look Like Treats? Retrieved November 13, 2017 from https://gretchenrubin.com/2014/03/30977/.

[360] Kuhland, J. (n.d.). What Is a Foam Roller, How Do I Use It, and Why Does It Hurt? Retrieved November 13, 2017 https://breakingmuscle.com/fitness/what-is-a-foam-roller-how-do-i-use-it-and-why-does-it-hurt.

[361] Hanh, T. N. (2006). *Understanding Our Mind.*

[362] Pullman, P. (n.d.). Questions & Answers. Retrieved November 13, 2017 from http://www.philip-pullman.com/qas?searchtext=&page=6.

[363] Browne, H. (1973). *How I Found Freedom in an Unfree World.*

[364] Thoreau, H. D. (1856). *Walden.*

[365] Holiday, R. (2016). *Ego Is the Enemy.*

Made in the USA
Middletown, DE
15 January 2018